Spying from Space

Number Twelve:
Centennial of Flight Series

Roger D. Launius, *General Editor*

Spying from Space

Constructing America's
Satellite Command and
Control Systems

DAVID CHRISTOPHER ARNOLD

Foreword by Lt. Gen. Forrest S. McCartney, USAF, Retired

TEXAS A&M UNIVERSITY PRESS
COLLEGE STATION

The paper used in this book meets the minimum requirements
of the American National Standard for Permanence
of Paper for Printed Library Materials, Z39.48-1984.
Binding materials have been chosen for durability.
⊗

Library of Congress Cataloging-in-Publication Data

Arnold, David Christopher, 1967–
  Spying from space : constructing America's satellite command and control
  systems / David Chritopher Arnold ; foreword by Forrest S. McCartney.
      p. cm. — (Centennial of flight series ; no. 12)
  Includes bibliographical references and index.
  ISBN 1-58544-385-9 (cloth : alk. paper)
  1. Space surveillance—United States—History. 2. United States. Air Force.
Satellite Control Facility. 3. Command and control systems—United States
I. Title. II. Series.
  UG1523.A76 2005
  358'.8—dc22
                                                                    2004012916

For my wife, Doreen, who let me go far, far away
to the exotic British Indian Ocean Territory, where
I served as operations officer at Detachment 2, 750th Space
Group, the Diego Garcia Tracking Station, giving rise to
this project.

Contents

List of Illustrations

Foreword

For the past fifty years, an important part of space history has been missing. It's not a glamorous part of space history, and it's been lying in the background, waiting for someone to tell its story. Finally someone has been willing to dig through the technical documents, talk to the people who built the military's system of satellite command and control, and uncover this piece of space history. This book isn't a story about rockets or satellites but is instead a story about a command and control system that made rockets and satellites useful.

One quiet night in 1961 we used that system of satellite command and control to change the world. I had the midnight passes on the console when we took the first operational photograph of the Soviet Union from space. I have that same picture, which I treasure, hanging in my office. Without knowing it—because they were not even briefed for the reconnaissance satellite program they supported—the men and women at the far-flung reaches of the world enabled Corona Flight 14 to take more pictures of the Soviet Union's nuclear program than were taken on all of the U-2 aerial surveillance flights combined. Without the system of satellite command and control, there could have been no military space program and, more importantly, no system of space-based reconnaissance that opened Americans' eyes to the real story of the "missile gap," which never existed. Moreover, in the process of reconnoitering the USSR from space, no one got shot at and no one died, even as the reconnaissance satellite program ushered in nothing less than a revolution in information gathering for the intelligence community.

As one of the three U.S. Air Force captains detailed to the Satellite Test Center in 1960 to learn to "fly" satellites, I was initially overwhelmed by the fantastic technology. In those days I had only my nuclear and electrical engineering background to fall back on. Unlike today, there was at that time no formal training program to teach new personnel to fly satellites—only on-the-job training. When I went to meetings, I gathered data, and someone might say, "Hey, here's a good book on that," so I just scrounged up my own library and figured out what made the best sense. My fellow air force captain Mel Lewin had an uncanny ability to put an enormous amount of data on a single slide. He was particularly helpful in getting the tools that I needed—the crutches and the crib sheets. I always carried a set of my own "cheat sheets" as prompts because we did a lot of rehearsals—almost every day—whether we had a vehicle on orbit or not. We took old tapes from previous flights and played them. When I was in the back room, I devised problems that I hoped would fool the guys who were trying to control the rehearsal vehicle. It got to be a challenge to see whether we could cope with the problems we threw at each other, and, boy, we thought of devious problems. All of that eventually paid off big time. As the three of us—Captains Mel Lewin and Al Crews and I—matured, so did the system of satellite command and control.

In prepass we briefed the station personnel and told them how we antici-pated the situation, what we wanted them to do, what to look for, and what we were concerned about. We were always concerned about acquiring the satel-lite with the reset monitor on. If I didn't see the reset monitor come on, I re-ally did not know where the Mylar control tape was, and I could be just before the fade point in the support, which would have cut the system off. So I gave a good prepass briefing on what I expected to see and what I wanted the sta-tion to do. The station then acknowledged and read the instructions back to me. The station acquired; they tracked; they gave me data. I asked for data. I told them what commands to send and when to send them. They sent the commands and gave me the read-back from telemetry, which told me what they were seeing. Then, after the support, they sent a postpass tape, which was a record tape of acquisition with system time against it, as well as azimuth, elevation, and range from the radar and the telemetry tapes. After the first series of orbits, we sent an airplane (either a C-47 or a C-54) up north to the Alaska tracking stations. The pilots picked up the tapes from Kodiak Island, flew over to Annette Island, picked up whatever tapes they had there, and flew all of these down to Naval Air Station Moffett Field, in Sunnyvale, California. The data people analyzed the tapes, and then I got ready for the midnight passes, which went from south to north.

At the time we had only thirteen commands that we could send. One com-mand, which a few of us knew was a payload command, was "image motion compensation" to try to synchronize the speed of the photographic film with Earth underneath it. The computers in the second building up from us at Menlo Park told us what payload commands to send. We had a separate phone that rang from the payload people, and, if you were not "cleared," you did not know who was talking to you. The person on the other end of the phone just said, "Send command four two times." I repeated the instruction, and then, during the support, I instructed the tracking station to send command four twice. Since the satellite supports ranged from a minute to six minutes, I had to track the vehicle, figure out what it was doing, decide what I wanted to do, get the commands in, and get them verified before the satellite went over the horizon. At times it was a lot of fun, to be honest with you.

Although flying satellites was the pointy end of the spear in the space program in those days, the bureaucrats in Washington also fought their own battles. When the Central Intelligence Agency and the Department of Defense established the National Reconnaissance Office (NRO) in 1960, the action came as a bitter blow to General Bernard A. Schriever and the staff of space experts that he had pulled together. The NRO siphoned off the reconnaissance programs of the "air force programs." The staff at Schriever's Air Force Systems Command, of which I was a member, was relegated to providing support to the NRO and taking on the new systems that were just beginning to evolve. As a result of the NRO's increasing prominence, the Satellite Control Facility became locked down. The flying programs closed and went underground, becoming just numbers as they too began to disappear behind a veil of secrecy.

However, organizations do not make things work. People make things work. We, in fact, were no smarter or dumber than Lockheed in the *Discoverer* days. It was not a question of whether the blue-suiters were smart enough to do the job. I think the smartest, most aggressive, and most highly motivated people are blue-suiters. I believed this when I was in the air force, I believe it now, and I wish I were still in the air force. So it was not a question of whether they were capable of doing the job. Rather, it was a question of the best use of the resource. In other words, as blue-suiters, how do you want to use the limited resources you have?

With a style that all historians of technology should emulate, Arnold brings the whole story together, from the technical developments to the bureaucratic infighting. In doing so, he describes the development of the system of satellite command and control from the glint in General Hap Arnold's eye to operational deployment. Even better, this young air force officer, who is a modern space and missile professional, has the keen ability to translate complicated technical developments into easily understood concepts, raising along the way some important questions about the development of large technological systems. He not only shows how engineers and managers made their decisions but also presents the alternatives to demonstrate that the military's system of satellite command and control need not have turned out the way it did. Above all, he shows that without a ground system for support, there could have been no space program. Arnold brings much-needed recognition to the thousands of Range Rats who enabled a revolution and quite possibly brought the world back from the brink of annihilation.

—Forrest S. McCartney, Lieutenant General, USAF, Retired
Indian Harbour Beach, Florida

Preface

In August, 2000, my house became a satellite tracking station. Sears sold me an eighteen-inch satellite dish in a box, and a subcontractor (of course) stuck it up on the side of the house. Then, to paraphrase Bruce Springsteen, the television had 157 channels but there was still nothing on. That diminutive dish turned the house, for less than two hundred dollars, into a passive tracking station for a geostationary communications satellite, while each remote tracking station in the Air Force Satellite Control Facility cost the American taxpayer millions (although they had many more capabilities and were more sophisticated than my small dish). The new, eighteen-inch system could do nothing more than receive, a capability that even nation-states did not have two generations ago. The revolutionary transformation that has occurred in two generations deserves study.

Two books that are contemporary with the initial development of satellite command and control are Shirley Thomas's *Satellite Tracking Facilities* and Eloise Engle and Kenneth Drummond's *Sky Rangers*.[1] I rescued two copies of these books from certain oblivion in the discard piles of local libraries, one in Farmington, Utah, and another in Columbus, Georgia. When these books were published in the early 1960s, space was new and exciting, and anything associated with it probably leaped right off of bookstore shelves. These two books, however, are little more than surveys of the various technologies available at the time to track satellites. They superficially cover a wide variety of topics from NASA's Minitrack network to the navy's space surveillance network. Because, at the time, "tracking" a satellite meant "command and control" as much as it meant watching an object cross the sky, these two books are just as devoted to radio tracking as they are to the visual observation of satellites. They were the last books devoted exclusively to satellite tracking until the twenty-first century dawned.

NASA's official histories have had little to say about the ground networks that enabled controllers to stay in touch with astronauts or to monitor their own satellite programs. The official history of the Vanguard program, the nation's first civilian satellite project, discusses its network of tracking stations, Minitrack, in some detail.[2] Minitrack, which was planned for one satellite program, accomplished very little after "Kaputnik," a nickname for the

December 6, 1957, failure of the Naval Research Laboratory's first attempt to leave the launch pad. Minitrack's long-term significance rests in its inclusion into NASA's many and varied manned and unmanned programs. The official history of the piloted Mercury program, *This New Ocean*, discusses the tracking network somewhat, but mostly as it relates to the obsession of flight surgeons for constant contact with the astronauts during all phases of spaceflight. According to the authors, however, the full extent of the tracking range and communications network was beyond the scope of their 681-page volume.[3] By the time one finally reaches the Gemini and Apollo programs, other technologies and factors play such an important role that the ground segment of these programs, largely built for Mercury and kept on into Gemini and Apollo, blend into the background.

Douglas Mudgway's history of NASA's own satellite command and control system, called the Deep Space Network, corrected some of the omissions of previous NASA histories. *Uplink/Downlink*, however, is an internalist history of a technology and therefore does little to enhance our understanding of the social construction of large technological systems. A typical nuts-and-bolts look at the way NASA developed its satellite command and control methods, in fact, continues the myth that the history of technology is about artifacts, not about the people who created these systems.[4]

An official NASA publication that does not ignore the history and development of NASA's ground network is James R. Hansen's story of the Langley Research Center, *Spaceflight Revolution*.[5] Hansen deftly incorporates the development of the tracking station networks into Langley's (and NASA's) overall story. His work includes anecdotes about survey trips, including a story about a team that set down in the Congo in 1966 to do a survey for a Mercury tracking station and found themselves in the middle of the first Congolese revolution.

Official U.S. Air Force publications, of which there are many volumes of organizational history, say even less about satellite command and control. In fact, nothing save *three* pages in David N. Spires's organizational history of the air force in space, *Beyond Horizons*, has been written about the men and women on the ground and the equipment they used to make the U.S. space programs possible.[6] Their contributions have remained in the background until now, even though the Air Force Satellite Control Facility was and still is an indispensable and dynamic organization that underwent many changes on its way to becoming the first, common-user network for space command and control.

Although a wide variety of information on satellite command and control is available, it is often hard to find because archivists have buried it in other topical collections. Further, the documents that deal with satellite command

and control also deal with a variety of other details regarding myriad satellite programs. Once the Air Force Satellite Control Facility became an independent organization and began recording its own official histories, more administrative details became available; however, these records ironically present even fewer technological details.

The largest collection of documents on the administrative history of the Air Force Satellite Control Facility lies in a vault in Colorado Springs at the Headquarters Air Force Space Command History Office (AFSPC/HO) on Peterson Air Force Base. AFSPC/HO's historians, although overworked, understaffed, and overcrowded because of a critical shortage of office space, took their valuable time to help me find what I needed. There are boxes and boxes and reams and reams of official documents and photographs on the history of the Air Force Satellite Control Facility, most of which unfortunately—and unnecessarily—remain classified. The nature of the collection is such that it is unique and literally unduplicated anywhere in the air force. Researchers should be aware that they will need to make special arrangements to view and use the collection because of its classified status, the nature of the history office as a functioning official military unit, and the complete lack of space for researchers in the history cubicle farm.

An equally valuable repository that *is* set up to handle researchers is the Air Force Historical Research Agency (AFHRA) at Maxwell Air Force Base in Montgomery, Alabama. AFHRA's sole mission is to help researchers both in and out of the air force write history. The collection is open to the public, and the archivists—who bend over backward to help—are pleased to have people look at their collections, which run the gamut from oral interviews and official histories to special studies, technical documents, and personal papers.

An equally valuable collection (but still difficult to use) is housed at the National Reconnaissance Office (NRO) in Chantilly, Virginia. This collection of declassified and redacted documents from the previously classified Corona, Argon, and Lanyard satellite programs is helpful, but it focuses almost entirely on the development of the satellites themselves, not on the system of command and control that made the satellites useful. Further, NRO's understandable obsession with security requires researchers to plan in advance and to understand that a lot of details are available elsewhere but are redacted here.

The Defense Technical Information Center (DTIC), the hardest nut to crack, acts as a repository of every technical report written under defense department contracts and is a great source of developmental details on satellite command and control; however, for most significant details it remains closed to most nondefense department users. Many documents in DTIC's collection on the Corona satellite program's "Subsystem H" remain unnecessarily classified. Although its collected works are searchable online, DTIC does not have a reading room and is set up to support the needs of the defense community, not of historical researchers. If you are interested in exploring the technology of satellite command and control in much greater detail, including down to the "black box" level, or if you enjoy wiring diagrams and organizational charts, then this is definitely a place you must visit online at http://www.dtic.mil.

By far the most valuable resource for this book has been the personal insights of the people who were there when it all happened. Until the declassification of the Corona program in the 1990s, many of the pioneers of the American military's space program *could* not and *did* not talk about their experiences. Because of this, many of the recorded official histories do not contain references to the early satellite programs. In addition, many of these people could not write anything down during their tenures; thus, much of the evidence remains oral history, sometimes tainted by fading memories and personal embellishments. Historians do not often have the opportunity to talk to the original participants, but historians of space history and other recent history topics certainly should not pass up this opportunity to meet the pioneers of their field of research. I felt privileged and honored to meet some of them and to talk with others on the telephone. In addition, using email I met and talked with others who provided astonishing details that have not been written down anywhere until now.

In this project I accumulated many debts that I can never hope to repay. The largest one is to my wife, Doreen, who has read every page at least twice, followed me back and forth across the country a few times, raised our daughter and our son, and never once complained. Only one name goes on the spine, but I want her to know that I will always consider this book, as I do our life together, a collaboration.

My mother, Linda; my father, George; my sister, Miriam; and my brother, Marc—teachers all—saw to it that my confidence never wavered and that I always had a full cup of encouragement on my desk. My father-in-law, retired air force technical sergeant and former missileer Walter McKnight, and my mother-in-law, Doris, made sure that my cup ranneth over.

Along with my advisor and mentor at Auburn University, Jim Hansen, are Lindy Biggs, Donna Bohanan, Amy Foster, Jeff Jakeman, Kristen Starr, Dan Szechi, Bill Trimble, and others on the faculty who helped make this project a reality.

The faculty at the U.S. Air Force Academy, led by retired Brig. Gen. Carl W. Reddel and Col. Mark K. Wells, who sent me on my way long before I thought I was ready, includes my good friends Michael Neiberg and John Jennings. Also in Colorado Springs, the staff of the Air Force Space Command History Office made this project possible with their willing and eager help. My thanks go particularly to Skip Bradley, Rick Eckert, Shelly Freeman, Karen Martin, and Rick Sturdevant, who helped tremendously, giving me virtually free run of their vault for the entire time I visited and even taking me to lunch a few times. At the U.S. Air Force Historical Research Agency I wish to thank Joseph Caver, who made my life easier, Milton Steele, who helped with photos, and Archangelo "Archie" DiFante's declassification efforts, which essentially brought this project to fulfillment.

It goes without saying that the men and women I interviewed, with the help of the Air Force Space Operations Association and the Air Force Space Command historians, made this project about people and not about hardware. I would especially like to single out Tom Haig, Forrest McCartney, and Bob Siptrott. In addition, I am indebted to the scores of official, unofficial, and additional-duty air force historians who recorded the endless bureaucratic and technological details that sent me well on my way to telling the story of this technological system.

A long, long time ago in a galaxy far, far away I worked very hard for then Col. Simon P. "Pete" Worden, who, *as a reward,* sent me 12,180 miles away from my wife to a small British island in the Indian Ocean. Under Charlie Scott and later Dave Folts I served as the operations officer for the Diego Garcia Tracking Station, call sign REEF. I will always treasure my year as a "Range Rat." The payback has far exceeded the investment. The men and women of REEF made the 369 days away from Doreen tolerable for her and for me and in a way gave rise to this project.

Spying from Space

Introduction
"Goldstone Has the Bird!"

[He] came up and shoved a piece of paper in my hands, on which were these magic words: Goldstone has the bird! . . . *Then someone turned up the loudspeaker, and we heard the president announcing that the United States had successfully launched an Earth satellite.*

—*Maj. Gen. John Bruce Medaris*
Commander, Army Ballistic Missile Agency

SOCIETIES SEND ARTIFICIAL satellites into orbit to collect data. Today, satellites perform a variety of data-related tasks: science, reconnaissance, navigation, weather observation, and communications. To accomplish long-distance relay of data, engineers and scientists use telemetry, which is simply the transmission of data from the satellite to Earth using electromagnetic signals such as radio waves. Satellite telemetry tells the amount of propellant remaining on board a satellite or the voltage level in its batteries; it can reveal the temperatures of certain critical parts or advise us when the engine starts or stops. Telemetry may also include mission data, such as pictures of far-away lands, or telephone calls, or navigation signals. "Satellite command and control," which refers to both the telemetry from and the command uplink to a satellite, provides the essential link between a satellite in its lonely orbit and the people who need its data.

The long and varied origins of space telemetry reach back into the nineteenth century, when wire links preceded modern radio methods of transmission. As early as 1845, the Imperial Russian army developed a "telemeter" for recording the speed of flight of cannonballs. When his paper was published in the 1912 *Transactions of the American Institute of Electrical Engineers*, American electrical engineer O. J. Bliss moved telemetry from the lab to industry. In that paper, Bliss described how to use telemetry to transmit information about the generation of electrical power. Not until World War II did telemetry and radio marry in missile development, a union that has proven fruitful and long lasting.[1]

Regardless of the mission, satellites gather data and send it back to Earth using radio signals, where humans interpret the telemetry, thus creating information. Space vehicles need human interaction to ensure that the vehicles function correctly and to tell them what to do or what not to do. Because of the nature of satellites, their missions, and their orbits, a satellite requires human intervention at many points in its existence. Radio connections between the spacecraft and the ground are necessary for retrieving the data. A satellite may transmit data obtained from its sensors, information regarding the status of its systems, or responses to queries sent from the ground. If no human receives and interprets its transmissions, however, the data are lost, and so might be the satellite. A station on Earth can send and receive data, give commands (such as to transfer to a redundant system or fire a thruster), determine satellite orbit, or ask the vehicle questions about its systems. The acts of sending and receiving information between a satellite and a ground station are the essence of satellite command and control. Communications, commands, and control, as well as the satellites themselves, are the basic elements of a space-based, data-collection system.[2]

Radio signals, which are used to transfer data, are line of sight, so a remote tracking station (RTS) can control and obtain data from a satellite only while the satellite is within view of a ground antenna. For low-orbiting satellites, line-of-sight periods are limited, sometimes as brief as five minutes. Consequently, RTSs must be widely scattered, yet also linked to a central control center. For example, as he flew over Australia, *Mercury* astronaut John Glenn was able to tell controllers on the ground that he saw the lights of Perth because the National Aeronautics and Space Administration (NASA) had a ground station in the western part of that continent.[3]

Satellite command and control is a tricky and complicated task, as difficult as any other aspect of satellite operations—and just as important. Imagine trying to find a vehicle the size of a school bus twenty-three thousand miles from a point on the other side of the globe without knowing precisely where it is or what radio frequency to use to communicate with it. Alternatively, imagine an airplane, flying overhead at the speed of sound. If the pilot ejects an object the size of a golf ball at sixty thousand feet, the apparent size and speed of the golf ball will be approximately that of a three-foot satellite at three hundred miles.[4] Now find the "satellite" against the background of space in less than five minutes and communicate with it; otherwise it might be lost forever. Such is the daily business of the ground network of space command and control.

Today, in support of its own and other agency's satellites, the U.S. Air

Force performs this vitally important command and control mission twenty-four hours a day, seven days a week, and fifty-two weeks a year with an accuracy rate of nearly one hundred percent.[5] In the beginning, however, when satellite command and control did not reach today's high rates of reliability, the air force performed satellite command and control for one agency: the National Reconnaissance Office (NRO), the nation's operator of reconnaissance satellites.

In the late 1950s and early 1960s, the air force developed a policy of acquiring a complete system with its development of the Advanced Reconnaissance System, which the Air Research and Development Command (ARDC) called Weapon System 117L (WS-117L). The reconnaissance satellite program office called the ground network for command and control simply "Subsystem H" because, when beginning to plan for the first space launches in the 1950s, the managers and engineers working for the air force understood the need for a complete space system.[6]

During the mid-1950s, the Western Development Division of ARDC funded WS-117L under Lockheed Aircraft Corporation as its prime contractor. Famous for its World War II fighters, Lockheed had never before taken on a space-related project. Seeing an opportunity, the aircraft manufacturer based its satellite proposal on the use of a booster missile already in production and on a new upper stage called Agena, which would orbit payloads for a number of applications, principally the reconnaissance of the Soviet landmass. U.S. Air Force Col. Frederic C. E. Oder, head of the WS-117L weapon system program office in Los Angeles, intended the program to demonstrate that the United States "could launch, control, get information from, program, and position a space craft."[7] The Corona reconnaissance satellite program, which sprang from WS-117L, did much more than that and provided intelligence for the United States for the next two decades.

From the beginning, the air force intended to make satellite command and control an exclusively military operation. In April, 1959, the service dedicated a unit to providing satellite tracking support, the 6594th Test Wing (Satellite), with three operating locations: Edwards Air Force Base (AFB), California; Chiniak, Alaska; and Annette Island, Alaska.[8] In late 1959 the air force added tracking stations at Vandenberg AFB, California; New Boston Air Force Station, New Hampshire; and Kaena Point, Hawaii.[9] Together the operating locations and tracking stations made up the Air Force Satellite Control Facility (AFSCF). These tracking stations and their command center in Sunnyvale, California, stand at the center of the story of the evolution of the military's system of satellite command and control.

Unfortunately, historians have obscured the importance of ground tracking stations to the American space program—civilian and military—even

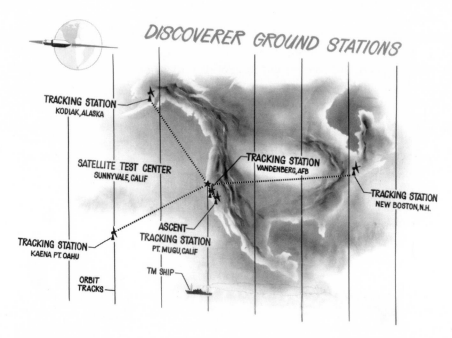

The Air Force Satellite Control Facility, 1960. Courtesy of the Air Force Historical Research Agency collection.

though they have written a large number of articles and books about American satellite programs.[10] Authors show their fascination with the missiles and the management styles that put the satellites into orbit, but so far they have ignored the tracking stations that keep the satellites viable while in orbit.[11] Some historians have written about the air force's contribution to space surveillance and missile warning but have paid little attention to an equally vital mission: satellite command and control.[12] This study attempts to fill in part of that void in space history.

Although historians have neglected satellite command and control, since 1945 scientists and engineers have understood the need for an integral network of ground stations for space operations. Without this ground segment, there would have been no verifiable space "firsts" like *Explorer 1* achieving orbit in 1958, which prompted Maj. Gen. Bruce Medaris to proclaim, "Goldstone has the bird!" about the large antenna in California. Just as the earliest developers of rockets and space vehicles faced their own special challenges, management and technological challenges have been a part of the history of military satellite command and control. Although developed haphazardly, the air force's satellite control network has been as vital to national defense as any satellite program and perhaps more so because the system now supports many different satellite programs. In short, without the military satellite command and control system, the Cold War would have been far more dangerous.

Before the end of World War II, Theodore von Kármán and other well-known American scientists produced *Toward New Horizons,* a report on their vision for the future of American air forces. From this report arose an air force that was wedded to technology. Gen. Henry H. Arnold, chief of U.S. Army Air Forces, already looked at the war as won and promoted the air force as a separate military service. Arnold wanted the aviation service to be prepared to fight the next war, which he assumed would be a technological war.[13] Arnold was right; technology played a pivotal role in the Cold War.

In the post-1945 period, the evolution of satellite command and control began with a report by Douglas Aircraft Corporation's research and development division (later the RAND Corporation) on the possibility of a "world-circling spaceship."[14] After World War II, RAND's scientists and engineers hurriedly produced the report because the air force did not want to be left out when they learned that the navy was looking into the usefulness of satellites. When the navy turned its attention to other projects, air force leaders filed away the RAND report for a decade. With the launch of Sputnik in October, 1957, and with the Cold War in high gear, the United States covertly accelerated its plans to develop a reconnaissance satellite.

Discussions about satellite command and control went on outside the air force also. The U.S. Navy's Advanced Projects Laboratory at Johns Hopkins University in Maryland developed an extensive satellite tracking network for Vanguard, the first American scientific satellite program. The United States in fact developed two separate but equal satellite command and control networks: NASA's public one and the military's not-so-public one, designed specifically to support the nation's top secret National Reconnaissance Program. During the 1960s, air force leaders pointed to the satellite command and control system developed for the reconnaissance satellite program as proof that the U.S. Air Force was the military's space service, supporting the new horizons of Arnold and von Kármán. However, the military satellite command and control system evolved in the 1960s solely to support the National Reconnaissance Program, without providing a unique space capability for the U.S. Air Force.

In 1967, well after the first successes of the reconnaissance satellite program, President Lyndon Johnson declared that "if nothing else had come out of [the space program] except the knowledge we've gained from space photography, it would be worth ten times what the whole program" had cost. "Because of satellites," Johnson said, "I know how many missiles the enemy has."[15] Gen. Bernard A. Schriever, leader of the air force's space and missile efforts during the 1950s and 1960s, tried to develop deterrence through strength and capability, not by a threat of mutually assured destruction.[16] As he said later, "I am looking for ways to avoid killing people. . . . We need to do something other than find ways to kill people better."[17] The U.S. Air Force's ground-based satellite command and control system, built as part of an integrated reconnaissance satellite program, helped remove the veil of secrecy from the face of the Soviet Union, thus reducing the threat of nuclear war between the superpowers.

1

The Inescapable Premise
Inventing Satellite Command and Control

No space program is feasible without an adequate ground environment.

—*National Security Council Memorandum 1859, January, 1959*

IN THE EARLY days of space operations, sending satellite telemetry over telephone lines—the most common means of transmitting data from the remote tracking stations to engineers in California—challenged engineers almost as much as launching the satellites themselves.[1] Telemetry in the 1950s and the 1960s, as it does now, contained important facts about systems status or for calculating a satellite's orbit, and engineers required the data for troubleshooting. The data, which were frequency modulated onto sine wave subcarriers, came down from satellites at high speeds, and the tracking stations recorded it all onto magnetic tape. After the satellite passed from view, the recorder operators rewound the tape and brought its speed down until the tape moved slowly enough to transmit on a low data-rate telephone line. The recorder operators in Alaska first made a voice phone call to the data center in Sunnyvale, California, and when the recorder operator there signaled "ready to record," the tracking station patched the tape playback in place of the telephone handset and then rolled the tape. Lockheed's satellite engineers often needed certain vital data on the tape, and transmitting with this method got the information to them faster than mailing the tape from Alaska would have.

Tracking station controllers called this system "Slow Poke" because the unattended tape usually played back at 1/32nd of the original recording speed, which thus required thirty-two minutes to deliver one minute's worth of telemetry. Most satellite supports at the Alaskan tracking stations on Kodiak

Island (station call sign KODI) or Annette Island (station call sign ANNE) lasted five minutes or longer and required more than two and a half hours to retransmit a single support's data. Fortunately, the trackers seldom re-sent a full set of data, so they did not object to tying up their only phone line to these isolated locations. Usually they sent only information that either the command center did not receive during the actual satellite support because of communications outages or that particularly interested the satellite engineers. Controllers at the tracking stations had contact with the outside world through only that one phone line and a 100-word-per-minute teletype machine. If during a transmission, the telephone operator in Sunnyvale needed to connect a northbound call and tapped the KODI or ANNE line to see whether it was in use, she might have only heard funny "beeps" and "boops" on the line. If she thought a line had actually failed, she might disconnect the call and log the line out to maintenance. Because KODI was then in the send-only mode, the station could not learn of the disconnection until the tape ran out hours later, wasting a lot of time. The tracking station controllers eventually let the phone operators know about the flaw in the procedure, and the phone operators learned about satellite data transmissions. Said one former operator at KODI, "Slow-Poke worked fine, but it sure was slow!"[2]

In those early days, everyone tried their best to make command and control work, inventing most things as they went along. As the former Lockheed program manager for the reconnaissance satellite puts it, "No one person can claim the responsibility for the design for something as complicated as [a satellite], the Agena [booster], or any large project like that. It's a group effort—there's management, there's specialists."[3] The system did not spring from one person's imagination—no "Eureka!" moment figures in its birth. Engineers borrowed from anywhere and everywhere, using teamwork to create the military's satellite command and control system.

By 1950 the larger air force organization had vested itself in existing technology, refusing to nurture an invention—space-based reconnaissance— that by its nature promised to contribute little to the organization and instead would challenge the status quo. The inventors of the military system of satellite command and control, therefore, distanced themselves from the mainstream air force research and development bureaucracy, Air Materiel Command, as well as the normal air force procurement system. The flying air force, uninterested in new technological systems for reconnaissance, did not contribute to the development of this new technology, which threatened obsolescence for piloted, airplane-based strategic reconnaissance.

In addition, the normal weapons procurement system simply could not bring a radical new weapon system online quickly enough for the American president, who wanted photoreconnaissance of the USSR in the dark days of the Cold War. Lockheed and the Central Intelligence Agency would take only nine months to get the covert *Corona* reconnaissance satellite program ready for launch, once given the go-ahead. Even today the air force has taken nearly twenty years to get the next-generation fighter aircraft ready for service, a time span President Dwight D. Eisenhower found impossible to accept in a national intelligence emergency like the ICBM race of the 1950s.[4]

Thus, a unique arrangement of free agents contributed to the development of a system of satellite command and control to support reconnaissance satellites. In the 1950s and 1960s the people who worked at the Western Development Division, the air force's center for space and missile research in El Segundo, California, did not invent systems development, but they raised it to a new level. They brought two major missile programs and a satellite reconnaissance program to fruition in just five years, using a developmental program they called "concurrency," and were spurred on to success by their self-determination.[5] These teams of scientists and engineers began their work in the 1950s by simply reading reports that others had written; they finished by creating a satellite command and control system to support the National Reconnaissance Program.

Independent Inventors Roamed Free

New and radical inventions occupied the minds of some airmen at the end of World War II. Gen. Hap Arnold stands chief among the air force visionaries. The Wright brothers taught Arnold to fly, and his distinguished career reached its culmination during World War II, when he was made a member of the Joint Chiefs of Staff while he was chief of staff of the Army Air Forces. Although he never served in an independent air force, General Arnold's vision and foresight created a powerful air and space force. His creative thinking gave people the opportunity to develop radical solutions to problems.

General Arnold fostered close relationships with various civilian academics, in particular Theodore von Kármán, one of the founders of NASA's Jet Propulsion Laboratory (JPL) at the California Institute of Technology in Pasadena. As the end of World War II approached, Arnold asked von Kármán and the U.S. Army Air Forces Scientific Advisory Group—a group of leading American scientists who advised Arnold—to develop a long-range vision for the postwar air force. Arnold speculated about "manless remote-controlled radar or television-assisted precision military rockets or multiple purpose seekers."[6] Von Kármán's science and technology forecast, *Toward New Horizons,* laid out his vision for the post–World War II air force. Summarizing his report in a December, 1945, letter to Arnold, von Kármán acknowledged that "scientific discoveries in aerodynamics, propulsion, electronics, and nuclear physics open new horizons for the use of air power. . . . The next ten years should be a period of systematic, vigorous development, devoted to the realization of the potentialities of scientific progress."[7] Von Kármán proposed a relationship between the air force, science, and industry that would provide young officers experience in science and industry and thus improve their capacity to make decisions later in their careers, much like Arnold's own personal experience. Von Kármán's report recommended the permanent establishment of a scientific advisory board and the creation of a major research and development command, both of which became reality in the newly independent service.[8] Once independent, the air force institutionalized the report's suggestions, thereby forging the scientific and technological orientation of the modern air force.

The U.S. Navy also had a small cadre of people who were willing to think in bold, new ways. In a simple, three-page report—including the cover page—the navy got the jump on the other services in the new medium of space. The navy's Bureau of Aeronautics (BuAer) issued report R-48 in November, 1945, "Investigation on the Possibility of Establishing a Space Ship in an Orbit above the Surface of the Earth," prepared by Lt. Cdr. Otis E. Lancaster and J. R. Moore. The mission for the ship would determine its orbit, but for reconnaissance of enemy positions, "all the necessary information could be obtained in a few trips over the target." Lancaster and Moore speculated that "television or automatic photography could supply the desired information, without personnel [on board]." They found especially interesting "a circular orbit, 22,300 miles above the surface of the earth, where the [space]ship would make one revolution per day. In this orbit, the ship may be kept over a designated point on the surface of the earth. Naturally, the higher the orbit above the surface of the earth, the more difficult it is to establish the orbit."[9]

Fortunately for the air force, Lancaster and Moore underestimated the technical requirements for their proposal. According to Robert Salter, a BuAer contractor at the time who reviewed the proposal, the navy wanted a single-stage-to-orbit vehicle, presumably to make worldwide ship-based launches possible. To achieve orbit using a single stage, however, required a thrust-to-mass ratio of around 95 percent, that is, 5 percent satellite and 95 percent booster, or "about the same mass ratio as an egg," given spacelift capability at the time.[10] (Even at the start of the twenty-first century, scientists and engineers have not been able to achieve such a lofty goal.)

Although brief, the Lancaster and Moore report did not ignore the need for satellite command and control, making it a significant first step. The Space-Missile Committee working under Lancaster and Moore assumed that an "experimental space missile" could be orbited at an altitude of about one thousand miles, suggesting that "one objective of constructing and launching such a missile" would be the "determination of the feasibility of radio track-ing and control."[11] The Space-Missile Committee considered the program only an introduction to the more general problem of satellites and needed a further elaboration of the bureau's organization and objectives for definitive progress. They never got their answer, though, as the navy moved on to su-percarriers and away from "experimental space missiles."

Some in the air force saw an obvious threat: If the navy developed a suc-cessful reconnaissance satellite, it would threaten the air force's monopoly on strategic reconnaissance.[12] The simple BuAer report directed only an exami-nation into the possibility of a satellite, but Maj. Gen. Curtis E. LeMay, deputy chief of staff for research and development for the air force, found out about the research and responded on a far-reaching scale. LeMay directed Douglas Aircraft's Research and Development Group (later the RAND Corporation) to investigate the possible uses of satellites. Released in May, 1946, RAND's response, "Preliminary Design of an Experimental World-Circling Space-ship," offered a comprehensive look at what satellites could do for the military and suggested three missions: meteorology, communications, and reconnais-sance. The report outlined four significant technologies for research and development: long-life electronics, video recording, attitude stabilization, and spacecraft design.[13] The flying air force, enamored with mammoth, long-range aircraft, largely ignored RAND's report when the navy competition disappeared.

Even at this very early stage, the 1946 report addressed the importance of tracking a satellite and calculating its orbital parameters, calling for a "series of telemetering stations [to] be established around the equator to obtain the data from the scientific apparatus contained in the vehicle."[14] The report rec-ommended that the first satellites be placed in orbit around the equator, where they could be repeatedly observed from dedicated ground stations. A radar-equipped ground station could measure both range and angle, com-pute the rate of change of altitude, and send a corresponding pulse to the ve-hicle. A beacon in the vehicle, which acted as a transponder, could also convey information from the vehicle to the ground. Nevertheless, RAND acknowl-edged, current radar techniques involving radar ranging or Doppler shift measurements did not offer adequate accuracy.[15] Engineers and scientists un-derstood the radar technology used in World War II, although they had yet to prove its utility for space vehicles.

The RAND scientists and engineers included in the report plans for a global network of tracking stations. For "orbital observation and telemeter-ing," a satellite required some twenty to fifty stations installed or positioned in a belt around the equator, across the Pacific, Ecuador, Brazil, the Atlantic, French Congo, Kenya, the Indian Ocean, and Malaya. The tracking system had to link all these stations with each other or with a central station by rapid communications so that engineers could maintain continuous tracking and telemetering of the "satellite missile," particularly to guide its return to Earth, which would be essential if it had a pilot.[16] RAND's estimate of the required number of ground stations proved to be a little high, but their idea of a centralized command and control system proved prescient.

RAND admitted that its scientists and engineers still had much research ahead of them. They barely understood the infant technology of transmitting telemetry from guided missiles to ground stations, although American engineers made great strides during the 1940s using captured German V-2s and other test missiles. Scientists and engineers could learn a great deal about satellite command and control from these activities, so they launched a number of missiles for their benefit. Eventually engineers developed, tested, and exercised an entire communication system that would be required in an actual satellite operation.[17]

In the 1940s and 1950s the air force reconnaissance community was wedded to long-range bombers flying reconnaissance missions: "When you wanted to take pictures of something, you just got in your airplane, went out, and turned on your cameras and came back and processed the film."[18] Senior officials who endorsed the idea of satellites for military purposes rightly sensed that the air force—committed to the existing aerial reconnaissance technology—would not nurture a new, space-based reconnaissance technology.[19] The mainstream air force rejected space-based reconnaissance as technically crude and economically risky and continued to champion piloted reconnaissance aircraft. President Eisenhower, on the other hand, needed the alternative of space-based reconnaissance to provide evidence that the Soviets lagged far behind in missile development because reconnaissance aircraft like the RB-29, PB4Y-2, and later even the U-2 could not reach every site in the USSR to search for missiles and bombers.[20] Eisenhower's pressing needs and the air force's stubbornness proved an asset for the space community in the short term but a detriment for the air force in the long run.

Inside the air force, a small but vocal minority of space enthusiasts argued that the notion of spacecraft and satellites had technical practicality. Espousing the cause of continuing satellite studies at considerable risk to their careers, leaders such as Maj. Gen. Donald L. Putt, air force deputy chief of staff for research and development; Gen. Hoyt S. Vandenberg, later air force chief of staff; and then Col. Bernard A. Schriever, military liaison to the Scientific Advisory Board, kept official interest in satellites and space programs alive. As Gen. Thomas Morgan later recalled, word came down from the highest levels in the air force that officers should not talk about such missions because space was a "nonuseful type of endeavor for the military to get into."[21] Yet, in for-

bidding officials even to speak the word "space," the air force merely acknowledged the radical character of the new invention.[22]

In the late 1940s, RAND scientists and engineers continued to develop
a basis for making satellite control systems a reality. Building on the 1946 report, RAND submitted twelve detailed, supplemental studies that aimed at
convincing the air force of the usefulness of the orbiting spacecraft. Finally,
in January, 1948, the vice chief of staff of the air force, General Vandenberg,
authorized the air force's Engineering Division to fund further RAND studies
of satellite operations. Vandenberg also issued a policy statement that staked
the air force's claim for space operations: "The USAF, as the Service dealing
primarily with air weapons—especially strategic—has logical responsibility
for the satellite."[23] Although the air force did not have a formally approved
space program at the time, some service leaders had an interest in the possibilities of space and never retracted General Vandenberg's statement. Building a satellite for any reason, let alone strategic reconnaissance, endured an
extended infancy in those postwar years.

In the early 1950s, organizations besides RAND investigated the usefulness of satellites. The first unclassified publication on satellites came from the
British Interplanetary Society (BIS) in 1951. Little more than a pamphlet,
The Artificial Satellite speculated on the possibilities for an unpiloted satellite
and even offered plans for an Earth-orbiting space station. Whereas RAND
envisioned military applications for satellites, the British Interplanetary Society's ideas of satellite applications emphasized scientific research: "The ex-
tension of radio-telemetering into free space will permit studies of radiations,
corpuscular and electromagnetic, emanating from outer space."[24] The society
recognized the need for telemetry, tracking, and control of space vehicles
and commented favorably on "the multiple-channel telemetering systems
used in the American high-altitude rocket programme."[25] BIS's pamphlet was
not nearly as remarkable as what RAND produced in 1951.

RAND's 1951 report, "The Utility of a Satellite Vehicle for Reconnaissance," became the first, detailed technical report in the evolution of satellite
command and control. RAND took a major step by stating the technical and
engineering possibilities for a reconnaissance satellite employing television
techniques for data readout to ground stations. RAND found its earlier satellite advice largely ignored, but its scientists and engineers did not give up,
preparing another report for the air force on "The Utility of a Satellite Vehicle for Reconnaissance." RAND personnel advocated television because
they recognized that satellites must transmit large amounts of imagery data,
and television seemed the easiest medium. In addition, in the early 1950s the
reentry and recovery capabilities needed to return an object from outer space
through atmospheric heating did not exist. Very heavy copper heat sinks con-

stituted the only available heat-reducing system. Weight put a tremendous strain on the launch and recovery capabilities of the time, so engineers tried to keep the satellite as small as possible.[26]

In building their technical case, RAND devoted most of its April, 1951, report to the type of orbit a reconnaissance satellite needed—for example, its speed, altitude, shape, and so forth.[27] Analysts suggested that the best orbit for reconnaissance of the USSR would be an 83-degree retrograde orbit at an altitude of 300 miles. At that altitude the orbit precesses one degree a day, giving the satellite repeated daily visits in the same sunlight over a certain point. It also gives the vehicle a longer line-of-sight communication time with ground stations.[28]

RAND also pointed out the need to convey the data recorded by the satellite back to the ground. Assuming that satellites could use television signals to broadcast the data to stations "sited either in friendly territories or on ships," transmissions still had to take place on a line-of-sight path because of the required radio frequencies, which were in the AM/FM range (530 KHz to 108 MHz). The maximum slant range (the line-of-sight distance) from a satellite in a 350-mile orbit to the ground would be about 1,400 miles, too far for effective data transmission using either AM or FM unless multiple channels could be modulated onto a single carrier wave (that is, joined together onto a single broadcast signal from the satellite to the ground). Further, this slant range required five stations off the Eurasian landmass, but such an orbit would still miss about 15 percent of the USSR because of the relatively low altitude. The possibility of eliminating unobserved areas increased when employing the technique RAND called "delayed broadcasting." The RAND team nevertheless underestimated the transmitting device technology as so bulky and complex that delayed broadcasting did not "appear to warrant any further investigation."[29] Significantly, the report illuminated most of the problems of using a satellite for reconnaissance and raised important issues in the area of command and control.

RAND's Robert Salter used personal connections at RCA to conduct research at NBC studios in Hollywood and determined early parameters of satellite command and control. On "the basis of a couple of martinis," Salter succeeded in simulating satellite photography. A year later, when Salter began working for eventual satellite contractor Lockheed, he took a few highly accurate pictures of Earth and put them on easels. Salter built degradations into the photos that he assumed matched those from space. Using image orthicons, which were vacuum tubes used in some television cameras, he scanned the pictures in a simulated satellite path and then transmitted them to Mount Wilson, near Los Angeles. Rebroadcasting the pictures back through the atmosphere, Salter recorded them using a kinescope, an early motion picture camera. A group of photo interpreters looked at the pictures to determine what they could see.[30]

RAND devoted considerable attention to the ground tracking stations. A station with an appropriately sized receiving antenna can theoretically track a satellite in a 350-mile orbit for about 3,000 miles, from horizon to horizon. A satellite would traverse that distance in approximately eleven minutes at an average angular tracking rate of 15 degrees per minute, requiring the antenna tracking system to be carefully tied in with the satellite's system. Engineers assumed the diameters of both the satellite's and the ground station's antennas to be one foot and sixteen feet, respectively, and that the ground station's antenna would be reasonably small enough to permit construction.

RAND's engineers preferred using a receiver in the satellite that would respond to a continuous wave signal from a ground beacon to direct the satellite antenna toward the ground station. Before the satellite appeared over the horizon, the ground station would begin transmitting its electronic "greeting." This "handshake" required the orbit to be established precisely enough to enable the ground station operators to predict the azimuth angle—the direction at which to point the antenna when the satellite "rises" above the horizon—to within one or two degrees. Once the two had made their radio connection, the ground station's receiving antenna could follow the satellite by means of a tracking receiver locked onto the television signal. RAND speculated that to make it all work, a beacon of about 1,000 watts of power would yield a broad enough beam to illuminate the satellite when it rose above the horizon.

Because of a ground station's size and the fact that it did not move much (whereas satellites moved a lot), considerations of circuit complexity and power consumption did not significantly affect the ground station design, which could take any of several forms. The ground station's sixteen-foot receiving antenna could have a single feed connected through a power receiver to two receivers for system redundancy. The search phase consisted of aiming the axis of the dish in the direction of the satellite's scheduled appearance and then oscillating the dish through its axis so that the axis of the scan would describe an arc centered on the direction of the satellite's orbit. When the satellite appeared, its tracking antenna would first contact the ground station's beacon, thus aligning the satellite's transmitting antenna with the ground station.[31] RAND believed that only a single ground station would be necessary, suggesting that its location be somewhere in Alaska, perhaps Fairbanks or Point Barrow, and believing that weather, communications, and transportation would all be sufficient even that far north.[32]

With the tracking problem seemingly solved, RAND turned its attention to the assimilation of the TV pictures after they arrived on the ground. The equipment required at any forward receiving station would not be complex and in fact would be similar to television broadcasting gear then in use. Any ordinary television receiver would probably suffice for monitoring for satisfactory picture quality. For recording, a station would need a second television receiver. Camera optics would reduce the image to the appropriate film size; RAND thought 35-mm film might be adequate, but if they lost a significant amount of detail, they could employ 70-mm film. Schedulers furnished each ground station with a plan for operations that was based on the satellite's orbit. A time coding scheme would be included with each frame that would indicate not only when the satellite took the picture but also when it arrived at the ground station. The central evaluation station—presumably the one at Hanscom AFB, Massachusetts, which already housed the air force's photograph interpreters, or later, the National Photographic Interpretation Center (NPIC) in Washington, D.C.—would receive the composite films from the forward stations and assemble the orbit into an integrated whole. The entire presentation system would be simple, rapid, reliable, state of the art, and practical, using well-known, photo evaluation techniques.[33] Anyone who was within the range of the remote tracking station could also easily intercept the signals. The report ended with a discussion of how the enemy might track the reconnaissance satellite, either actively with radar or passively with cameras similar to the air force's own Baker-Nunn camera, which was used for ground-to-space observations (an entirely different type of satellite tracking).

In sum, the scientists and engineers of the Scientific Advisory Group and RAND Corporation roamed widely to find solutions to the problems they encountered. Von Kármán's report to Gen. Hap Arnold presented a vision for the air force in space. Arnold's successors, although stymied by a conservative organization, turned the vision into reality by seeking out independent research organizations. RAND's reports on the utility of an artificial satellite became the first detailed technical reports in the evolution of satellite command and control. However, unlike aerial reconnaissance, the air force did not have an exclusive interest in satellite command and control.

Invention of Satellite Command and Control outside the U.S. Air Force

During the 1950s, the United States had several organizations besides RAND researching the usefulness of a satellite and the technology of satellite command and control. These organizations all had to overcome the same problems and questions that RAND faced in its research; among the most important of these was "What do you *do* with a satellite once you've got it in space?" Without exception, everyone came to the same conclusion: Gather data. The Minitrack and Microlock satellite tracking networks—which scientists and engineers developed in the 1950s for the Naval Research Laboratory and the Army Ballistic Missile Agency and which were both innovative but essentially conservative inventions—proved the viability of satellite command and control, while simultaneously improving and expanding existing telemetry systems.

After World War II Johns Hopkins University's Applied Physics Laboratory (APL) broke new ground in telemetry systems. Working for the navy on the Bumblebee series of guided missiles, APL made enormous strides in the late 1940s, establishing many of the standards for radio telemetry and introducing subcarriers on radio frequencies to enhance data transmission capabilities. By the time telemetry matured, engineers and scientists had continuously enhanced and increased the flexibility of ground station equipment. Recording techniques, especially, progressed from making a phonograph record to recording on magnetic tape.[34] Scientists and engineers outside APL borrowed their methods and used them for their own satellite programs.

S. Fred Singer, a young Princeton physicist whose doctoral committee had included nuclear physicist J. Robert Oppenheimer, offered his Minimum Orbital Unmanned Satellite of the Earth (MOUSE) to the American Rocket Society in April, 1955. In his discussion of the technical problems associated with the launch, control, and instrumentation of MOUSE, Singer made sure everyone understood the ramifications of telemetering, including—for the first time in a satellite proposal—channels and frequency modulation. He suggested a polar orbit for MOUSE as the most economical by storing data on board the satellite and then releasing it over either the North or South Pole. Because polar orbiting satellites passed over the poles and therefore over polar-based tracking stations on every orbit, this plan called for a minimum number of ground stations. Singer's strategy would thus obviate the need for the large number of tracking stations required to support an equatorial orbit, which other proposals advocated. Singer drew the same orbital conclusions RAND had drawn, but an international treaty made Antarctica off-limits for anything but purely scientific research, so for RAND's proposed reconnaissance satellite the South Pole sat too far away, both physically and politically. Singer understood that his proposed test satellite could not perform the types of missions—like reconnaissance—that required a high degree of orbital precision. He noted that engineers could accept deficiencies in optical visibility and the accuracy of the orbit for a satellite with geophysical or astrophysical research applications. Such a scientific satellite required only extremely simple propulsion, guidance, and control in comparison to satellites meant to fulfill more ambitious functions like space-based strategic reconnaissance.[35] Singer's proposal, the first significant proposal for a scientific satellite discussed in nongovernmental circles, caught on with the scientific community, but not with the U.S. government.

Scientists and engineers often publicly discussed how best to build the needed tools for communicating with satellites. At the February, 1957, Astronautics Symposium in San Diego, cosponsored by the Air Force Office of Scientific Research and the Convair division of General Dynamics, prime contractor for the Atlas ICBM, experts from Lockheed, RAND, and the Jet Propulsion Laboratory gave papers on satellite tracking. The conference attendees concluded overall that no additional major breakthroughs would be required for an adequate communications system for space travel. Using systematic exploitation of the techniques and devices already known, electronics engineers could achieve a level of communications system performance that would satisfy space travel requirements for years to come.[36]

Max Fishman, a researcher at Lockheed, suggested at the conference that the size of the transmitters and receivers on the satellites themselves might be the biggest problem in satellite command and control because early designs placed a premium on "legroom." Increasing the bandwidth of the communication link (that is, the amount of data that could move across communications signals) with a satellite dictated greater transmitter power, increased receiver sensitivity, or increased antenna size. The simplest solution called for increased antenna size on the ground and a decreased number of operating frequencies, which Fishman achieved with a fixed base, steerable antenna system.[37] Fishman's ideas eventually found their way into the air force's tracking stations.

After years of engaging in little more than intellectual discussions, governmental officials found their indifference to satellites fading in the glare of the International Geophysical Year (IGY). First discussed by the scientific community as early as 1954, this international project of a concentrated, coordinated exploration of Earth's cosmic environment was planned to run from July, 1957, to December, 1958. Publicly, the United States denied that a race with the Soviet Union to orbit a satellite for the IGY forced its decision to go ahead with a satellite program. Privately, the United States staked its technological reputation on a research and development project called Vanguard. Vanguard would develop a grapefruit-sized, scientific satellite that utilized a radio tracking plan called Minitrack, which the Naval Research Laboratory would run.

On March 26, 1955, the National Security Council ruled that the American scientific satellite program should not use ICBMs or IRBMs. The army's proposal depended on the new Jupiter IRBM then under development, but the Vanguard engineers planned an entirely new rocket for their satellite. Then in August, 1955, the Stewart committee, the scientific review panel that was charged with selecting the American entry for the IGY, formally selected Vanguard as the scientific satellite program. According to Homer J. Stewart, chair of the panel, Vanguard's Minitrack network had a direct bearing on the decision to accept Vanguard over the army's Project Orbiter, which planned a visual instead of an electronic tracking network. Vanguard's brand-new missile, perceived as untainted by either the air force's or army's long-range missile development programs, also helped sway the Stewart committee.[38]

Vanguard's electronic tracking system used radio interferometry. Essentially, two ground receiving stations tracked the signals broadcast by a satellite; by comparing the phases of the signals, each of them separately received, scientists could accurately calculate the angles to the spacecraft and therefore calculate its orbit. In a sense, radio antennas work much like our ears in that they are able to locate the source of a sound by determining the phase differences in the sound waves, which arrive at each antenna at slightly different times.[39] Vanguard originally included an optical tracking plan, but this method, although accurate, had limitations. By using the best equipment, trackers could observe an object in orbit with the sun only at five degrees below the horizon, that is, just before sunrise or just after sunset; even then, visual tracking required clear and relatively cloudless weather.

Vanguard's tracking system became the nation's first dedicated satellite control system. In the early 1950s, Vanguard engineers under Milt Rosen at White Sands, New Mexico, built and field-tested a tracking system for their Viking missile tests. John T. Mengel and his associates came up with a 13-ounce transmitter for the Vanguard satellites, far smaller than those carried aboard their Viking rockets but employing the same system. Mengel gave the tracking system the name Minitrack. Minitrack consisted of a quartz-crystal-controlled and fully transistorized oscillator aboard the spacecraft. Its 10-milliwatt output operated on a fixed frequency and had a predicted lifetime of ten to fourteen days.[40] In addition to the tracking function, Minitrack included antennas and receivers to read the data transmitted by the satellites—in other words, ground telemetry stations.[41]

Vanguard faced political limitations on its tracking network that made it useless for reconnaissance satellites. Because they planned to launch Vanguard from Cape Canaveral, the satellites had to go into an orbit limited to 35 degrees above or below the equator. An orbit with such an inclination could prove useful for not only tracking reasons but also political ones. Vanguard satellites would not track so far north that it would invade the "space" above the USSR, but they could still help set a precedent for freedom of navigation in orbit above Earth, a major American concern before the first satellite launch.[42] Therefore, to track the satellite, the Vanguard team planned to establish a "picket line" of Minitrack stations along the roughly equatorial orbital path, eventually placing stations on the islands of Grand Bahama, Antigua, and Grand Turk, as well as in South Africa, Australia, and South

America. These stations, including one in the United States, would be leased with the help of the navy and the Department of State. These seven stations had a 90-percent chance of tracking every pass of the planned 300-mile orbit.

The system introduced the concept of control from a central location. Bendix Corporation built the ground station equipment, including the radio-frequency receivers, power supplies, operating consoles, phase measuring equipment, analog and digital recorders, and quartz-crystal oscillator clocks. Melpar, Inc., built the AN/DPN-48 radar beacons for tracking. Observers at the tracking sites sent information by teletype to the Vanguard Computing Center in downtown Washington, D.C., where technicians fed the figures into an IBM-709 "electronic calculator," leased to the government at $900,000 for six weeks (including a backup capability at IBM's headquarters in upstate New York).[43] As the stations collected observations along various points of the orbit and controllers transmitted them back to Washington by teletype, technicians fed the data into the computer that calculated Vanguard's orbit. The software included corrections for atmospheric drag and the wobble of the orbit due to Earth's bulge. It could give a minute-by-minute position 150 times faster than Vanguard actually flew.[44] The program centered its communications network in Anacostia, in Washington, D.C., from which teletype connections stretched to Cape Canaveral and all of the tracking stations, as well as to the Vanguard Computing Center. From one central location, then, scientists were able to follow and control the whole progress of Vanguard's tracking and data acquisition. Thus Vanguard became the prototype for future satellite systems.[45]

Just before going operational in late 1957, the system faced its first test. All the Minitrack equipment operated on the IGY frequency of 108 MHz, which later became the edge of the civilian FM radio band. In October, 1957, the Soviets' Sputnik satellites operated at 20 MHz and 40 MHz, the same as American ham radio frequencies. Minitrack engineers scrambled to get as many stations as possible retuned for this de facto operational test and to send new oscillators and instructions out to all of the ground stations. Most of the stations never got accurate data on Sputnik, but the stations at Lima, Peru, and San Diego, California, picked up useful tracking data on both *Sputnik 1* and *Sputnik 2*, which launched a month later. The IGY committees had chosen 108 MHz because it would give a more accurate indication of direction for tracking purposes, but the Sputnik frequencies nevertheless yielded information about the ionosphere and its effects on radio frequencies.[46] Sputnik demonstrated that the nascent American tracking system worked, although it had little flexibility.

Vanguard's Minitrack became the nation's first ground-based, space tracking network, but engineers had designed it for only one satellite program and operated it at only one frequency at a time—both major shortcomings. Mini-track operated full-time as a worldwide satellite network, but only in a limited fashion. Minitrack had 35 full-time tracking and data acquisition facilities in operation, and another 15 that were shared or part-time facilities, but the entire network supported a single satellite at a single frequency. In addition, virtually no capability existed for polar orbits, and Minitrack could support only about half of those orbits with inclinations greater than 51 degrees, thus making it virtually worthless for a satellite reconnaissance system reconnoitering the USSR. The only satellite programs fully supportable included those at 35-degree inclinations and transmitting at 108 MHz, like the Vanguard satellite itself. The meager data acquisition capabilities included only low-bandwidth capabilities and also required the use of magnetic tape to record and send data by mail to the central office. Teletype transmitted only the most rudimentary data in real time. Eventually, Minitrack's shortcomings became so pronounced that NASA and the DoD proposed the creation of a national tracking program on the "inescapable premise that no space program is feasible without an adequate ground environment," at a total cost of $41 million for FY 1959.[47] When Vanguard finally orbited successfully, Minitrack served it exceptionally well, but its shortcomings limited its usefulness for an American system of satellite command and control that could support reconnaissance satellites.

Other important developments in satellite command and control occurred on the West Coast. Engineers at JPL generated a number of technical innovations that proved significant in their contributions to the programs that would follow. The receiver in JPL's Microlock—a phase-locked loop tracking system capable of picking up minute signals at great distances (e.g., under ideal conditions, a 1-milliwatt signal 6,000 miles away)—was as an impressive innovation. As adapted in 1955 for the army's Project Orbiter studies (which eventually became Explorer, the first American satellite to achieve orbit), Microlock separated out five telemetry channels. Explorer also included a tape-playback system that made it possible to store and then transmit data when in view of a ground station, which Explorer would not be for most of its orbit. In 1958, *Explorer 3* even contained a miniature tape recorder that moved at the slow speed of 0.005 inches per second, using less than three inches of tape per orbit. This recorder is the archetype of the satellite-based, store-and-forward systems in use today. When a satellite neared a tracking station, a ground signal turned on the satellite's playback head and its high-powered transmitter. In less than five seconds, the satellite sent all its data on the tape, erased it, and reset.[48] Many of Jet Propulsion Laboratory's innovations found their way into satellite programs over the years.

For the scientists and engineers at the Jet Propulsion Laboratory, the problems of tracking Explorer called attention to the need for a worldwide

tracking system. On a dry lake one hundred miles from Pasadena, a huge revolving dish 85 feet in diameter rose out of the Mojave Desert at Goldstone,
California. In those days, because only minimal ambient radio "noise"
reached out that far from Los Angeles and because of the dry desert weather,
Goldstone proved ideally suited to set up the Deep Space Network, soon to
provide support for all aspects of American civilian spaceflight and to become
a vital part of JPL's activities. The Jet Propulsion Laboratory engineers received approval for foreign stations in Australia, Spain, and South Africa.[49]

The American Mercury space program also required a worldwide tracking
network to support its astronauts. Of all of those efforts, NASA had the most
difficulty in establishing a new tracking network from scratch. When flight
surgeons decided they needed to have constant contact with the astronauts,
Mercury program engineers realized they had to create a worldwide tracking
and communications network with gaps of no more than ten minutes. They
knew that the technically immature Minitrack network already in place had
too many gaps in its coverage to meet the flight surgeons' criterion and thus
was inadequate. In February, 1959, the Space Task Group at NASA Langley
put together an ad hoc team that built a telemetry, tracking, and control
network within two years.[50] NASA, therefore, built its second worldwide tracking network to serve the needs of its piloted, low-declination space program.
The Mercury network stretched from the Mission Control Center at Cape
Canaveral to eighteen communications relay stations on three continents,
seven islands, seven foreign countries, and two ships. It used 177,000 miles of
hard-wired communications lines, most of which were leased; 102,000 miles
of teletype; 60,000 miles of telephone lines; and more than 15,000 miles of
high-speed data circuits, all cross-linked and connected to NASA's Goddard
Center in Maryland, where two IBM 7090 computers calculated orbits in real
time.[51] NASA estimated the total cost for the system in 1959 at $41 million.

For the fifth launch of a Mercury spacecraft on board an Atlas booster
(MA-5), the tracking network performed flawlessly. Unfortunately for Enos,
the chimpanzee sitting inside, the same was not true for the incorrectly wired
systems inside the spacecraft, which shocked him repeatedly even though
he did his tasks correctly. The tracking network's first challenge in real time
came near the end of Enos's first orbit, when the trackers noticed that the
spacecraft's clock ticked eighteen seconds fast, and they sent a command to
reset it. The stations in the Canary Islands and Western Australia detected
other problems, but the Woomera, Central Australia, station could not con-
firm them. In late 1961, NASA approved the tracking network for human
flight and prepared MA-6, John Glenn's *Friendship* 7.[52] This tracking network
formed the nucleus of NASA's tracking network for piloted spaceflight all the
way to the moon flight.

The Minitrack and Microlock tracking networks—and their offspring used in Mercury—improved upon and expanded the existing systems; engineers did not invent radically new systems. The later Air Force Satellite Control Facility began its evolution as part of a radical new system of satellite reconnaissance but became essentially a conservative system as well. Ideas about satellite command and control developed similarly inside and outside the air force, but engineers built the networks differently because the space programs had different missions. In effect, therefore, the United States had two tracking networks: one civilian and in the open; one military and in the background.

Invention of Satellite Command and Control in the USSR

Unlike the United States and because of the nature of the totalitarian state, the Soviet Union did not have the artificial distinctions of civil and military space programs. The USSR's space program served state purposes, whether scientific, military, or propagandistic. Interestingly, though, little differentiates the Soviet and American space programs with regard to their general purpose and direction. Both included elements of scientific exploration, technology development, national image building, practical uses, and military support applications. For example, between 1957 and 1981, the U.S. Defense Department conducted about 57 percent of the nation's space flights, including 44 percent for military-only reasons; by 1981, the Soviets had conducted about 66 percent of their successful space flights for "strictly military purposes." Budgetary comparisons are harder to make, but it might be safe to assume that they equate roughly as percentages of gross domestic product, perhaps weighted more to the USSR.[53]

Regardless of the purpose, the Soviet space program had to have a tracking network just like that of the United States to verify space "firsts" and to maintain command and control over satellites. In this regard the Soviet tracking network did not differ from the two U.S. tracking networks. As in the United States, the Soviets developed their tracking network from the systems that were originally designed to evaluate the success of missile test flights.

Historians have already written much about the advanced state of rocketry in the Soviet Union in the years before and after World War II. Even in Imperial Russia, Konstantin Tsiolkovski had speculated about multistage rockets and space stations. Sergei Korolev and his compatriots also tried to create the Soviet space program they wanted within the system they were using, much as has been suggested about Wernher von Braun during and after World War II.[54]

While von Braun and others worked hard on artificial satellites in the United States, Korolev and others did the same in the USSR. The Technical

Documents Liaison Office at Wright-Patterson AFB in Dayton, Ohio (the center of the U.S. Air Force's weapon system program development offices, including reconnaissance satellites until 1956), obtained and translated a copy of a Soviet technical report nominally written by A. Shternfel'd [*sic*], called simply *Artificial Satellites* and classified as top secret. The report covered a variety of subjects on the application and operation of satellites. In these highly technical chapters, Shternfel'd speculated that "three or four ground stations" would be sufficient for the continuous maintenance of communications "with a space radiosonde-satellite flying around the moon." As American engineers and scientists already knew, "[s]ince the operator controlling the space rocket-sonde would be on the earth, telemetering and telecontrolling would have to be provided with a device to compensate [for] the earth's rotation."[55] In fact, the Soviets accomplished much more than just researching and writing about the command and control of artificial satellites.

Contrary to popular opinion, in creating their system of satellite command and control, Soviet space engineers used advanced science and technology. In 1953, in an address to the World Peace Council in Vienna, the president of the USSR Academy of Sciences noted that "Science has reached a state when it is feasible to send a stratoplane to the moon [and] to create an artificial satellite of the earth."[56] Soviet scientist G. I. Pokrovskii speculated that although a satellite the size of a billiard ball would be of sufficient size to be observed from Earth, a "satellite several decimeters in diameter" could be more useful.[57] Soviet scientists and engineers published papers and gave talks in an effort to share knowledge, "provided, of course, this [research] will be directed to the good of mankind, for the progress of science," but also in an effort to show the world that the Soviets' science and engineering capability matched "that of most great countries."[58] Thus, even before the international propaganda success of *Sputnik 1*'s 1957 launch, Soviet scientists and engineers had begun planning for a tracking network, just as their American counterparts had.

The unique Soviet political structure also affected the organization of the Command-Measurement Complex (KIK), which has served every single piloted, interplanetary, scientific, and military space mission from 1957 to the present time. A government decision in January, 1956, following "fierce interministerial wrangling," placed the responsibility for developing a satellite command and control network onto the shoulders of the military.[59] Engineers, scientists, and military officers expended a major effort in creating a ground infrastructure to track and make contact with *Sputnik 1*. After fierce competition between the Academy of Sciences and the Ministry of Defense for the contract to build the telemetry, tracking, and command network, the defense ministry took on the job of satellite command and control. Overseen by Deputy Director Yuriy Mozzhorin, KIK initially comprised seven major stations spread across the USSR—at Tyura-Tam, Makat, Sary-Shagan, Yeniseysk, Iskhup, Yeilzovo, and Klyuchi—euphemistically called "scientific measurement installations" in order to justify the high ranks and salaries of the commanders and personnel, as well as to provide a cover story for the military's involvement.[60]

Scientists and engineers in the USSR positioned their satellite tracking stations in a way that kept their locations secret; at the same time, however, they provided an acceptable environment for communications, power, and living arrangements. At each site the military established new units with their own seal, banner, and guard. They placed the stations in the arid desert or steppe on both sides of the flight trajectories from the Baikonur launch site in Kazakhstan. The stations became independent units with their own supplies, technical support, and financial resources, employing five or six officers and thirty to eighty conscripts. Officers' families lived with them but had no schools or other support facilities. Life at the tracking stations, as in the American systems, grew monotonous when the personnel were not supporting a launch. At first newcomers would feel elated because of the apparent freedom and independence of the isolated sites. Then they would become bored and often volunteered for transfers to anywhere else.[61] In one case, a lieutenant colonel who was appointed commander of one such outpost committed suicide rather than accept his assignment.[62] Although their satellite tracking sites existed in the same sorts of isolated environments, American commanders mostly dealt with alcohol abuse as their main problem.

Soviet engineers, scientists, and military officers created a ground infrastructure capable of centralized satellite command and control. Each station relayed all the tracking and telemetry data to the Coordination-Computation Center, established in Moscow in early 1957, under the command of Pavel A. Agadzhanov.[63] In addition to its responsibility for the missile-tracking network, the ministry of defense was accountable for the tracking, telemetry, and command network for all Soviet satellites. Despite rumors to the contrary about women doing all the calculations by hand, computer facilities in the USSR could easily determine the initial trajectory of a space launch with a high degree of accuracy. Like their competitors in the United States, the Soviets did data processing for orbital calculations as early as 1961 using an advanced digital computer capable of 20,000 operations per second, with another computer probably capable of around 50,000 operations a second. These computer capabilities easily rivaled those of their counterparts in the American space program of the 1960s.[64]

The size of the USSR presented unique problems for the developers of command and control. The Soviet Union stretched two and a half times the width of the United States, but only nine of every twenty-four hours of a satellite's orbit passed over the Eurasian, ground-based tracking network. When tracking requirements became more stringent for the piloted space program—as they did in the Americans' Mercury program—the Soviets added six new ground-based tracking stations. The lack of a global tracking network capable of continuous observation and communication with satellites became the chief limitation on Soviet capabilities for satellite command and control and necessitated another solution.[65] The Soviets filled in the gaps in their tracking coverage primarily with tracking stations on ships, by positioning them at strategic points around the world (similar to the one NASA later used to fill in holes in its coverage, though on a much wider scale). Perhaps reluctant to negotiate or unable to achieve agreements for placing tracking stations in foreign countries as NASA and the American military had, the Soviet Union relied on fully equipped, self-contained, floating tracking stations, which first set sail during the ICBM tests of the late 1950s as part of Pacific Ocean Hydrographic Expedition Number 4.[66] As in the U.S. programs, the satellite command and control ships developed out of the missile-testing program. By the mid-1960s, the tracking ships, including *Kosmonaut Yuri Gagarin* and *Akademik Sergei Korolev,* each displaced at least 17,850 tons, and each had a crew of 121 plus a science team of 118. American ships like the USNS *Hoyt S. Vandenberg* and USNS *Henry H. Arnold* exhibited similar displacements. *Gagarin* reportedly made frequent port calls to Havana.[67]

As in the United States, Soviet engineers sometimes had to improvise in the development of a satellite command and control system. In 1959, when Korolev first began developing interplanetary spacecraft to fly to Mars and Venus, he proposed a dedicated site to build a deep space tracking station, comparable in capability to NASA's deep space tracking network. Because they had a deadline of just eight months, Korolev came up with the ingenious idea of mounting the dishes using leftover parts from the Soviet navy. Construction workers dug a huge crater out of the rocky ground, poured in a foundation, took the revolving gun turret of a former seafaring battleship consigned to the junkyard, and placed it on the foundation. Then workers placed the open framework of a railroad bridge over the turret. The solid hull of a scrapped submarine, to which they fixed the antennas, covered the bridge itself. Eventually the station, located at Yevtaporia on the Black Sea, consisted of three complexes separated by several kilometers: one designed to send commands, and the other two to receive telemetry. Each complex had eight antennas, each one with a diameter of 16 meters and a surface area of 1,000 square meters and a total maximum range of 300 million kilometers. The facility became fully operational on December 30, 1960.[68]

Thus, the Soviet Union created a single satellite command and control network rivaling the two American tracking networks, creating perhaps an economically more efficient network that was able to serve both the civilian scientists and the defense needs of the military, one just as limited by the constraints of politics and society as its American counterparts. Soviet scientists and engineers created their satellite command and control network according to the sociopolitical needs of their highly controlling national system.

Summary

Although separate from the mainstream, the air force did not invent satellite command and control on its own; a variety of scientists and engineers, free from the constraints of large industrial or governmental organizations, developed solutions to the issues that engineers and scientists encountered when working on the problem of satellite command and control. The air force, for example, received assistance from a group of scientific advisors who represented the best minds in the nation and from the RAND Corporation to answer the questions the air force could not resolve alone. Gen. Hap Arnold gave Theodore von Kármán wide latitude for his report, *Toward New Horizons*. Later, Douglas Aircraft's RAND group produced a series of reports on the utility of a "world-circling spaceship," which eventually became the first technical reports in the history of satellite command and control. In addition, General Schriever had unprecedented autonomy in developing the ICBM and the reconnaissance satellite. He did not give details about his programs through normal air force channels but instead reported with the highest national priority directly to the secretary of the air force and the president of the United States.

The inventors of satellite command and control in the United States—scientists and engineers at RAND Corporation, the Naval Research Laboratory (Vanguard's Minitrack), and the Jet Propulsion Laboratory (Explorer's Microlock)—distanced themselves from their larger organizations. Large organizations that are vested in existing technology rarely nurture inventions that by their nature contribute little to the organization and even challenge the status quo, so the air force went outside—to the Scientific Advisory Group and the RAND Corporation—and found answers to questions it could not answer by itself. These scientists and engineers roamed widely and developed solutions to the problems they encountered, according to their own unique situations. RAND's series of reports on the uses for satellites became the first technical reports in the history of satellite command and control and specifically endorsed the idea of satellites for strategic reconnaissance, which fell within the air force's purview.

Ideas about satellite command and control developed similarly inside and outside the air force, but scientists and engineers in the United States built their networks differently because their satellite programs had the very different mission goals of science and military reconnaissance. During the next developmental phase, engineers transformed the invention proposed by the RAND reports into a system of satellite command and control that could support a space-based, satellite reconnaissance system.

2

Of Vital Strategic Importance
Developing a Satellite Command and Control System

*We cannot be fearful of failures and thus attempt only the sure
things, which result only in a short-term gain.*

—*Brig. Gen. Homer A. Boushey*
Air Force Deputy Director of R&D

IN THE EARLY 1950s, nobody knew how to build antennas capable of tracking a low-Earth-orbiting satellite; the air force and its contractors learned
as they went along. During construction of the earliest ground stations to
support the national satellite reconnaissance program, mechanical problems
plagued the command and control antennas on the ground. Because the analog transmitters on board the satellites sent only weak signals, the tracking stations needed big reflectors to acquire the transmissions. Enormous antennas
on the ground also compensated for the limited power available on the satellites. Lockheed and Philco, the Philadelphia-based radio company that served
as Lockheed's subcontractor on the tracking stations, mounted the big parabolic dishes—some 70 feet in diameter—to ensure movement in all three
axes. In high winds technicians had difficulty pointing an antenna with accuracy and stability because the dishes vibrated and oscillated, especially those
that Lockheed furnished. Philco furnished antennas that one former program officer recalled had been "built like battleships." Making the pedestal
for the modified World War II–era SCR-584 radar antennas from inch-and-a-
quarter-thick boilerplate, Philco undertook a major challenge in installing
and outfitting them. In fact, Philco built only two or three of these expensive,
heavy antennas. Because of their great mass, these antennas often came to a
stop accompanied by the screeching of motors and grinding of gears. The
drive motors could just barely move the antennas at a rate that allowed it to

A typical Discoverer/Corona *launch. Courtesy of the Air Force Historical Research Agency collection.*

track a low-orbiting satellite like the reconnaissance satellite, which moved from horizon to horizon in roughly five minutes.

As the technology improved, it became evident that the spacecraft could transmit a stronger signal, meaning that the ground antennas could be lighter. The air force and Lockheed went to a lighter ground antenna, the AN/TLM-

18, which was 60 feet in diameter but with a mesh reflector instead of a solid steel dish. Lockheed supplied and reworked some of the base structures for the TLM-18s several times in order to make them three-axis tracking antennas. After some delay, Lockheed finally completed an expert technical installation of the expensive antennas.[1]

To develop a technology for satellite command and control, engineers constructed test environments that became successively more complex and more like the world that the system would encounter in actual operation. In doing so, the large organization that was inventing and developing the system assigned subprojects and problems to different types of professionals. As engineers strove to develop a support scheme for the reconnaissance satellites, they continued to give the military's system of satellite command and control everything it needed to function in not only the new physical environment of space but also the social environment of politics and high technology.

Incorporating Economic, Political, and Social Characteristics into the System

While developing the technical components of the military's system of satellite command and control, the air force's Western Development Division, aerospace corporation Lockheed, and radio corporation Philco incorporated in their invention the political characteristics it needed to survive in the maze of government agencies. This unexpected intersection of society, politics, economics, and technology, which result in a transformation of one technology's function, exemplifies what historians have come to understand as the social construction of technology. Satellite command and control, therefore, changed from a relatively simple idea into a complex technological system infused with various factors. The Air Force Satellite Control Facility's inventors introduced economic, political, and social changes during its development as it grew and became indispensable to American military satellite command and control.[2]

In 1951, Air Research and Development Command (ARDC) authorized the RAND Corporation to make specific recommendations for the start of developmental work on a reconnaissance satellite system. RAND recommended in Project Feed Back that as a matter of "vital strategic importance" the air force should begin studying the "use of an efficient satellite reconnaissance vehicle."[3] After reading the Project Feed Back reports that addressed matters such as orbital mechanics and satellite photography of Earth, Major William G. King Jr. became convinced that these capabilities could be realized in the near future. The RAND studies and King's own earlier observation of ballistic missile launches at both the White Sands Army Proving Ground in New Mexico and the Joint Proving Grounds in Florida persuaded him that the

United States could perform military missions in space. King subsequently helped establish the official Advanced Reconnaissance System Program Office. After briefing the secretary of the air force, King used $2 million for systems concept studies of military satellites.[4]

RAND sold ARDC on the idea of satellites by proposing them as a system designed to test the feasibility of building a satellite, complete with estimates of costs, development time, and critical design criteria. In early 1953, ARDC's program office for the Advanced Reconnaissance System recommended the acceptance of the RAND proposal for letting a system design contract within one year. Unfortunately, from December, 1953, to January, 1954, ARDC did little beyond documenting the reconnaissance satellite proposal as Project Number 409-40, "Satellite Component Study," engineering project MX-2226, ARDC M-80-4, Project 1115; tentatively assigning it the designation Weapon System 117L; and giving it the unclassified name "Advanced Reconnaissance System."

Although convinced of the utility of a satellite for reconnaissance, King still had to sell it to the air force as an operational system, not just a fancy research project. Strategic Air Command (SAC), the air force's nuclear command responsible for President Eisenhower's doctrine of massive retaliation, expressed interest in the uses of the Advanced Reconnaissance System. In mid-1955, King traveled from ARDC headquarters in Dayton to SAC headquarters in Omaha, Nebraska, to speak about the Advanced Reconnaissance System. At the start of King's "sales pitch," someone yelled "Attention!" and everybody stood up. In walked SAC Commander in Chief General LeMay with "half-a-dozen of his horse holders." King usually introduced his presentation by saying, "I'm here to tell you about the Advanced Reconnaissance System, the ARS. 'The arse.' Now, some of you people don't know your 'ARS' from a hole in the ground, and I'm going to straighten you out." He often got a laugh, but this time, with the hard-nosed, cigar-chewing General LeMay sitting right in front of him, King decided not to use his "arse" joke. A young major in front of an air force legend, King started his presentation a little awkwardly, but he thought the general was paying attention. Afterward, King knew for sure that he was. LeMay walked by King and said, "How did you fellows justify your TDY [travel money] to come in and tell me such crap?"[5] LeMay, a career pilot and the person responsible for strategic aerial reconnaissance as SAC's commander in chief, roundly rejected the idea of satellite-based reconnaissance, which he had actually initiated in the air force when he served as chief of research and development (R&D) for the air service. Later, LeMay became a supporter of satellite-based reconnaissance, but at the outset satellite systems required a tough sell.

Unfortunately for the space enthusiasts, the air force did not commit itself to fight for the embryonic satellite program. No operational air force command bought into the idea of a reconnaissance satellite, so it fell to ARDC to define and develop the entire Advanced Reconnaissance System. Even though the air force decided on November 27, 1954, to support a reconnaissance satellite program, and even though ARDC published System Requirement Number 5, covering satellite reconnaissance, the air force still allocated no funds at all for development. The ARS remained a research project until March 16, 1955, when Air Force Headquarters published General Operations Requirement number 80, which called for the development of a satellite reconnaissance vehicle for use by a combat command.

In the 1950s, politics and space never strayed too far from the other. The first American policy statement on space came from the National Security Council (NSC) on May 20, 1955, in the classified document NSC 5520, "Draft Statement of Policy on U.S. Scientific Satellite Program." President Eisenhower was intensely interested in the discussions of the National Security Council, often attended meetings, and took an active role in the deliberations, which considered three satellite programs in early 1955, including WS-117L.[6] The policy statement stressed the political benefits of having the first satellite launched under the auspices of the International Geophysical Year (IGY). According to the NSC's report, DoD studies indicated that the United States could launch a small scientific satellite weighing 5 to 10 pounds into orbit using adaptations of existing rockets.[7] This small project fit well within President Eisenhower's vision for space. The United States had an official American IGY entry, Vanguard, but the country still had no national policy on satellite reconnaissance.

The NSC also recognized the need for "tracking facilities" as part of the overall cost of the program despite the small American IGY effort. Unfortunately, it is not entirely clear from the NSC statement just what "tracking" meant. It might have meant just watching satellites through passive, visual means, or it may have actually meant command and control of space vehicles. The NSC concluded that if they decided to embark on a space program promptly, the country would probably be able to establish and track such a satellite within the two-year period from 1957 to 1958. The NSC estimated that $20 million would guarantee a small scientific satellite for the IGY, allowing for "adequate . . . observation costs," implying visual observation. That estimate included $2.5 million for "instrumentation for tracking" and another $2.5 million for "logistics for launching and tracking."[8] Looking carefully at Annex A, the technical appendix to NSC 5520, the details become clear what "tracking" the scientific satellite meant; the NSC, still largely concerned with passive, optical tracking of the IGY satellite, understood the advantages of "electronic techniques" for tracking.

The NSC insightfully recognized the need for satellite command and control and its political consequences for the entire U.S. satellite program. Any satellite fixed in a highly elliptical orbit, for example, 200 miles by 1,000 miles, passes completely around Earth in about ninety minutes. If controllers selected an orbit over Earth's poles or one inclined to the equator, a satellite passed successively farther west of the launching point on each revolution because Earth rotates under the satellite's orbit. Significant for command and control, an individual tracking station set up for inclined orbits cannot be in an observing position for every revolution. Therefore, as we have already seen, the optimum location for tracking polar orbits is at or near the poles because they do not rotate from a satellite's orbit and instead pass underneath the satellite on each orbit.

Despite the great idea, polar tracking stations had their own political problems. In 1955, the United States had a base near the North Pole, at Thule Air Base in Greenland, a Danish possession. At that time the air force based thousands of American airmen and B-52 bombers at Thule, where they flew on hair-trigger nuclear alert. The United States also had a presence on Antarctica, at the South Pole, which American policy and later the 1959 Antarctica Treaty protected from any military activity. Neither polar-based option seemed useful for scientific purposes because of the poles' distance from the continental United States and the difficulty in reaching them, both physically and electronically. A more inclined orbit, however, especially one inclined at 90-degrees and nearly polar, substantially reduced the usable data per station for scientific experiments based on passive, optical observations.

An orbit around the equator made for a better political solution in the mid-1950s. Such an orbit, at low latitudes, did not pass over hostile territory and placed a tracking station in a position to observe most satellite revolutions. The usefulness of the IGY scientific satellite and the selection of a desirable orbit depended on the degree to which the satellite could be both acquired and tracked by electronic or optical techniques. NSC 5520 suggested, therefore, that the United States set up tracking stations to gather data on the new satellite at the Navy Air Missile Test Center, Point Mugu, California; the Naval Ordnance Test Station, Inyokern, California; White Sands Proving Ground, New Mexico; the British-Australian Guided Missile Range, Woomera, Australia, and at a number of astronomical observatories, presumably for passive, optical observations as Earth rotated under the satellite.[9] While the NSC debated the political issues related to a scientific satellite, the air force continued to plan for a tracking system for a reconnaissance satellite, which needed polar orbits.

Based on the RAND studies in early 1955, the Advanced Reconnaissance System program office in Ohio issued a request for proposal (RFP) that was targeted at specific companies to whom the air force would issue development contracts. When the RFP for WS-117L went out, the air force gave the ARS a new program name: Pied Piper. Lockheed, Glenn L. Martin Co., and RCA all decided to submit proposals. The air force offered Bell Labs and IBM, two other electronics firms, money to study the idea, although both declined.[10] The air force provided $1 million to Lockheed, Martin, and RCA for research, which gave the corporations plenty of latitude.

Observers outside the air force assumed that RCA, a big electronics firm heavy in data processing, had the upper hand over the two, old-school airplane companies, Martin and Lockheed. These observers did not take into consideration the fact that the airplane companies had an important advantage over RCA: They had been involved in selling systems to the air force for years, so they understood the air force's procurement system much better than RCA did. Martin and RCA recommended an electronic video system, not too far removed from RAND's original proposal for a readout satellite, but the narrowness of their proposal hurt them both.[11] The air force accepted neither RCA's nor Martin's bid.

Lockheed's president, L. Eugene Root, on the other hand, enlisted some of the best minds in the burgeoning space industry to help his company's proposal. A former RAND employee himself, Root recruited Robert Salter, Bruno Augenstein, William Fry, and Sidney Brown from the original team of RAND's "world-circling spaceship" engineers and scientists. Augenstein eventually became chief scientist of Lockheed's satellite program and then moved on to the defense department, working under Harold Brown, defense director of research and engineering during the Kennedy and Johnson administrations. James W. Plummer, a Salter protégé, later served as under secretary of the air force and director of the National Reconnaissance Office in the Nixon and Ford administrations. Other engineers and scientists joined Lockheed, and together they made a difference for the airplane manufacturer that was trying to make its way into the realm of space contractors.[12]

Because of its unique combination of experienced scientists and engineers, Lockheed took a broader approach to the problem of satellite reconnaissance and included both video and film reconnaissance systems in its proposal to ARDC. Louis Ridenour, formerly of MIT's Radiation Laboratory and the first chief scientist of the air force, presented Lockheed's proposal to ARDC and very much impressed the review board. Lockheed included in its proposal a host of other functions for the satellite system besides visual (photo) reconnaissance, including infrared surveillance and communications surveillance. Lockheed also wrote the proposal in the ARDC format for development plans, spelling out the system requirements, their plans for developing the system, their approach to training personnel, their strategy for maintaining and operating the system, and even their proposed locations for

the tracking stations.[13] According to Robert Salter, Lockheed's proposal orig-
inated the requirement for launch facilities at Camp Cooke, on California's
central coast, not far from El Segundo, "which Schriever liked because he
wanted something up there. He received that with open arms."[14] In short, unlike the competition, Lockheed put forward a complete satellite system to the
air force. General Schriever recalled later that "it turned out that the companies which had been engaged in aircraft weapon development were among
the most competent companies in the country for undertaking this new work
[space]."[15] Either way, Lockheed clearly stood out from its competitors.

In the days before Sputnik, reconnaissance satellite advocates had to convince national political and military leaders not only that such a satellite could
serve national defense but also that the air force had the R&D capability for
the program. In 1956, the air force tried to speed along development by colo-
cating all space and missile development in El Segundo, California, which
moved the space program away from the aeronautical systems center at Wright-
Patterson AFB. Despite the move, the entire reconnaissance program budget
still came to only $4 or $5 million for studies, analyses, and experimental work
in laboratories.[16] For quite some time the Western Development Division tried
to convince its investors, the Eisenhower administration, to approve a full-scale
development.

General Schriever's deputy in El Segundo, Osmond J. Ritland, arrived in
April, 1956, as a colonel. Schriever immediately assigned Ritland the task of
reporting on the status of the reconnaissance satellite program to the president's scientific advisory board. Ritland gathered together a combined air
force-industry team, made up mostly of air force engineers, experts in photography from Eastman Kodak, and specialists in satellite hardware from
Lockheed. They presented the status of the reconnaissance satellite, still a research program, and recommended that the air force vigorously pursue an
operational reconnaissance satellite (identified then as a "data readout system," which the air force would later call the Sentry program). Ritland and his
team left the meeting with the impression that they had convinced the government to accelerate the program. Still, nothing happened because Air
Force Secretary James H. Douglas Jr. felt that the engineers still "overesti-
mated" the roles that satellites in orbit might play.[17]

In June, 1956, General Schriever officially announced that the review
board had selected Lockheed over RCA and Martin as the prime contractor
for the WS-117L program, still known as Pied Piper, but then the reconnaissance satellite system suffered another setback. On April 2, the Western Development Division had published a development plan for WS-117L, calling
for full, initial operational capability by 1963 and R&D costs of $153 million.[18]
The air force approved the development plan for Pied Piper on July 24, 1956,

but allocated a mere $4.7 million, only 3 percent of Lockheed's estimate.
In November, new Air Force Secretary Donald A. Quarles told the Western
Development Division to cease development on the scientific satellite idea.
"Don't bend any metal," Quarles told them, knowing that the United States
already had a very public, scientific satellite program with its own tracking
network, Vanguard.[19]

Domestic political debates about space prevented major funding for the
reconnaissance satellite program. The United States had yet to decide which
organization should have responsibility for space. Senior air force leaders
wanted to make sure that the government and the public thought of the air
force as the nation's space service. In a November, 1957, speech to the National Press Club, Air Force Chief of Staff Gen. Thomas D. White, echoing the
theme that Gen. Hoyt S. Vandenberg had first articulated in 1948, once again
asserted the air force's claim to space:

> In speaking of the control of air and the control of space, I want to
> stress that there is no division, per se, between air and space. Air and
> space are an indivisible field of operations. . . . Ninety-nine percent of
> the earth's atmosphere lies within 20 miles of the surface of the earth.
> It is quite obvious that we cannot control the air up to 20 miles and re-
> linquish control of space above that altitude . . . and still survive.[20]

Thereafter, White frequently used the term "aerospace" to make his point that
the air force should be the service that would implement all military missions
above Earth's surface.

White's efforts to claim space for the air force did not stop with speeches.
The air force released the 1959 edition of *Air Force Manual 1-1* (AFM 1-1),
United States Air Force Basic Doctrine, with references to "space" as an operational air force mission. Issued under General White's signature, the manual
used "aerospace power" in place of the old term "air power." AFM 1-1 also
abandoned the idea of gaining a "dominant position in the air" in favor of an
objective of obtaining "general supremacy in the aerospace":

> The aerospace is an operationally indivisible medium consisting of
> the total expanse beyond the earth's surface. The forces of the Air
> Force comprise a family of operating systems—air systems, ballistic
> missiles, and space vehicle systems. These are the fundamental aero-
> space forces of the nation. . . . That nation, or group of nations, which
> maintains predominance in the aerospace—not only its military
> forces but also in its sciences and technologies—will have the means
> to prevail in conflict.[21]

Because air power and space power both operated above Earth's surface, the air force took the position that the United States should vest control of these areas in a single military service that, whatever its official name, would be *the* aerospace force. Thus by 1959, the air force had convinced itself that it should take the lead in space operations, but it had not convinced anyone else, especially not the supreme political and military authority in the United States, President Eisenhower.

On October 4, 1957, everything changed. RAND, which had defined the feasibility of using a satellite for reconnaissance within the current state of the art in its April, 1951, secret report, stepped again to the forefront. RAND's report had languished in the "back of the files" until Sputnik's dramatic October launch, when, said RAND's space pioneer Scott J. King, "You never saw a file opened so dammed fast in your life!" King remembered people saying, "'What the hell did RAND say back there? Let's get cracking on this thing.'"[22] Recalled General Schriever, "When Sputnik went up . . . everybody was saying, 'Why the god dammed hell can't you go faster? Who's in charge here?'"[23] The air force accelerated the reconnaissance satellite program but did not move it into the fast lane. Instead, the service spent funds on its major strategic nuclear buildup and pushed the development of ICBMs, all the while leaving satellites at a lower priority.

The air force's Scientific Advisory Board, which had first suggested the study of pilotless aircraft in *Toward New Horizons,* urged rapid acceleration of the reconnaissance satellite program. In a May, 1956, report, the board recommended a "VIGOROUS SUPPORT AND EXPANSION" [*sic*] of the reconnaissance satellite program because

> To launch a group of satellite vehicles and maintain them in orbits several hundred miles above the earth seems to all of us a great enterprise linked to the traditions of . . . the Wright Brothers' airplane. . . . The instrumented earth satellite is one of the most exciting adventures in the Air Force research and development program.[24]

In a December, 1957, memo to Air Force Chief of Staff Gen. Hoyt S. Vandenberg, Scientific Advisory Board chair (and National Advisory Committee on Aeronautics chair) Jimmy Doolittle urged the acceleration of the reconnaissance satellite development program.[25] In a planned speech before the Air War College in 1957, Air Force Undersecretary for Research and Development Trevor Gardner also urged a more rapid development of "the so-called space satellites."[26]

When the CIA got involved, the entire nature of the reconnaissance satellite program changed, but the Air Force Satellite Control Facility did not. The

CIA had had the U-2 for overhead reconnaissance for some time, but that air-craft had limited capability, and President Eisenhower employed it only re-luctantly. Eisenhower also did not want to admit publicly that the United States had an active reconnaissance satellite R&D program, particularly after Soviet Premier Nikita Khrushchev rejected the "Open Skies" proposal. As a re-sult, the Western Development Division deputy commander, Col. Ritland, sat down with Richard Bissell at the CIA and created the Discoverer cover story about a bioenvironmental satellite test program. The two had successfully created the U-2 reconnaissance aircraft and teamed up again on the recon-naissance satellite. The new, covert, CIA-led reconnaissance system received a quick go-ahead for development. Publicly, the air force now was authorized to develop a prototype demonstration satellite capability using a Thor IRBM with an upper stage, whose stated aim was to provide a demonstration of launch, orbit, and recovery. Privately, the CIA acted as the overall program manager, using the air force's resources and contractors to do the job, a re-turn to the arrangements of the U-2 development program. Thus, although the air force started it, it was primarily the CIA that funded the reconnaissance satellite program, hiding it in plain sight.[27]

Reconnaissance satellite advocates and their associates embodied in WS-117L the political characteristics it needed to survive in the maze of govern-ment agencies. In addition, it had the sponsorship of a major American defense contractor, Lockheed, and a major government development agency, now renamed as the Air Force Ballistic Missile Division (AFBMD) in El Se-gundo. As the invention changed from a relatively simple idea into a complex system, the military's system of satellite command and control experienced economic, political, and social changes in its development, ultimately grow-ing and becoming indispensable to American satellite command and control.

Systems Engineering in the Air Force Satellite Control Facility

In 1954, General Schriever's Western Development Division began using a particular management scheme to develop the Atlas ICBM, which it called "concurrency." The new management system stemmed from the realization that neither industry nor the air force then had a sufficient in-house ability to undertake the broad technical management of ballistic missile weapon sys-tems, while the urgency of the international military situation called for strong measures to expedite the program. Schriever, therefore, surrounded himself with an unusually competent group of scientists and engineers who were capable of analyzing systems, supervising the research phases, and con-trolling the experimental and hardware phases of the ICBM program. As the aerospace industry's competence increased, a number of companies appeared on the scene fully capable of managing the development of weapon systems of similar complexity.[28]

On the other hand, the air force's in-house capabilities to plan, analyze, and procure complex systems did not reach the point where the service could direct the development of such systems without contracted assistance from companies with exceptional scientific and technical competence. This problem also extended to the air force's space programs, which Schriever handled in El Segundo. Technical assistance, therefore, had to come from a civilian contractor with a privileged position. The problem became one of balancing the urgent need for rapid development with the lack of technical skill in the air force while giving no favoritism to one contractor over another. The air force itself recognized that any appearance of impropriety would endanger its relationship with the contractors it would need to build a successful space and missile program.[29]

The air force did not use systems engineering in the WS-117L program, although one former program manager wishes it had.[30] Because of this important context, it is worth investigating the character of systems engineering and technical direction as well as the way the concept affected the technological style of the Air Force Satellite Control Facility. The concept is still important today in the Air Force Satellite Control Network; in fact, the network could not operate without the stations' network integrators, who are experts in station technical configuration.[31]

General Schriever and the leaders of ICBM development understood that the air force did not have the expertise to build a major space system. In the 1950s no one in the air force had a strong background in ballistic missiles. They also knew that no single company in the United States had the overall ability to develop and manage the ICBM program on its own. To solve this dilemma, they found companies throughout the United States with the most expertise in the various subsystems of guidance, propulsion, and so on. The ICBM principals also believed that no company had the management skills to develop the ICBM. Even these missile zealots knew the air force could not transition completely from airplanes to missiles; the ICBM was simply another weapon system for strategic and political warfare.[32] The missile development leadership decided to recruit some of the best brains in the United States into a new type of management organization, a specifically technical supervisory group. The Ramo-Wooldridge Corporation, which had split off from Hughes Corporation, had a nucleus of about fifty, highly technical people who had been involved in the initial study of the ICBM. Schriever decided that together they could provide the needed management skills for the ICBM program as an associate contractor.[33]

Simon Ramo served as executive vice president of Ramo-Wooldridge, later Thompson-Ramo-Wooldridge (TRW). He knew that the ICBM and the reconnaissance satellite had complex technical problems covering a large number of disciplines that the technical direction contractor had to pull together. To meet this need, he recruited people from various fields—aerodynamics, control, heat generation, and so on. Ramo also recruited a peculiar form of generalist that he thought of as a "systems engineer," someone who could understand enough of each of the pieces and communicate ideas well. In other words, these systems engineers became the integrating contractor by understanding the trade-offs and determining what to give or add so that the engineers could make the weapon system compatible and harmonious.[34]

To reduce the possibility of a conflict of interest, TRW split off the part of the company that was engaged in manufacturing and created a wholly owned subsidiary called Space Technology Laboratories (STL), with retired air force Gen. Jimmy Doolittle as chair. Schriever, Ramo later said, wanted STL to be a transitional activity that would do the systems engineering and technical direction for the space and missile programs.[35] STL recruited people from all over the country and at one time had more than twenty-five people on two- or three-year leaves of absence from top American universities working in California on the ICBM problem.[36] In theory, STL obtained the best talent, drew on their expertise, and then returned them to their universities.

While the air force built the space and missile program, Space Technology Laboratories played the primary role in describing the various tasks—without building anything. For instance, what did the reentry contractor do? STL's contract included defining those tasks. The air force, that is, General Schriever, always made the final decision, and he had some good colonels helping him. Then a separate group, consisting only of military people, made up a list of contractors eligible for competition and invited them to bid on a particular project. STL made a detailed presentation about the task and answered the questions from the visiting contractors. Ramo personally involved himself heavily in these presentations. STL listened to the recommendations of the invited contractors and then carefully read their proposals. STL commented on the substance of the proposals, analyzed, and rated them. After the presentations, STL's experts stepped back. Because the military had additional criteria for the selection, they made the final choice. For example, the air force considered a company's record in previous, particularly recent, procurements. How did it adhere to the niceties of contract control? How did the air force auditors view the company? Then, everything else being presumably equal, the air force awarded the contract to the company that needed it the most and had people to assign to the project.[37]

Colonel Osmond Ritland joined the missile development team in Los Angeles in 1956 as General Schriever's deputy. Ritland felt that the decision for

Space Technology Laboratories to oversee the systems engineering and technical development made sense—that is, until STL decided to get into the hardware business as well. STL proposed the first Delta stage, built from the Thor vehicle, but Schriever's system forced STL to turn the drawings over to another contractor, in this case Douglas Aircraft, which built the launch vehicle. When Schriever got permission to proceed with WS-117L production, STL wanted part of the production business. It found the answer in creating Aerospace Corporation, a new, noncompetitive organization, because STL, the technical direction contractor, a for-profit company, had insight into profit-making opportunities. Aerospace Corporation became responsible for the ballistic missile and space-oriented engineering, research, and planning projects that STL had previously performed. By January, 1961, seven months after incorporation, Aerospace Corporation's staff totaled about 1,700 employees and the company added 900 more over the next five months, including 600 technical people.[38] The new, nonprofit Aerospace Corporation, a captive, government-controlled organization, had sole responsibility for systems engineering and technical direction, with no authority but to make recommendations.[39]

The systems engineering and technical direction contractor provided valuable continuity in this major weapon system development program. Air force officers moved every three years, sometimes faster. Now a retired Philco employee, Howie Althouse moved from operations and maintenance to system integration in 1966 and spent the next twenty-nine years in integration and engineering, providing continuity and direction for the program. "The last [five] years of my management career [were] spent trying to provide direction and remind the customer what the job was! All the customer seemed to be able to focus on was budget[; they] had no idea what the job was!"[40] According to one former military operator, the air force relied on the contractors because the military service did not have the capability itself: "The guys in the blue suits were way over their heads" in part because of the military's philosophy of giving young officers more responsibility early in their careers than most of their counterparts in industry. Said retired Col. Mel Lewin, one of the first air force officers to operate a satellite, "We were operating at a level far beyond that which we would be operating if we had been out in industry. Most of us were pretty young. I think we needed industry and I think they did a good job." Developing a space command and control capability at that time with military engineers would have been difficult. The air force simply did not have people with an adequate background in the nuts and bolts of satellites.[41] A former military satellite operator put it this way: "If you're not violating the laws of physics, you can do anything with enough resources. You can go to the moon in ten years. This country did that. The challenge is trying to get the job done on limited resources. That's the challenge of the Air Force today."[42] Doing the job with limited resources continues to be the challenge both inside and outside government today, and the purpose of integrating contractors is to ensure it gets done right.

Not everyone believed that systems engineering and technical direction would be the solution to all of the air force's technical problems. According to retired Col. Tom Haig, contracting out system engineering and technical direction robbed air force personnel of the opportunity to assume true responsibility and authority in engineering situations—circumstances requiring an engineering background—and kept them from doing good, original, and responsible work. Instead, systems engineering and technical direction made engineers into managers:

> There is no reason why you can't write a contract with a contractor for the technical direction part of a program, as well as the production part, within his own company and use your own engineers, then, as participants in this program and as people who do their engineering and direct the contractor properly. I'm completely convinced that the "blue suiters" that I have met are at least the equal to anybody I ever met in STL, Aerospace, or Ramo-Wooldridge.[43]

In Haig's mind, the air force could not retain engineers it had paid to put through school in the first place, thus wasting time, money, and effort. The whole Ramo-Wooldridge concept of a systems engineering and technical direction assignment outside of the direct line between the producer and the government had been highly detrimental to the air force, Haig felt, and far outweighed its benefits. "Aerospace turns right around and . . . talks a guy that's in the air force into resigning or retiring and then hires him, and then the air force pays for him at double or triple the salary over there at Aerospace Corporation. It's stupid. It's a dumb system. And the air force is the only service that really does this."[44] The army departed from its arsenal system at Huntsville but then stopped using systems engineering and technical direction contractors. The navy also does not now use systems engineering and technical direction contractors; only the air force does so and continues to believe in the practice, which is consistent with the close cooperation between the air force and industry that has existed since the birth of the military airplane and continued through *Toward New Horizons*.

Haig also believed that the systems engineering and technical direction concept made satellite systems development larger and more costly than necessary. Removing the experts from overseeing the contractor led to vast increases in costs. When he left the weather satellite program four years after starting it, only fifteen people worked in the program office. The office had grown from five to fifteen people, mostly because five officers from SAC, the planned eventual operator of the satellites, constantly rotated through the office to learn the system. The office also had more secretaries. "God, we'd gotten up to four secretaries," recalled Haig, "so we still had about six productive people, about five SAC people, and four secretaries to handle the increasing amount of paperwork as we moved toward 'normalization,'" the placing of the weather satellite program under standard government procurement regulations.[45] Haig achieved operational capability for the weather satellite program with one secretary, four air force engineers, and a contractor that built the satellites, and without a systems engineering and technical direction contractor at any time while he ran the program.

After he retired in 1968 as assistant director for R&D for the NRO, Haig had occasion to visit his old program office in California. It had grown to 120 military and civilian people and an equal number of Aerospace Corporation employees. They managed exactly the same program but had no development work because the contractor had already built the ground stations by that point. In addition, the program office had no more booster development work to do. The program office only *monitored* the contract for the satellites. Unfortunately, they managed the program so poorly that the National Reconnaissance Program went without weather satellite support for more than two years. (The National Reconnaissance Office originally intended the weather satellites to fly ahead of the Corona vehicles so that the camera operators could set the cameras to take pictures of targets on the ground rather than cloud formations, meaning less wasted film.[46]) According to Haig, "What happened was that they 'normalized' everything. They went back under the 375-series [procurement] regulations, and in five years they had had six program directors. The air force was assigning nonengineer fighter pilots as program directors to get that on their records so they could be promoted."[47] General Ritland had pointed out— although he could do nothing about it—that a single officer in charge of a satellite program office for a reasonable period of time could do a better job than if the leadership style changed four times under four different officers. Each officer had a tendency to impose different directions on a given program. Even the personality involved in a change slowed a program down while the people got used to the new leadership. Ritland believed that such rotation consumed time and led to inefficiency but air force policy favored these transfers in order to expose officers to different experiences, broadening their careers.[48]

During his visit, Colonel Haig wanted to learn the details of the latest sensors going on the spacecraft at that time. When he asked a program officer whether he knew about the devices, the officer pointed to the shelves behind him and said, "It's all there in those books." "Have you read the books?" Haig asked. "Oh, no, I don't have to read that shit," the officer answered.[49] Haig started the weather satellite program office with only a handful of people, and he knew everything about the spacecraft. Lou Ricks, an air force captain in the office, knew everything about ground operations and in fact simplified the whole tracking procedure by creating a lot of nomograms (i.e., charts that represent numerical relationships between multiple variables; they are used for predictions) and tables, entirely eliminating the necessity for a computer to do the tracking. Ricks got the angles from the tracking stations for the first couple of passes, put them through his nomograms, and came up with the orbital parameters; this sort of tabular statement is called an ephemeris. Then he predicted the next satellite pass over a tracking station and refined his ephemeredes after two or three supports, achieving greater accuracy each time.[50] This method was certainly easier than using a massive number of punched computer cards, but Ricks's system still relied on the expertise of one person to do the job.

Similarly, the father of the solid-fueled Minuteman ICBM felt the same way about systems engineering and technical direction, calling it "the biggest mistake ever made."[51] Before leaving the Air Force Ballistic Missile Division in 1958, Col. Edward N. Hall, who had been in Los Angeles since 1954, wrote a severe, fifteen-page, typed, single-spaced memorandum. In it he suggested that Johannes Kepler had reduced the physical laws of ballistic missiles to mathematics long before the Cold War, making ballistic missiles far simpler than bombers or even most jet fighters. Hall felt that the importance of having a ballistic missile to counter a Soviet ICBM drove the air force's adoption of the systems engineering and technical direction method. However, by continually deferring to "relatively naïve" groups of scientists and encouraging them to believe they possessed a unique competence in the development of complex weapon systems, the air force destroyed its own ability to carry out its assigned task of defending the nation.[52]

Certainly the answer lies somewhere in between. Looking at both sides of the issue reveals the technological style driving the creation of the Air Force Satellite Control Facility, which is why it is important to look at the systems engineering and technical direction method in this context, too. They contributed greatly to the creation of the air force system of satellite command and control by integrating not just blue-suit operators and contractors, but also contractors outside the normal procurement system into its construction. The air force thus achieved a space-based reconnaissance capability faster than they could have done it without industry's cooperation.

Assigning Problems to Others

Before further expanding the invention into an operational satellite command and control system, the Air Force Ballistic Missile Division and its partner, Lockheed, had to determine how to handle an increasingly large number of projects and subprojects. Its origin as Subsystem H of Weapon System 117L meant that the Air Force Satellite Control Facility supported an R&D program to demonstrate the air force's capabilities for the launch, command, control, and recovery of instrumented space vehicles for reconnaissance. In January, 1958, a few months after *Sputnik 1*'s launch, the reconnaissance satellite system received formal but covert government approval, and in March, 1958, the air force issued a contract to Lockheed for five ground stations.

The air force divided its satellite project into three distinct satellite programs but identified the command and control function separately from all three. This function consisted of a control center, called the Satellite Test Center, and a number of remote tracking stations with all the equipment and software required to track and control satellites during ascent, orbit (called "on-orbit"), and recovery operations. Lockheed planned to put the test center near its facility in Sunnyvale, California. The air force agreed to Sunnyvale because of Lockheed's major presence there and the room available there for growth at the time. Close quarters at the Air Force Ballistic Missile Division headquarters prevented the locating of an operational activity in Los Angeles. The AFBMD called the small group of air force people in Sunnyvale a Field Test Force. Originally located in a Palo Alto Lockheed facility, two people staffed the Field Test Force: one air force lieutenant colonel and one Lockheed engineer. Subsequently, AFBMD designated them as a separate military unit reporting to General Schriever; Lt. Col. Charles A. ("Moose") Mathison served as the first commander.[53]

To handle a satellite's requirements, engineers had to add specific equipment, subsystems, and the remote tracking stations to the Satellite Test Center's network. At first, an antenna connected to a specific receiver interfaced with its own program-specific control, display, and command equipment. Telephones and a 100-word-per-minute teletype circuit connected the ground sites to the Satellite Test Center in Sunnyvale. Computers both on the ground and in orbit on spacecraft remained a few years in the future. The equipment at existing remote tracking stations required hours or even days to reconfigure and check out for each of the several programs the air force was developing. The unwillingness of contractors involved in the development of satellite hardware to cooperate with Lockheed, particularly in the sharing of information, also caused problems because they suspected that Lockheed would gain an advantage in future satellite procurement competitions.[54]

Nevertheless, a cooperative mood settled over the Air Force Ballistic Missile Division in the late 1950s as the air force tried to get the Atlas ICBM built in record time. In testimony before Congress, General Schriever called the ICBM a "team effort of industry, science, and the military." The same mood applied to the air force's relationship with its prime satellite contractor, Lockheed. Cooperation did not mean a lack of competition. Schriever spoke generally about competition in 1956 congressional testimony:

> [Our] philosophy in the program has been competition in two senses: competition among contractors and competitive approaches. We feel that this will get us there sooner, better, [and] cheaper and will also provide us a technical backup in case one of these things should fall on its face—which is always a possibility.[55]

Given the limited budget they had to work with and the national urgency they had added to their goals, cooperation—indeed partnership—between the air force and the prime contractor added to the chances of success.

Not everyone believed that the contractors worked in the government's best interest. A Lockheed subcontractor, Fenski, Federick, and Miller, installed a projection system meant to allow the satellite operators to gather information in three dimensions. Wearing polarized glasses, not unlike those that teenagers wore in movie theaters in the 1950s, satellite operators could see three-dimensional (3D) images projected on the screens through two slide projectors. The machine etched the flight of a launched booster on the surface of a smoked glass plate with a little stylus. As the stylus went through, it cut off the smoke, projecting a 3D image of the superimposed trace.

Air force Col. Tom Haig, responsible for the ground station portion of the satellite command and control system, believed that 3D carried to the brain only about 2 percent of the information that 2D did, making the new display system a useless tool for making decisions. When Haig arrived in Sunnyvale for a familiarization tour of the control center, the Fenski, Federick, and Miller technician had been trying to install the 3D system for almost a week. What Haig saw appalled him. He talked to the technician, who thought the system would never function. With his mechanical engineering background, Haig also believed the 3D system was "a monstrosity" that could never work. Haig went back to his office in El Segundo and wrote a memo instructing Lockheed to cancel the subcontract, recover all of the funds, and remove the equipment. When Gen. Schriever approved Haig's request, Lockheed knew Haig had arrived in the program. Although he had certainly saved the government "maybe several hundred thousand to maybe a couple million [dollars]" by simplifying the satellite control center, Haig also made the control

Satellite Test Center, main control room, 1960. Courtesy of the National Reconnaissance Office collection.

room functional instead of "a fancy, elaborate place. . . . They made it fancy enough, God knows, but at least we took that part out."[56] Despite the large amounts of money floating around AFBMD and the reconnaissance satellite program's status as a national priority, officers still tried to save tax dollars.

The air force also had its share of unsavory characters that made cooperation difficult. When Philco integrator Althouse transferred to the station integration office at the New Boston Tracking Station in New Hampshire, he encountered some disagreeable officers. The contractors had cubicles in a building with an air force major and his staff who acted as the contract monitors. The major distrusted the contractors and listened in on their phone conversations with the home office, read company correspondence left on desks, and stayed late every night. The contractors retaliated several times by leaving phony memos and noting the specific location where they had placed things the night before. After the major moved on, Althouse finally felt he could work without having to look over his shoulder.[57]

At other times the whole unit, contractors and military, enjoyed stationwide picnics or ball games. At the New Boston tracking station, a team effort in the

conservation program won air-force-wide awards for safeguarding the environment. In addition, over the years, a basewide effort transformed some of the
2,800 acres into a recreational park for the military community in New En-
gland, not an easy task on the site of a former World War II, B-24 *Liberator* practice bombing range. The military got the state to stock several ponds with trout,
and at the station they raised pheasants for hunting, made camping spots, allowed firewood cutting, and built a trap and skeet range. The contractors had
access to all of these recreational opportunities, too, but nonbase personnel
did not, which annoyed some of the locals. Today, because of their efforts, the
base provides a military recreation area as well as a tracking station.[58]

Despite the unusually cooperative atmosphere, the situation began to look
to some senior air force leaders like Lockheed had its hands full with the development and testing of the Agena booster, the control center, and all of the
tracking sites, in addition to serving as prime contractor for the reconnaissance satellite itself. To make matters easier, Lockheed contracted much of the
tracking station work out to radio company Philco. In 1958, Philco and Lockheed made a verbal agreement to cooperate with each other and started work.

*New Hampshire tracking station Christmas tree, 1962. Notice Santa's sleigh being towed
by a Thor-Agena launch vehicle. Courtesy of the Air Force Space Command History Office
collection.*

White lab-coated Lockheed engineers preparing for the first Corona contact at the Cooke (later Vandenberg) Air Force Base tracking station, 1959. This is the typical operation in 1959, in the very high frequency building. The control room in the background occupied one end of the room. At right are the antenna positions and equipment (with the R-1162 operator in the foreground and tri-helix operator second from right). At left is the ground station and recording equipment. Courtesy of the Air Force Historical Research Agency collection.

Althouse admitted that Lockheed and Philco got along "like teenagers!"[59] However, merely shaking hands eventually hurt Philco because the company had thought it would get to staff all of the remote tracking stations. When the air force awarded the contracts for the tracking stations individually, Lockheed got the prizes—Vandenberg and Hawaii—leaving Philco with the remote sites of Annette Island and Kodiak Island in Alaska and the tracking ship *Private Joe E. Mann* in the Pacific Ocean (the contractor did not have New Boston ready for operations), which were considered less than first-class locations. Philco went ahead, though, and sought employees for these assignments because the company had people with a reputation for going to remote locations without a lot of fuss and doing a good job.[60]

Even though the air force trusted Lockheed to do the job, the Air Force

Ballistic Missile Division believed that difficulties in the development of satellite command and control could soon overwhelm the contractor. Maj. Arnell "Stormy" Sult, the deputy director of the Command, Communications, and Control Directorate in Los Angeles, monitored the technical development and operation of the Satellite Test Center and the tracking stations. General Schriever, therefore, gave Sult the task of leading a team of officers to review the progress of development and operation of the control center and tracking stations.

By now, the air force had three separate satellite programs: Midas (missile warning), Sentry (photoreconnaissance), and Discoverer (the biomedical research cover story for the CIA's Corona photoreconnaissance satellite). Concern about how the separate satellite programs should share in the expense of operating the Air Force Satellite Control Facility also entered into the picture. Sult's team spent three weeks visiting Lockheed and Philco, dissecting each contractor's duties and organization, and estimating the assets at each tracking station. Armed with that information, Sult and his supervisor, Lt. Col. Gene Allison, assembled a formula based upon the average time each of the three types of satellites used the antennas during a support at the various tracking stations. This procedure, along with the value of the stations' assets, determined how much each satellite program office should budget for the use of the AFSCF. General Schriever called this the "Sult formula."[61]

The satellite program offices agreed to the recommendations, although the Midas office expressed unhappiness with the formula for deciding their share of the operational costs. Midas, which orbited at 1,500 to 2,000 miles, had the longest contact time with the tracking stations of any of the three programs, so it had to budget the most for AFSCF support. Sult reported his findings and recommendations to Schriever and his staff:

> 1. Lockheed was overloaded and should be relieved of some of its responsibilities in the Air Force Satellite Control Facility
>
> 2. Lockheed should retain the Control Center development and operation
>
> 3. Lockheed should retain responsibility for manning and supporting the Vandenberg Tracking Station, inasmuch as it would also support the Thor/Agena launches from VAFB
>
> 4. Philco should become a prime contractor to be responsible for development, installation, manning, and operation of the remaining and future tracking stations. Philco also had contract responsibility for some of the transmitters and receivers that were integrated into the Agena upper stage booster.[62]

Schriever then asked Sult to apprise Lockheed and Philco of the approved plan for splitting the satellite command and control "pie." Lockheed sent a contingent to the Los Angeles headquarters for Sult's briefing. They listened attentively but obviously disagreed with what they heard. Afterward, Lockheed's program director, Fred O'Green, met privately with Schriever, probably to try to persuade him to overturn some of the recommendations. When the recommendations went into effect, Philco successfully outbid Lockheed and achieved a major boost to their status in the air force's space program.[63] In addition, Philco's status meant that the military's system of satellite command and control had now reached a new level of importance and was worthy of its own prime contractor.

Friction between the contractors increased with Philco's elevation to equal status with Lockheed. For example, Lockheed resisted Philco's attempt to increase the size of its effort; the two companies bickered and contested continually, according to several former program officers. At the monthly "Black Saturday" sessions, in which the contractors' representatives and the military's program officials got together and went over all aspects of the programs for the previous month, everybody "lied like crazy." As they evolved, the Black Saturday sessions helped smooth out relations between the contractors, kept the control center to a reasonable size, and helped straighten out a horrible computer mess.[64] The air force also kept the contractors in line by staying directly involved.

Although the contractors competed and certainly tried to protect their turf, they did not collude. When Gen. Bill King led the Air Force Satellite Control Facility, he wanted a better measurement of station performance, so he ordered records kept. He ordered the field test force director, the representative from the satellite's program office on duty while a satellite orbited (similar to a mission director), to record a score for the stations during individual satellite support operations. They used a check sheet of questions that were answered with a simple "yes" or "no": "Did the command message reach the station and the validation come back?" "Did the station come up on the satellite on time?" "Were the ephemeris [orbital] data transmitted in?" Some officers worried that the scoring system might ruin the morale at the stations. King went forward, anyway, because he believed it was important to know which stations could adequately support the satellites and which ones could not, and if he had to relieve somebody, he would have the information necessary to back it up. Resistance to the idea of comparing the stations against each other began with King's own vice commander and reached down into the stations, but the scores turned out as King expected. In his estimation, the level of professionalism in the AFSCF meant he had to evaluate the stations' performance; the satellite program offices that had the use of stations had to know whether they could trust them. King thought that comparing the stations with their peers could improve assistance to the customers—the satellite programs.[65] The Air Force Satellite Control Facility's mission, after all, was service.

In sum, therefore, to help Air Force Ballistic Missile Division accomplish the important task of satellite command and control development, they assigned subprojects and problems to different types of professionals. AFBMD assigned the overall Advanced Reconnaissance System to Lockheed; Lockheed, in turn, farmed out many projects the airplane company did not have the expertise to handle on its own. As the satellite command and control system grew larger, Lockheed called in even more subcontractors to handle more aspects of the contract. Finally, the air force stepped in and made the difficult decision to replace Lockheed as prime contractor. As times changed and as air force officers grew in their knowledge and experience of space operations, the service Lockheed provided came to be less indispensable. In the late 1950s, though, Lockheed provided the air force a service it could not have developed on its own.

Constructing Test Environments

Not only did the inventors of the air force system of satellite command and control embody the Air Force Satellite Control Facility with the political and economic characteristics it needed to survive in its environment, but engineers also constructed test environments that became ever more complex and more like the world that they believed the system would encounter once it was operational. Then, in response to an urgent request from Air Research and Development Command Headquarters for a test plan covering the IGY period, in January, 1956, the Western Development Division issued a preliminary development plan for WS-117L's initial test phase.[66]

The initial test phase for the ARS included both the research, design, development, and provision of all of the components and subsystems for an orbiting vehicle system and the necessary facilities for launching, acquisition, tracking, communicating, and ground testing. The plan included ten orbital tests of the vehicle, beginning in August, 1958, using the Atlas ICBM as a booster, and launching at a rate of one vehicle per month for a total of ten vehicles; six were expected to reach orbit. The first two tests would be from the eastern test range in Florida; the remainder, from California.

Preliminary research studies indicated that the problem of signal acquisition had more to do with the space-to-ground link than the ground-to-space link. For ground acquisition and tracking, engineers planned to use the AN/FPS-16 instrumentation radar, which was still under construction. The entire AN/FPS-16 system, including the 16-foot parabolic reflector, the

Original radar vans at the Cooke (later Vandenberg) Air Force Base tracking station, 1959. The setup at this point is not that different for tracking satellites than it is for tracking missiles. Courtesy of the Air Force Space Command History Office collection.

transmitter, and the receiver, needed modifications to enable it pick up the relatively weak signals coming from space. Engineers confidently predicted that they could construct a receiver for the ground stations with adequate sensitivity and a space-borne transmitter with adequate output power within the "state of the art."[67]

To get the program operational as soon as possible, the air force planned to use as much off-the-shelf equipment as possible. Engineers, therefore, developed a ground-to-space command link and a space-to-ground telemetry link using techniques that had been around for some time and that employed mostly recycled equipment. They understood the reception of ICBM telemetry and the transmission of information to ICBMs, such as commanding a missile to self-destruct when ground controllers saw it going awry during ascent. An incident that occurred at the New Boston tracking station during a critical command upload revealed the off-the-shelf nature of the WS-117L program. The station used a GE-125, punched-paper tape reader to send commands to orbiting satellites. Before a scheduled support operation, the optical reader failed when the light bulb that read the holes in the paper tape burned out. Joe Schraml, a station operator, made a call to logistics, which had no spare bulbs. Controllers informed the chief of operations, Alex Czernysz, that the station could not provide support because a bad bulb made the reader inoperative. When Czernysz looked at the burned-out bulb, he thought it looked familiar. He went outside, took the dome lamp bulb from his 1958 Mercedes 220S, and screwed it into the optical reader. It fit. With minutes to spare, New Boston completed the satellite support with a foreign-made part.[68]

The system engineers had successfully studied a variety of technical configurations meant to provide the best support with the least difficulty in the fastest manner. Yet engineers and technicians did not just shove together off-the-shelf parts in the hopes that they could provide an adequate capability in a hurry. Engineers designed the remote tracking station equipment systems to meet the requirements of a particular type of satellite—the early Corona vehicles—and its particular instrumentation. They thought out and systematically designed the Air Force Satellite Control Facility to provide immediate support for important national security needs, rather than using the ARS to advance the state of the art in telemetry technology.

Engineers also studied several geographical configurations for the WS-117L tracking stations in order to determine the best arrangement for data acquisition. To retrieve intelligence pictures, the air force at this point preferred a data readout instead of the physical recovery of the film from space (which the CIA eventually opted for); the stations thus required the engineers to take into account a number of considerations. Using systems analysis, Lockheed's engineers N. N. Berger, N. E. Tabor, and L. Lutzker studied the accuracy requirements of the tracking network and revealed a need for greater accuracy in angle determination for orbit predictions. To achieve adequate satellite acquisition on the first orbit, the tracking radar had to observe the satellite at an elevation angle of 10 degrees or higher for at least two minutes. What's more, in order to achieve data readout times that were long enough to retrieve all of the intelligence data, a station in the northwest continental United States was inadequate because it could not "see" a satellite often enough or long enough.[69]

In addition, all three tracking stations—small budgets limited the planned system to three operational stations—had to be in the United States or its possessions. Hawaii, a station planned for the test phase, could not completely serve operational needs because, although it could gather useful data for orbit prediction, its distant southerly location could not support long-enough data readout times. In addition, in the event of hostilities, Oahu could be "susceptible to enemy attack, destruction, or even capture." In Oahu's favor, excellent supply and logistics—important considerations—kept it in the running. Therefore, another consideration entered into the analysis: The sites had to be close to military airfields, railheads, and all-weather transportation facilities with water, telephone, power, and housing. Such issues made Pretoria, South Africa, a good location. Maj. Stormy Sult visited the proposed site, traveling on *Air Force 2* to get there, but, because of security considerations, Pretoria ultimately did not make the list. Nevertheless, remotely locating the stations introduced other factors as well, such as dependents' living arrangements, length of duty tours, additional pay for undesirable locations, and difficulty in recruiting and retaining experienced personnel.[70] As they wrote the report, the planners added more and more requirements for the tracking station locations to meet.

In their considerations of tracking station locations, Berger, Tabor, and Lutzker also discussed various countermeasures the Soviets might take to prevent the United States from retrieving reconnaissance data from space. They considered electronic jamming of a 60-foot antenna from 30 miles at sea or from 50,000 feet impractical because of the power required and the size of an effective jamming antenna. Interference posed a more serious problem, though, because the jammer required knowledge of only the frequency the tracking station transmitted on, which was not a secret at all. Overall, the consequences of a compromised system posed a grave problem because, if the Soviets learned of America's capabilities from space, that information could provide the USSR with the information it would need to effect countermeasures. To prevent national security compromises, the stations had to be more than 600 nautical miles from Soviet territory.[71] Another reason for the Alaskan and Hawaiian sites was that the air force had no definite idea how difficult it might be to get to orbit, and Alaska could be the first place to pick up the satellite's ground track over American soil, assuming a launch from California.[72]

In addition, both natural and human forms of interference could be just as problematic as Soviet-generated jamming. The site had to allow 360-degree radius search and acquisition at elevations of 2 degrees or higher, a separation of 10 to 15 miles between the tracking and data-receiving antennas, and enough distance from major airfields to prevent interference similar to television flutter, or "ghosting." They also had to be far enough from heavily populated urban or industrial areas to provide protection from interference from rotating machinery, radiating home radio and television receivers, and other devices. For example, human-made interference struck the weather satellite program during the Cuban missile crisis. On Monday, October 29, 1962, operators failed to read the data from a weather satellite over Eglin AFB, Florida, after a weekend of successful supports. They located the source of interference almost immediately: In order to command the satellite, they had to aim their transmitter almost directly across the housing area at Eglin. On Monday, traditionally washday, the engineers traced the interference that was emanating from the base housing area to the continual use of washers, dryers, vacuum cleaners, and televisions. Weather satellite program manager Col. Tom Haig convinced Eglin's wing commander, Brig. Gen. A. T. Culbertson, to throw the power switch to base housing whenever a satellite passed overhead. Culbertson inserted information into the base news bulletin about periodic power outages, and the interference disappeared.[73] Turning the power off in base housing worked for a temporary situation such as the Cuban missile crisis, but the air force had to locate permanent tracking stations to avoid this type of human-made interference.

Finally, with their analysis complete, Lockheed planned to situate the northwest station in Alaska; station two anywhere in the Midwestern United States north of the center line of the nation; and station three anywhere in the Northeast United States north of the Mason-Dixon Line and sufficiently remote to prevent human-made interference. They settled on Annette Island, Alaska; Ottumwa, Iowa; and New Boston, New Hampshire. These locations, sufficiently remote to prevent human-made interference but not too distant to prevent adequate logistics, already had sufficient supplies of power and water, offered adequate housing, and made Soviet countermeasures less likely.[74] Lockheed estimated the cost of each station at $10.967 million, including $4.977 million for facilities and $5.99 million in equipment, or more than $32 million for the three tracking stations. The total estimate for the WS-117L facilities, including testing, tracking, and launching facilities, was $112.7 million in 1957 dollars.[75]

When considering the amount of equipment and the number of personnel needed, the costs for each tracking station began to add up. In the earliest configuration of the Kodiak, Alaska, tracking station, for example, the system of command and control required two antennas: (1) a three-pulse, very long-range tracking (VERLORT) and commanding radar, and (2) a tri-helix, telemetry-receiving antenna. In addition, a 100-word-per-minute teletype machine and an "analog voice circuit" (that is, a telephone) provided off-station communications. Teletype messages told the Kodiak operators the launch and support schedules, and then the operators passed telemetry readouts after each support back to Sunnyvale. Real-time telephone calls served adequately for everything else. The air force could encrypt the teletype, but all voice transmissions went in the clear. Because a learning curve existed in the United States and the USSR, because the air force went to great lengths to publicize its space program, and because the air force could not hide these electronic secrets, eavesdropping on satellite command and control operations became common. From his days in Alaska, Marv Sumner reports that a Russian fishing trawler drifted 13 miles east of Kodiak, "probably listening to all of our voice and commanding."[76] The VERLORT radar transmitted three pulses during each pulse of the spacecraft: a contact pulse, called a main bang, a command pulse, and an execute pulse. In this form of analog commanding, the time-position of the middle pulse varied at a sinusoidal rate. Four tone frequencies went into space, transmitted in pairs for a possible list of six commands, and later expanded to fifteen commands. Digital commands had three discrete time slots—one each for ones, zeros, and *s*'s. The *s*'s kept the system synchronized and the radar power steady when the ones and zeros did not go out. Analog commanding instructions came to the station by real-time voice, and station operators inserted them into the transmission stream; digital commands arrived at the station on the teletype as punched-paper tape before the satellite support.

At Kodiak, the telemetry antenna and its equipment van sat on a hill (called T-Hill or "Readout Ridge") away from the radar and teletype equipment. The radar automatically tracked the satellite in angles and measured the range to deliver tracking data. The van had receivers, demodulators, tape recorders, and displays for processing the raw telemetry. A large *X-Y* plotter with preprinted paper maps in the site control room displayed the tracking data. As the antenna moved, the controllers described the support progress over the telephone to California and then mailed the maps south daily. All of the data left T-Hill on the telephone or in the mailbag. After a satellite support, a technician wrapped and addressed the magnetic recording tapes, strip-chart recordings, and handwritten data sheets and took them down the hill to the mailroom. The teletype operator typed lists of special readouts for postpass transmission. A third antenna, a single whip on the roof of the van, received an unmodulated RF carrier from the satellite at 216 MHz and measured the one-way Doppler data, printed out on a punched-paper tape, which a controller took to the teletype room and transmitted to California. Even this simple system could handle lots of information, although not quickly.

In California, the CIA gave the responsibility of setting up the reconnaissance satellite program to its only officer in Palo Alto, Charles Murphy. On active duty with the air force but assigned to the CIA, Murphy had been a B-36 Peacemaker navigator and a key player in the development of the U-2 reconnaissance aircraft. To ensure adequate daylight in the USSR target area, Murphy used the ARS to determine the best time of day to launch. He also ascertained what altitude to launch into to get the best pictures. Coordinating with analysts at the National Photo Interpretation Center, he learned what scale meant to photo interpreters, how they liked to have targets illuminated, how much sun they needed, and what type of effects shadows produced. People had thought about and been meeting these needs for aerial reconnaissance for a long time, but mission planning for satellites differed because the camera system, instead of flying several thousand feet in the air, orbited 100 miles above Earth, which made the planning factors quite different. Murphy eventually decided that the intelligence community should use the Corona camera as a search system, not a spotting system; that is, it would be better to take pictures of wide areas and search the photos themselves rather than try to take pictures of particular things that may or may not be present. Using the search method, photo interpreters discovered that many of the targets of America's nuclear weapons did not lie where the planners had thought. In fact, in Murphy's opinion, the original mapmakers had placed the targets so far off their actual location that an American nuclear strike on the USSR might not have been successful. Using this knowledge, Murphy determined new launch windows and began turning the satellite program into a useful tool for gathering intelligence about the USSR.[77]

The Subsystem H engineers, using largely off-the-shelf equipment, managed to cobble together a satellite command and control system before the first reconnaissance launch, achieving successes and failures as often as any other aspect of the early reconnaissance program. With the test phase essentially over, the Air Force Satellite Control Facility prepared to expand its role in the air force's space program.

Summary

During the developmental stage, before the military's system of satellite command and control came into actual use, satellite command and control changed from a relatively simple idea into a complex system infused with various economic, political, and social factors. To accomplish the important task of supporting a complicated reconnaissance satellite program, the Air Force Ballistic Missile Division and Lockheed called in subcontractors to handle more of the system's development. As they worked, these associates embodied in their invention the characteristics it needed to survive in the maze of government agencies. The Subsystem H engineers accelerated the development process by modifying off-the-shelf equipment to create a satellite command and control system that would be ready before the first launch and that was also vital for the early reconnaissance program.

By the end of 1958, the tracking stations had been built, installed, tested, and station personnel waited the first planned launch, which was set for early 1959. With the covert program established and because of the importance of the Advanced Reconnaissance System, managers decided to get the systems operational as soon as possible rather than extend the testing. Therefore, with the abbreviated period of testing essentially ended, Air Force Satellite Control Facility engineers moved into developing the techniques necessary to support satellites that were critical to national security.

3 Getting Off Dead Center
Innovating for a Single Customer

The money flowing in from the NRO and the CIA made satellite command and control work.

—Brig. Gen. William G. King Jr., USAF, Retired
Former Commander, Air Force Satellite Control Facility

THE FIRST ATTEMPT to launch a reconnaissance satellite on board a Thor/Agena booster came on January 21, 1959. While the Thor booster sat quietly on the launch pad, the Agena upper stage malfunctioned when small, solid rockets that forced propellant into the rocket engine's fuel inlet fired prematurely. After inspection, the Agena turned out to be a total loss. Engineers referred to this launch attempt as *Discoverer* Ø.[1]

On February 28, 1959, the air force finally launched *Discoverer 1*, which carried only a light engineering payload. Although at least one tracking station claimed to have heard it in orbit, the Air Force Satellite Control Facility presumed that it crashed near the South Pole. *Discoverer 2*, the first mission to reach orbit, failed when controllers lost it on the seventeenth orbit because a bad command sequence ejected the capsule at the wrong time, causing it to crash near Spitzbergen, Norway. Efforts to recover the capsule ended when aerial reconnaissance revealed that the Soviets had probably recovered the capsule, which carried a pair of mice, not a camera.[2] The first camera-carrying mission, *Discoverer 4*, failed to reach orbit when the Agena burned out prematurely. A string of failures followed. For example, *Discoverer 5*'s camera batteries failed in orbit; the range safety officer blew up *Discoverer 10*; and *Discoverer 11*'s reentry vehicle ejected, but the spin-stabilization rockets exploded during reentry. The first successful mission, *Discoverer 13*, came in August, 1960, a year and a half after the first launch. The very next mission,

Inside the original radar vans at the Cooke (later Vandenberg) Air Force Base tracking station, 1959. Courtesy of the Air Force Historical Research Agency collection.

Discoverer 14, included the first air-recovered film capsule and returned more imagery of the USSR than the twenty-four previous U-2 flights combined.[3]

True to the engineering culture of the day, James Plummer, Lockheed's Corona program manager, looked on every launch as a successful engineering test regardless of whether it provided reconnaissance of the USSR: "We didn't look at those as twelve failures, we looked at those as twelve successes. We were learning new things every time in every part of the missile and the recovery and all of the things that we had to do. . . . If it hadn't been for President Eisenhower's support for the [CIA's approach to the program], of course it would have been cancelled."[4] *Discoverer 14,* the first completely successful reconnaissance satellite mission—from start to finish—included an aerial catch of the capsule and processed reconnaissance information. Corona continued to serve national reconnaissance needs until the 1970s.

Before the brilliant successes of the satellite program, the creators had to develop their invention into a complex system of manufacturing, sales, and service facilities. Through clever innovation, the engineers and managers created an essentially conservative invention—satellite command and control—

from a radical system: satellite-based reconnaissance. In essence, the method developed for the Advanced Reconnaissance System (ARS) simply improved conventional radar tracking and missile telemetry techniques. Going beyond their original mandate, the Subsystem H principals—the Air Force Ballistic Missile Division and Lockheed—tried to develop command and control as much as possible. They strove to increase the size of the system by creating a structure that was larger and more capable than the one originally envisioned for a single satellite program.[5] In addition, once the design stabilized, the inventors faded from the focal point of the activity into the background in favor of the new management organization, which was officially designated as the 6594th Test Wing (Satellite), with the single purpose of supporting the national intelligence program.

At the urging of the contractors and the air force, those who were presiding over Subsystem H began to expand the size of the system. Numerous players carved out their own spheres of influence, thus preventing Lockheed and the air force from truly controlling the new satellite command and control system. By 1961, managers, both contractors and military officers, had replaced the inventors of satellite command and control. After successfully arguing that a military service organization should be responsible for command and control of the WS-117L program, not the operational nuclear command, the air force retained satellite command and control as a critical function for the air force's test community to perform.

Making Satellite Command and Control a Conservative Idea

In the conservative mid-1950s, some government officials viewed satellite-based reconnaissance as a radical invention that was too experimental and unproven for an important national defense role. Yet no one viewed satellite command and control as especially difficult to accomplish because it used proven techniques borrowed from the ICBM test environment. The air force developed satellite command and control—an essential part of the reconnaissance satellite program—as much as possible and in the process expanded the scope of that system.

Despite the military unit designations, operations in the Air Force Satellite Control Facility had a decidedly nonmilitary flavor. Geographically separated from each other, operations ran much more like a corporate undertaking than a military one, reflecting the influence of Lockheed and its partners. Newly arriving air force personnel in California wore civilian clothes so as to not stand out among the people entering and leaving the various Lockheed buildings. The air force even issued a specific directive on proper civilian attire: "A business suit, shirt, and tie compose the normal attire worn by businessmen. The coat may be removed within the office of work. Female officers will follow accepted standards of business and professional women when wearing civilian clothing and accessories."[6] From this unquestionably non-military start and because a mixed group of military personnel and contractors working side by side made up the field test force in Sunnyvale, the use of first names among the engineers became standard. When controllers established the voice network for a satellite support, the test controller in Sunnyvale and the operations controller at the remote tracking station could be either a member of the military or a contractor.[7]

Military protocol did not bother American leaders from Eisenhower on down who wanted to obtain photographs of the Eurasian landmass as soon as possible. Air force leaders like General Schriever believed that the ARS could provide a significant boost to intelligence capabilities. In meetings between Air Research and Development Command (responsible for all air force R&D), the Air Force Ballistic Missile Division (responsible for air force space and missile R&D programs), and Strategic Air Command (the air force's nuclear command), officers agreed that the minimum essential capability to handle operational pictures from any R&D flights could be speeded up by using the California launch facilities and the Satellite Test Center for operational satellite control, reading out the data at the New Boston and Vandenberg stations, and using the Air Recovery Service's force in the Pacific to recover film capsules ejected from space.[8]

Therefore, with the tracking equipment undergoing installation and a preliminary budget in hand, Schriever's team set about producing a development plan for WS-117L. Taking into consideration the upcoming International Geophysical Year, the January 14, 1956, development report reinforced the cover story that the air force had a satellite program for R&D, not operational reconnaissance. The Air Force Ballistic Missile Division (AFBMD) tried to grab a piece of the space prestige pie by answering a request from air force headquarters to present a possible development program for the initial test phase of the ARS that would permit the launching of an orbiting vehicle during the IGY.[9] In Schriever's cover letter to the development report, he made it clear that the ARS was a part of the U.S.'s IGY program. Later he even suggested renaming WS-117L the "American Space Observatory" in celebration of the IGY, only barely concealing the satellite's real purpose.[10] Renaming never actually occurred, but AFBMD kept looking for ways to expand its role in the space program.

Lockheed's development reports over the next several months document its efforts to begin expanding the command and control system to make it useable by the time of the first launch, planned for late 1959. In March, 1956, Lockheed produced its first report on the air force's Pied Piper reconnaissance satellite. This program consisted of a satellite vehicle containing equipment to perform visual, electronic, and infrared reconnaissance, together with the necessary system of ground stations and the data-processing centers (the Satellite Test Center and the center planned for photo interpretation).[11] In April, 1956, the air force followed up on Lockheed's work and submitted a development plan for WS-117L. The plan called for a 300-mile altitude, near-polar, circular orbit. An internal timer would tell the camera when to take pictures of "an area of interest." At this point designers planned WS-117L as a readout system that would take pictures over the USSR and transmit them when over a U.S. ground station.

Clearly there could be no reconnaissance satellite program without a command and control capability, and Lockheed used this requirement to increase the size of the system under its control. Lockheed planned a master computer for the "south central continental USA" WS-117L intelligence center, to be located presumably near Fort Worth, Texas, although the air force had not yet made a final decision.[12] Lockheed anticipated that "a nucleus of contractor personnel to provide a stable organizational structure with full exploitation of accumulated experience" would staff the center. The training of military and contractors' personnel could be accomplished there as well to provide more people to handle this "unique large-scale data handling system."[13] Lockheed was already thinking ahead to the operational system.

The budget numbers also illustrate how the reconnaissance satellite program threatened to take over air force R&D. The WS-117L plans estimated the total cost at $74 million.[14] Total government R&D expenditures reached only $3.446 billion in 1956, so the estimation for WS-117L equaled 2 percent of that budget.[15] By 1959, the earliest date for which figures are available, the Department of Defense's (DoD) spending for space had reached only $489.5 million, but $74 million equaled 15 percent of the total space budget.[16] The AFBMD submitted a budget for the entire project at $95.5 million, including $13 million requested for the fourth quarter of FY 1956.[17] Schriever later recalled that his budget for WS-117L was $10 million in 1957 dollars, a mere one-fifth of 1 percent that was then being spent on U.S. government R&D and just under 10 percent of what Lockheed said it needed to complete the project.[18] CIA Director Allen W. Dulles later authorized the release of just $7 million—which he intended for "covert procurement"—for Project Corona in FY 1958.[19] During a time of lean budgets and other national priorities, WS-117L therefore endangered a large portion of the U.S.'s total R&D effort for space even before Sputnik.

Lockheed, the primary contractor for the Advanced Reconnaissance System, did not let the numbers stop them. In fact, when Congress left budgets undecided, Lockheed continued work on the reconnaissance satellite program

Data receiver antenna at the Cooke (later Vandenberg) Air Force Base tracking station, 1960. Courtesy of the Air Force Historical Research Agency collection.

using its own money until the air force resolved the situation.[20] Lockheed produced the next version of the WS-117L development plan in November, 1956. The company named itself as the contractor for the "vehicle intercept, control, and data stations," tentatively selected for installation in the "Northeastern USA, Northwestern USA, South Central USA, and in the Hawaiian Islands." The report conceived of the four stations only in general terms. Each one contained "tracking equipment, [an] orbit computer, [a] command transmitter, [a] recording system for reconnaissance data, and a telemeter-type receiving station."[21] The initial test phase included research, design, development, and provision of all of the components and subsystems for both an orbiting vehicle system and facilities for launching, acquisition, tracking, communications, and ground tests. Command and control began to come to life—but only on paper.

Other innovations in space and missile design helped move the reconnaissance satellite program along even faster. Because of the army's work in the Jupiter missile program and scientist Carl Gazley's work at RAND, ablative reentry techniques emerged on the satellite stage, proving both practical and, more important, lightweight. As physical recovery of objects from space became an option, RAND scientists eagerly introduced an innovation to the air force—recoverable satellites. In a research memorandum titled "A Family of Recoverable Reconnaissance Satellites," Merton Davies, Amrom Katz, and others described a group of reconnaissance satellites that provided both an early and a continuing photographic reconnaissance capability to augment the WS-117L program. Davies and Katz had seen their original ideas, first published in the late 1940s, go nowhere, especially not into space. The first proposed system included a water-recoverable vehicle, the basis for the Corona program until the 1970s.[22] Engineers now had the information they needed to bypass the problems they had encountered in developing the data readout satellite.

The latest RAND report did not ignore the importance of command and control either. R. T. Gabler wrote an appendix to "A Family of Recoverable Reconnaissance Satellites," called simply "Tracking." He included command and control for three main purposes: to determine an orbit accurate enough for photography; to command the reentry of the capsule; and to establish the reentry area, suggesting two or three tracking sites along a line normal to the orbit, spaced about 200 miles apart to allow a little orbital overlap and making orbit prediction more accurate. Three stations placed at a high northern latitude, if spaced about 200 miles down a longitudinal axis, met the necessary minima to support the reconnaissance satellite, which the air force already planned to launch into a polar orbit. The vehicle had to carry a transponder for ranging while on orbit and a radio beacon for locating it after splashdown. Gabler suggested frequencies, types of transponders, and tracking radars. He also recommended using existing AN/FPS-16 tracking radars to command the satellite at 200 Hz and another antenna to receive from the satellite at 500 Hz. The total radio weight aboard the spacecraft would be between 10 and 15 pounds.[23] The RAND report omitted nothing. Now the air force needed only enough funding to make the project a reality.

In late 1957—after Sputnik—the AFBMD authorized Lockheed to develop a plan to accelerate WS-117L, and on December 5, 1957, General

Schriever approved the proposal. Robert Gross, Lockheed's program manager, told the air force that "Lockheed would draw on its entire facility as necessary to expedite the WS-117L development." The Thor IRBM was also chosen as a booster over the still-unproven Atlas ICBM. In the most significant program change, Lockheed agreed to the physical recovery of reconnaissance photographs from the orbiting vehicle rather than an electronic readout of scanned pictures on a video link, thus finally accepting RAND's capsule recovery proposal. Lockheed wanted immediate authorization to proceed and provided the necessary hardware and services the air force typically provided its contractors. Given that President Eisenhower had established the highest developmental preference (called "DX priority") for WS-117L, giving it the same national urgency as the ICBM, Lockheed expected the air force to expedite the approval of subcontracts.[24] With WS-117L's new lease on life, Lockheed asked that the air force waive military specifications for drawings in connection with Philco-supplied equipment. Instead, they would use "specifications in accordance with good commercial practice." They also asked for the authority to proceed immediately from design to fabrication of ground support equipment, without the air force's design approval. Finally, Lockheed asked the air force either to provide concrete foundations for the TLM-18 antennas at the interim tracking stations or to permit Lockheed to procure them directly from the antenna subcontractor.[25]

Location requirements for the ground stations now changed because of RAND's proposed capsule recovery plan. Alaska entered the picture, as did California's central coast, while Northwestern USA and South Central USA departed. For the tracking function alone, especially on a first orbit, a near-polar location offered the most advantages. A site at about 65 degrees north latitude in Alaska, as RAND had previously determined, was also the best point at which to initiate recovery, which might then be 1,500 miles south. Hawaii remained in the picture because of the choice of the Pacific for the recovery zone.[26] The program began to expand even faster.

As a result, the total cost for WS-117L ballooned to $95.1 million, an increase of almost 25 percent. Subsystem H, the largest chunk of the program, gobbled up $24.6 million, in part because it required dozens of people-supporting structures in places where the government did not already own buildings. Lockheed convinced the air force that "the vital national importance of successful acceleration of the WS-117L program, and the inherent developmental difficulties associated with this complex Weapon System" justified the increase.[27] The speeding up of WS-117L gave Lockheed another opportunity to expand the segment of the program under its control.

Because the air force needed to be prepared for the start of launch rehearsals in November, 1958, they planned to begin construction on the tracking stations in May, 1958. In April, 1958, Schriever signed the first monthly status report for WS-117L, announcing that the first test of the ARS would take place in late 1959 from Cooke AFB on board a Thor IRBM. It also stated that the system now required five acquisition and tracking stations, which would probably be located at Cooke AFB; a site near Oxnard, California, which was downrange from the Cooke launch site; Kaena Point, Hawaii; Anchorage; and Sitka, Alaska. The interim facilities consisted of one 60-foot-in-diameter TLM-18 telemetry antenna and a receiver building, a tracking radar, and "associated structures." Van-mounted tracking and transmission facilities could be supplied for the stations in Alaska by November.

Development continued as the program received a new name. In the May, 1958, status report General Schriever reported that the Advanced Research Projects Agency, nominally responsible for all military space projects, had renamed the video reconnaissance portion of the ARS vehicle "Sentry." Sentry now referred only to the video reconnaissance portion of WS-117L, not to the recoverable portion, which had already become the highly covert Corona program. The new name did not refer either to the biomedical satellites of the Discoverer program (which the air force used for the Corona cover story) or to the plans for an infrared ICBM detection satellite, which the air force called Midas. Schriever also stated that the contractors were planning to have the Cooke and Hawaii tracking stations completed by September 1, 1958. The air force agreed to the two sites in Alaska because of uncertainty about how accurate they could get the Corona orbits.[28]

The June, 1958, status report offered more encouraging news, including important shifts in program development. General Schriever reported that the AFBMD had formed an Air Force Bioastronautics Division in California to function as a consultant and liaison group for all biomedical activity in the ARS program. This action reaffirmed the Discoverer cover story of a biomedical test program.[29] General Schriever also said that the air force had decided to recover capsules returning from space at approximately 10,000 feet by using Fairchild C-119 *Flying Boxcars.* Just as significant, engineers described their progress on the ground equipment as it rapidly approached the prototype stage. By using printed circuits, they had managed to save some development time. They also explained the techniques they intended to use to command the initial "call-down" of the capsule for recovery.

In addition, New Boston, in New Hampshire, had been selected as the northeast control site, while a location in the central part of the United States was still to be determined. Construction began at the other sites. Finally, Lockheed also completed the design of the Interim Development Control Center in Palo Alto, California (later called the Satellite Test Center), although the location for the Central Intelligence Center remained "unresolved."[30] The locations for the ARS Intelligence Center had moved to SAC headquarters at Offutt AFB, near Omaha, Nebraska, but the CIA objected to the decision. The air force envisioned SAC as the primary intelligence information user and operator of the ARS satellites, so the location made sense to the air force, but not to the CIA.[31] Although satisfied with Omaha as the choice for the operations center, Roy Johnson, director of the Advanced Research Projects Agency (ARPA) and manager of the overall military space program, wanted Air Research and Development Command (ARDC) rather than SAC to run the satellite program.[32]

On July 1, 1958, AFBMD published a new development plan for WS-117L with the title "New Horizons." Less than a year after formal program approval, the air force completed "beneficial occupancy" of the interim telemetry tracking facilities at Cooke, Kaena Point, Annette Island, and Kodiak Island. The New Hampshire site suffered from a lack of funding; when the money finally arrived, the system integrators did not have enough time left in the relatively short northern construction season to complete the facility.[33]

By the end of 1958, the interim tracking stations had been built, installed, and tested, and their crews anxiously awaited the planned launch of *Discoverer 1*, set for late 1958. As the technicians sat and trained for the first flight, the managers began to increase the size of the air force's satellite command and control system.

Expanding the Size of the System under Control

Instead of bestowing the space budget on the air force like a parental trust fund, President Eisenhower created ARPA to prevent any one military service from monopolizing the nation's money. He ordered the agency to manage and direct selected basic and applied R&D projects for the DoD. Eisenhower also directed ARPA to focus on high-risk technology that offered the potential for a dramatic advance in traditional military roles and missions. Pied Piper certainly fit into both of those categories. Secretary of Defense Neil H. McElroy formed ARPA on February 8, 1958, as a new office for space technology R&D with complete authority to direct the expanding U.S. military space program. ARPA director Johnson construed his mission very broadly, considering his organization to be a "fourth military service," in effect a military space agency.[34] In the area of space systems other than launch vehicles, the DoD's R&D board had assigned military satellites to the air force in 1950. Now, with the creation of the new agency in 1958, program direction came from ARPA, not the air force or ARDC headquarters.

In October, 1958, trying to minimize the implications of aggression suggested by the military's participation in the national space program, ARPA director Johnson directed the air force to cease using the term "weapon system" when referring to satellite programs. The IGY showcased the scientific uses of satellites, he reasoned, and using the term "weapon system" for a satellite program, even a reconnaissance satellite program, could stir up unnecessary commentary. Such actions by ARPA made the air force fearful that the agency might take over its space program.[35]

The air force's fears, however, proved unfounded. Defense Secretary McElroy gave ARPA the responsibility for all U.S. space programs, both military and civilian, but the AFBMD in Los Angeles remained the executive agency for the air force's space programs. Program leadership came from ARPA for the next year and a half, but in fact the air force retained overall control of the reconnaissance satellite program; one more layer of bureaucracy stood between the air force and the defense establishment. So, although it appeared from the outside as though ARPA had taken over the air force's space program, the agency actually did little beyond supervising a few space studies, choosing instead to reassign most former air force space projects to field units such as the AFBMD. Even so, ARPA had a short-lived political role in advanced satellite reconnaissance because of the creation of a new, separate civilian agency responsible for space.

Upon the recommendation of his science advisory committee, chaired by James R. Killian, President Eisenhower submitted legislation to Congress and signed into law the *National Aeronautics and Space Act of 1958*, creating the National Aeronautics and Space Administration (NASA). In the realm of space exploration, NASA inherited existing scientific satellites and planetary missions from the National Science Foundation and ARPA and later piloted spaceflight as well. The *National Aeronautics and Space Act* divided U.S. space activities between the public, civilian NASA world and the more secretive military world.

Finally, ARPA lost its dominant role in December, 1959, when the DoD divided the responsibility for the various military satellite missions among all three services, redesignating the fledgling military space agency as solely an R&D agency. On March 6, 1961, new Secretary of Defense Robert S. McNamara further hurt ARPA's attempt to become the military's space service by assigning research, test, development, and engineering for all military space programs—satellites as well as launch vehicles—back to the air force, except for "unusual circumstances." Any DoD agency could then conduct preliminary research. McNamara also stipulated that the services had to submit proposals for space development programs to the director of Defense Research and Engineering (DDR&E).[36] McNamara assigned the task of developing communications satellites to the army; responsibility for navigation satellites (primarily the Transit satellite navigation program) to the navy; and control of reconnaissance and surveillance satellites to the air force. ARPA officially released WS-117L to the air force, but in reality the operational reconnaissance satellite program had already been reassigned to another secret DoD agency.[37]

More significant for this study, President Eisenhower authorized the creation of an agency whose very existence remained secret until 1992. Deeming overhead reconnaissance too important to leave to the generals, on August 31, 1960, the DoD had created the Office of Missile and Space Systems under Assistant Secretary of the Air Force Joseph P. Charyk, who reported directly to the secretary of defense. In January, 1961, the DoD and the CIA jointly rechartered the organization and renamed it the National Reconnaissance Office (NRO), classifying its existence. NRO became a separate agency responsible for the consolidation of all DoD "satellite and air vehicle overflight projects for intelligence" and "for the complete management and conduct" of these programs, thus fitting the military's space program into America's top-down Cold War paradigm.[38] The NRO developed techniques of procurement and program management, which the CIA dominated and which frequently involved overspending. The NRO also obtained a share of the military space program, taking a huge bite out of total space activity and shrinking the amount of space work under "normal" military development procedures and control.[39] Designated as the prime customer for all overhead intelligence, the NRO also assumed operational authority for overhead reconnaissance, taking away the air force's authority for operating the nation's reconnaissance satellites. The NRO's new power refocused air force space activities only on launching and tracking satellites, not on gathering intelligence. For that, whether the nation knew about it or not, the NRO had primary responsibility.

The U.S. space program now had three branches: one concerned primarily with space science and political prestige (NASA); one, with military support missions (the defense department); and one, with reconnaissance operations (the NRO). Later presidents and secretaries of defense formally endorsed these divisions, which largely remain in effect today.

Even though the reconnaissance satellite program appeared to be on track for a 1959 launch, some senior engineers intimately involved with the program wanted to make sure that it did not get off track even slightly. Edwin (Din) Land, head of the Scientific Advisory Board Reconnaissance Panel on Reconnaissance from Satellite Vehicles and inventor of the Polaroid instant film-developing process, chaired a meeting of the air force's Scientific Advisory Board panel on reconnaissance satellites, held in Boston near the Corona camera maker, ITEK, in October, 1958. ARPA director Roy Johnson and Lockheed's Corona program manager James Plummer both attended. Lockheed began the meeting by giving a complete update on the Corona program, which received favorable reviews from those present. Land stated to all present, although clearly aimed at ARPA's Johnson, that the goals for Corona included an operational system designed to achieve limited objectives—photoreconnaissance of the USSR—and that no one should tinker with the program as their own "pet R&D project." Land believed that the secret program should be governed by its security and cover requirements—the Discoverer biomedical story—to prevent its exposure. Johnson objected and suggested slipping Corona into fall, 1960, in order to speed up the development of the Sentry program, what one officer present referred to as "super-Corona." Land stated his view that simultaneous development of Sentry interfered with developing Corona into an operational system.[40]

ARPA objected to the time required to develop a new satellite program because Johnson saw Lockheed and the AFBMD as in too much of a hurry. ARPA *authorized* the air force $136 million in FY 1958 for the satellite programs, representing only 63 percent of the requested $215 million, but initially *released* only $22.7 million on June 20, 1958, increasing that amount to a slightly larger $30.7 million in mid-July. General Schriever asked the air force to release another $40 million in late July (for a total of $70.7 million), but Secretary of the Air Force Douglas released only half that amount. Schriever asked for $20 million more in August, 1958, which he received. Schriever informed Douglas that a work stoppage might occur on WS-117L if Lockheed did not receive funding by January 20, 1959. Douglas then reduced funding for the overall program again, from $148.2 million to $96.6 million, excluding facilities, which he cut by $800,000. He tentatively planned FY 1960 funding at $148.0 million, but only for Sentry and Discoverer because ARPA declared Midas separate from the other two. Schriever funded Midas on a month-to-month basis with mostly AFBMD funds, so work continued on it. Even given these relatively large sums of money, Johnson did not authorize the air force to begin operational development of the WS-117L program.[41]

Despite the apparent setback, the air force scheduled the first launch attempt for December, 1958, as the system began to come together. The complete ground communications links between the tracking stations and the Palo Alto control center underwent a series of tests to ensure their operational readiness. The air force and Lockheed had a simple objective for the first flight: to prove that the booster and the ground support equipment worked and to check the telemetry, tracking, and control equipment. Other objectives included testing the interstation communications network and the crews' proficiency with the equipment and procedures. This would be the air force's first operational experience with satellite command and control.[42] Even NASA's brief experience with the Explorer program did not compare to the air force's ambitious, first Corona launch, but the attempt heralded bad tidings.

Despite the rapid progress in the development of a reconnaissance satellite, at this early stage in national space policy some Eisenhower administration officials saw such reconnaissance as contrary to the "peaceful purposes" directive because satellite overflight of foreign territory might violate international law, as the U-2 program had. The government assured the satellite program's security, which it considered of the "utmose [*sic*] importance from the political standpoint" through the CIA's actual responsibility for the program. Because any changes would have to come from the president, any recommendation the air force made to take over the program completely would "have to be of sufficient importance to have the President change his mind" about the CIA-led program, which the CIA did not deem likely. Disagreeing with the CIA's position, the air force planned aggressively for exploitation of the imagery and to "request complete control of the program [from the CIA] following any relaxation of the security policy."[43] Although no relaxation of the security policy would come until the 1990s, the air force successfully made its point that only it provided a satellite command and control capability for national defense.

ARPA used the new secrecy surrounding the military's satellite programs to expand the scope of its control over WS-117L at the air force's expense.[44] When the air force asked ARPA to declassify certain aspects of WS-117L, ARPA director Johnson denied the request. He knew the air force wanted to publicize its space program and that Lockheed even had a publicity program ready to advertise its participation. After discussions with the state department Johnson ordered the air force and its contractors to make no further reference to WS-117L, reconnaissance satellites, or even the "launching of very large satellites."[45] The state department had concerns that such publicity could disturb the general question of the international political framework in which the United States would place reconnaissance satellite programs. Moreover, the National Security Council was still considering that subject. Still trying to make its case as the nation's space service, the air force generally ignored Johnson's order to keep quiet and continued to greatly publicize its space activities and plans with press releases and magazine articles.[46] The promotion eventually so upset President Kennedy that, according to one staffer, apparently "every time the Air Force put up a space shot and any publicity was given to it, he just went through the roof."[47] Given the growing importance of space and satellites to the entire defense department, every interested group tried to appear as though it played a role.

ARPA tried to reduce the scope of other agencies' involvement by introducing a new level of secrecy to the military's space program, which the air force did not want. After the dramatic recovery of *Discoverer 13*, General Schriever met President Eisenhower to show off the reentry vehicle, the first object recovered from outer space. Because of the diagnostic nature of the mission, the bucket contained nothing other than an American flag, but ARPA officials closed the doors and sealed up the room to prevent too many details about the mission from "leaking out."[48] This action upset General Schriever because it restricted publicity about this first air force success after a string of thirteen failures. Schriever became more upset following the next Discoverer mission one week later. He later recalled, "I didn't know that they had a camera on *Discoverer 14*. Here I was, standing around, four-stars, giving them all the support," but ARPA officials neglected to tell Schriever the details of the mission.[49]

Already people thought about laying plans for a common-user satellite command and control network in the DoD with the Air Force Satellite Control Facility at the core. ARPA planned to use the Discoverer tracking facilities to support all other space programs. The total overall cost for FY 1960 stood at $64.1 million. In an effort to reduce costs, the defense department and NASA, the nation's other operator of such networks, tried to devise a satellite command and control system that would work for both of them. Secretary of Defense McElroy and NASA administrator T. Keith Glennan agreed to pool their resources and to reduce costs by carefully coordinating the requirements of all potential users of a tracking and data acquisition system. The entire network would not be built at once, only common parts necessary for R&D, although, as each matured and became more sophisticated, DoD and NASA expected to eventually go their own ways.

To increase the likelihood of cooperation, DoD and NASA agreed to global tracking, data acquisition, communications, and data centers for space flight. They recognized that NASA's requirements primarily supported R&D flights, whereas the military's requirements supported R&D as well as operational flights and intelligence gathering. The two agencies agreed to use the same facilities, including those at Goldstone and the NASA sites in Africa, Australia, Spain, and Japan. The NASA Vanguard center would also freely share data with the air force's Spacetrack facility at the Cambridge Research Center in Massachusetts. They also agreed to participate in worldwide communications networks. They would monitor developments by hosting a technical committee for the continuing study of global tracking, data acquisition, and communications problems.[50] At the May 13, 1959, meeting of the National Security Council, President Eisenhower gave priority "above all others for R&D and for achieving operational capability" to space projects that had "key political, scientific, psychological or military import," including the "DISCOVERER (satellite guidance and recovery)" program.[51] Everyone, including President Eisenhower, now understood the importance of satellite command and control for the national space effort.

In summary, then, the AFBMD and Lockheed, presiding over Subsystem

H, developed satellite command and control as much as possible in order to expand its role in the reconnaissance satellite program. Methods to make the system operational included cutting corners on paperwork; switching to physical recovery from data readout; using older equipment; and having the air force do as much of the legwork for Lockheed as possible. Lockheed and the air force, trying to control the new system on their own, dealt with other agencies, each attempting to take over part of the system. The Advanced Research Projects Agency, obviously interested in expanding its authority, used budgetary gimmicks, satellite program-renaming regimens, and other means to assert control over WS-117L. Yet, always in the background, the CIA pressed to get Corona ready as soon as possible and pushed the developers along.

Managers Wrest Control from Inventors

While the air force tried to increase the portion of the military's space program under its control, the Air Force Ballistic Missile Division dealt with a movement within the air force to bring WS-117L to readiness as soon as possible by turning it over to an operational command, namely SAC. AFBMD believed that an operational program conducted concurrently with a developmental program would unnecessarily divert resources from R&D and thus prevent the timely delivery of a fully developed system. If the air force needed additional satellites, facilities, or other provisions for operational or training reasons, it might extend R&D unnecessarily.[52] To advance their agenda, managers—both contractors and military officers—started to replace the inventors of satellite command and control.

Some in the AFBMD such as Col. Osmond Ritland, its deputy commander, believed that the operation of the reconnaissance satellites by a combat command, especially the all-nuclear SAC, might unnecessarily and unwarrantedly restrict the use of the overhead images of the USSR. The organization and operation of WS-117L in that framework, some worried, might lead to the exclusion of many desirable applications for a satellite system other than the collection of military intelligence. Even though the United States had a real, urgent, and lasting requirement for photoreconnaissance of the USSR, and while a satellite system could help fulfill this requirement, WS-117L could do more than gather military intelligence, he argued. An agency with a wider scope of understanding could also collect electronic, photographic, and visual data. In that case, the interpretation of the data would decide its final use. If a command such as SAC operated the system, the command's requirements—in this case, targets for nuclear weapons carried by bombers and missiles—would always come first and might even exclude other interests, such as those of the CIA, the Atomic Energy Commission, industry, the scientific community, or the United Nations. The United States could also employ such systems to transmit radio or television signals for propaganda purposes, collect weather information by observing worldwide cloud cover, track hurricanes or icebergs, support global navigation, collect data from airbursts of nuclear weapons, provide scientific and technical information, and enable worldwide mapping.[53]

CIA veteran Colonel Ritland recommended, therefore, that a service agency such as the AFBMD control the system to ensure that a single organization without a combat mission could meet the requirements of all agencies. The team involved in gathering, transmitting, and receiving data, independent of their interpretation and use, he believed, would be better able to support WS-117L. Ritland wanted to have one overall agency because the ground components of the system involved the greatest investment in dollars, research, and industrial personnel and would therefore be the most expensive part for a similar program to duplicate. Furthermore, because one set of collected data could be of use to several information consumers, Colonel Ritland believed that a single service agency such as AFBMD could serve many other agencies as well.[54] Ritland's suggestion that the air force create a service organization that could fully and expeditiously exploit the potential of WS-117L provided flexibility for future U.S. positions on space sovereignty in that it did not require subordination to an organization with an overpowering, single-purpose mission and a requirement for the application of resources.[55] The dynamic nature of the forces that operate in space distinguished the medium as unique. With the R&D community involved in the operational side as well, the researchers could be constantly on the alert for novel programs and original techniques to take full advantage of the new opportunities that space operations offered.[56] To the inventors of the satellite command and control system, staying involved seemed to be paramount.

Ritland also borrowed from the state department the argument that operation of WS-117L by SAC might "embarrass the United States in future international negotiations concerned with space sovereignty." America's declared space policy called for "peaceful uses of outer space," so placing the nuclear SAC in charge of a major U.S. space program seemed politically unwise. Knowing the many possible applications for a satellite system, Ritland did not want the air force to "confuse space operations with space warfare." Although a combat command may use a satellite either directly or otherwise just as they use aircraft, other military and nonmilitary users of space have "a much wider and more enduringly constructive interest in space." To avoid restricting future decisions, the initial organization and operational concept for WS-117L, Ritland suggested, should begin as a system operated by the military as a service to others as well as to itself.[57] Operation by the military made sense in that only the military had the resources, organization, and experience necessary to support such a program in the late 1950s.

To make known the point that the AFBMD provided space R&D services for the United States, the agency publicized its undertakings. Given the go-ahead for a satellite program, in 1958 the air force prepared an initial press release for the Discoverer series of test launches, masking the true Corona reconnaissance satellite with the biomedical research cover story. The press release described the new satellite as important for developing systems and techniques that would be employed in the production and operation of space vehicles, thus introducing the fallacy of WS-117L as a simple test program, not one with immediate operational goals. The air force's public affairs specialists included in the release a series of questions that they themselves answered and that were as significant for what they did not say as for what they did. Of particular interest are the bald-faced lies:

Question: Is the Discoverer a reconnaissance satellite?
Answer: No.
Question: Is it part of the Weapon System 117L—or Sentry—or Pied Piper program?
Answer: No. . . .
Question: If the Discoverer is not part of WS117L, and if it is not a reconnaissance satellite, will it make a contribution to a reconnaissance satellite program?
Answer: Ultimately, the Discoverer, like any satellite that achieves orbital capacity, can be expected to make a contribution to *every* other satellite program. However, reconnaissance as such is still very much in the research stage and must, of necessity, be considered in terms of future development. . . .
Question: Why is Discoverer being placed in a polar orbit?
Answer: Polar orbit is the only one from Vandenberg AFB with hardware presently available. Eastward launch from Vandenberg is prevented by safety considerations. Launch to the west would entail an unacceptable speed penalty.
Question: Why is a low altitude orbit being used?
Answer: High altitudes are not possible with the weight-thrust rationale [*sic*] established for Discoverer. Because of testing instrument requirements, a rather heavy payload is contemplated.
Question: Why not launch the Discoverer from Cape Canaveral?
Answer: The facilities at Cape Canaveral are overloaded. One of the purposes in constructing a missile range on the West Coast was to reduce the burden on the Atlantic Range.[58]

In addition, as this press release illustrates, to those seeking to wrest satellite command and control from its inventors, the issue of secrecy dominated. The air force believed in the logic behind itself as the organization to control Corona and its associated command and control network.

Any further air force attempts at publicity died in June, 1959. ARPA director Johnson terminated the photographic recovery (E-5) portion of Sentry, the official name for the reconnaissance mission of WS-117L, because "it duplicated, rather than complemented, other planned programs," although he did not mention which specific ones.[59] Johnson officially and publicly cancelled the reconnaissance satellite, but the essential elements (such as satellite command and control) remained because the cover story for Corona—the Discoverer biomedical research program—was already well established.

The air force underscored its position in discussions over the location of the central intelligence-processing center—not in the Washington, D.C., area, but near Omaha. In its early development plans, the AFBMD and Lockheed assigned responsibility for the Advanced Reconnaissance System Intelligence Center (ARSIC) to Eastman Kodak, producers of the film for Corona's camera, and the government, providers of the facilities. AFBMD saw ARSIC primarily as solving the problem of data handling on such a large scale that machine and personnel demands exceeded realistic values. In the April, 1956, development plan Lockheed wanted the ARSIC to be "managed and operated by contractor personnel to provide a stable organizational structure with full exploitation of accumulated experience."[60] Lockheed attempted to use the ARSIC to minimize redundancy and accelerate the interpretation of reconnaissance data. Not everyone thought the location of the ARSIC near SAC headquarters such a good idea. The intelligence community remained reluctant to grant access to their work, requirements, methods, and organization to nonoperating intelligence people.[61]

Development plans included putting the ARSIC at Offutt AFB, Nebraska, because the air force wanted to assign SAC, the presumed user of the photos to be gathered, as the operating command for WS-117L. The air force chose SAC as WS-117L's operator because it wanted to move the system away from Washington, thus preventing the navy from expanding its role in the military's space operations, and because it expected the overall satellite tracking mission to eventually include an antisatellite mission ("tracking" at this time meant command and control as well as detecting and following so-called silent satellites, which referred to friendly but inoperative satellites and all Soviet satellites).[62] The air force also planned to collocate the central tracking and data acquisition station in Nebraska and to staff it with military personnel as soon as possible.[63]

Believing in the "urgent need" for information generated by the missile threat from the USSR, Gen. Thomas Power, SAC's commander in chief, called any delay of the schedule "inconceivable" and wanted the air staff to provide the money required to have the satellite ready by July, 1962, and the Midas satellite by July, 1963, "even at the expense of other programs." Power's proposal included restricting facilities construction and equipment to the minimum necessary for the Samos and Midas programs only because he thought it "absolutely essential" to get those projects "off of dead center."[64] He wanted a "basic, operationally useable system. The sophistication and any required increased scope of activities should come later."[65] Power's goal was to obtain as much information as possible as soon as possible.

Air Force Chief of Staff Gen. Thomas D. White also believed it essential that the air force operate WS-117L but understood that SAC would not be the only user of the intelligence data. He asked General Power for patience because of problems "other than operational" in WS-117L and made it "abundantly clear" that the air force would not be allowed to implement the operations concept that designated SAC as the main operator. In particular, General White cancelled SAC's plan to have the ARSIC at the old Martin bomber plant near Omaha. "Operate" in General White's mind meant "launch, injection, command and control on orbit, data retrieval, data reduction as required, and dissemination of this new data to designated users" but did not include data exploitation to satisfy the air force's needs. "Other agencies," White told Power, would exploit the data. The air force could operate WS-117L as "a national asset responsive to all participating agencies."[66] The new managers began to assert themselves, but they still had to be aware of the real drivers behind satellite-based reconnaissance and command and control: the CIA and the NRO.

Some outside the air force, aware of the relationship of the reconnaissance satellite program with non–air force agencies, participated in the debate over who should manage the command and control system. In an interoffice memo Reuben F. Mettler of Space Technology Laboratories, a division of Ramo-Wooldridge, the prime systems engineering and technical direction contractor on WS-117L, demonstrated how the transition from developmental to operational status in satellites would differ from that for ballistic missiles. Mettler believed the division of responsibility between the developing agency (the Air Force Ballistic Missile Division) and the operating agency (SAC) required new ways of thinking. First, he knew that WS-117L might actually produce operational information from the first launch, well before the system had sufficiently matured to put the conventional "operational" label on it, let alone turn it over to SAC's checklist-driven operators. Second, he expected that continued developmental improvement of various components or subsystems would prevent a stable configuration of the satellite system. He suggested a more conservative approach, turning over satellites to SAC one-by-one after AFBMD had performed certain prescribed tests once a vehicle reached orbit. If it passed, the vehicle could be turned over to by-the-book SAC, who would then command the satellite on and off as required and operate the readout stations; if the satellite failed the tests, AFBMD could continue to use the vehicle for special developmental purposes.[67] In his own way Mettler suggested that the AFBMD delay as long as possible the turnover of the command and control system to the operational air force.

In a reply to Mettler, General Ritland, now commander of the AFBMD, acknowledged the one-by-one turnover of satellites but considered it unnecessary. Ritland assured Mettler that the AFBMD had established ground rules with SAC and the Air Defense Command (who would operate the missile launch warning satellites of the Midas program) concerning certain specified R&D objectives. In essence, before WS-117L could be made operational, the basic configurations, facilities, and procedures had to be well established and proven or AFBMD would not turn over the programs under their control to an operational command.[68] This is how the air force had always conveyed new weapon systems to operational commands; clearly, in the case of WS-117L, not everyone thought this was a good plan.

Herbert York, assistant secretary of the air force for R&D, agreed with Mettler. York believed in the necessity of thoroughly testing all of the system's elements in order to evaluate a particular method of reconnaissance. In fact, he asked the secretary of defense to stop the expenditure of funds for personnel training and acquisition of land for new facilities, including refurbishing the Martin plant in Omaha and data links from Vandenberg to Sunnyvale. In fact, York recommended to new Secretary of the Air Force Dudley C. Sharp a budget cutback for the reconnaissance satellite program by funding only one tracking and acquisition station.[69]

Air Force Vice Chief of Staff Gen. Curtis LeMay settled the debate temporarily. In an August 5, 1959, letter to ARDC and SAC, the former SAC commander in chief assigned his old command the responsibility of operational planning for employment and control of the Advanced Reconnaissance System but classified that knowledge as secret. Moreover, because the air force expected WS-117L to have operational potential right away, LeMay wanted SAC to be responsible for the data obtained from space and for providing information and data necessary for its continued development.[70] LeMay did not assign a specific timetable to the turnover of the program to SAC from ARDC.

To keep the eventual plans secret, the air force advertised the Air Research and Development Command as the WS-117L developer and operator and indicated that ARDC would activate the system and make it operational. The air force gave Air Defense Command operational control over Midas.

The air force did not release its actual goal to staff the reconnaissance system with SAC and ARDC personnel or its intention to eventually transfer the entire system to SAC, including the Air Force Satellite Control Facility and almost all of its subordinate units, which the air force classified top secret and placed on a strict need-to-know basis.[71]

Publicly, to develop and operate the system, the air force created a new service organization in April, 1959, to "support military space development and operational employment" of military satellites. Air Research and Development Command organized the 6594th Test Wing (Satellite) under the leadership of Lt. Col. Charles A. ("Moose") Mathison to "[e]xecute development, test, and evaluation programs in support of the DISCOVERER, SAMOS, and MIDAS programs" in order to develop and achieve "the initial USAF military capability to operate and maintain" them. The 6594th Test Wing (Satellite) set as its number-one goal the capability to "operate and maintain the SAMOS and MIDAS systems *with assigned military personnel* to include launching, tracking, data acquisition, data processing, data reduction and recovery for orbital space vehicles in accordance with the approved operational program schedules."[72] The new management had now taken its place.

In the April, 1960, edition of *Air Force/Space Digest,* Brig. Gen. Charles H. Terhune Jr., new vice commander of the AFBMD, talked about "the last great frontier." He described the Sunnyvale-based 6594th Test Wing (Satellite) as "the nation's first organization set up exclusively to satisfy the launch, tracking, acquisition, and recovery requirements of a satellite program." An AFBMD news release issued in October, 1960, said nothing about Strategic Air Command or, in fact, Air Defense Command. It described Project Samos simply as "a research and development program to determine the capabilities for making observations of the earth from satellites." It also made clear that the Vandenberg, Hawaii, and Kodiak tracking stations had primary responsibility for on-orbit telemetry, tracking, and commanding, while the Satellite Test Center received all orbital data and exercised command and control over Samos.[73]

Also in the April, 1960, edition of *Air Force/Space Digest,* General Terhune described the blue-suit operations in Sunnyvale. The goal of operations now included achieving "at the earliest practical time" the ability to operate and maintain—with military personnel—the command, control, engineering data-processing and computing facilities associated with the Satellite Test Annex in Sunnyvale and the tracking stations in Alaska, California, Hawaii, and New Hampshire.[74] Tracking, control, and communication with orbiting vehicles would be performed by staffs of NCOs, whom the air force considered similar to the troops who serviced fighters, bombers, and cargo planes. Civilian engineers would perform R&D, but when the systems became operational, the jobs would revert to military personnel.

Even at this early stage, using uniformed personnel to perform all of the operations and maintenance tasks proved problematic. The standardization division of the 6594th Test Wing (Satellite) undertook a study of the feasibility of air force maintenance of the Programmable Integrated Computer Equipment (PICE), a large magnetic core buffer that used Control Data Corporation's CDC 1604 computer and stored data from external sources to make it available upon request—what we would today call computer memory. The standardization office found it reasonable to proceed with a training course for air force personnel, who would ultimately assume maintenance responsibility for the PICE system. PICE's condition, still in "engineering status," meant that contractors had neither delivered certain peripheral equipment or handbooks nor established any official procedures, making it doubtful that the air force could assume full maintenance capability before January, 1962.[75] The system inventors demonstrated their reluctance to give way to the new management.

The responsibility for operating the tracking station under contract to ARDC belonged solely to Lockheed. In Hawaii, during the second half of 1960, the air force assigned military personnel at the 6593rd Instrumentation Squadron to work with the civilian contractor "in training and recovering orbiting vehicles." The station's contractor personnel integrated enlisted air force technicians into the subsystems that composed the tracking station, including the antennas, data readout, and communications networks. Air force personnel willingly assumed the positions Lockheed allocated them. According to one partial observer, from the beginning Lockheed workers accepted the air force technicians but were concerned about their own job security. Much to their relief, the air force staff showed the Lockheed employees that they would work with the contractors, not replace them. The air force team came under the direct supervision of Lockheed managers and rapidly moved around the station to supplement their operational knowledge, capability, and effectiveness.[76]

At the Satellite Test Center in Sunnyvale, earlier corners that had been cut for Lockheed in the area of documentation began to hurt the air force in the transition to blue-suit operations, preventing the new management from taking over as smoothly as it wanted. When air force personnel assumed the responsibility for flight test operations in data processing, they had a good deal of trouble finding written work that explained the specifics for accomplishing the mission. After discussing the matter with Lockheed personnel assigned to the section, the air force technicians learned that very little existed in writing concerning the operation, including no job procedures whatsoever. They partially solved the problem by sitting down with their Lockheed counterparts and thoroughly reviewing every process. The information they garnered enabled

Raising the 6593d Instrumentation Squadron's first fifty-star flag at the Hawaii tracking station. William E. Mileski, Lockheed station manager, presented the flag to Lt. Col. Charles D. Fisher, Jr., the station commander. Courtesy of the Air Force Space Command History Office collection.

them to write job procedures, develop task checklists, and prepare an interim manual on computer procedures for flight operations.[77] The contractors remained a part of the operation to help with procedures because the air force believed they did not have enough information to operate the system alone.

When Secretary of Defense McNamara assigned the air force the duties of research, development, testing, and evaluation of space programs and projects on March 6, 1961, the service took a step closer to management of the military's space operations. DoD directive 5160.32 effectively made the air force the DoD's executive agent for all space development programs, regardless of which service ultimately used it. The directive essentially reversed the decision to assign the responsibility of space systems development to the using agency, which Neil McElroy, McNamara's predecessor, had issued in September, 1959.[78] The air force now had to direct all field operations actively, including operations in Sunnyvale, a step beyond merely supervising the contractor's work.

On April 1, 1961, the air force stepped to the forefront of the military's space program, and Lockheed stepped back when the service took over the operations and maintenance of all ground-space equipment at the tracking stations from Lockheed and its subcontractors. The air force ordered the 6594th Aerospace Test Wing (Satellite) to develop "the capability to operate and support, with military personnel, selected elements of satellite systems." However, the directive left an out: "Where contractor operation or support is more economical and effective, it will be used." Therefore, Air Research and Development Command gave the operation of the satellite control facilities and the direct supervision for all technical and logistic support to the 6594th Aerospace Test Wing (Satellite). This change represented a major shift in air force policy because to this point Lockheed had been the operator, while the 6594th only monitored Lockheed's operations.[79] Now the military managers of the Air Force Satellite Control Facility stepped in to take charge from the experienced contractors, who nevertheless remained because "contractor operation or support [was] more economical and effective."

The air force now played a more direct role in the operations and maintenance of the stations, although the personnel remained mostly the same. The AFSCF prepared and published operations and equipment integration procedures as well as long-range planning information and directed the briefing of the crews on mission requirements. At New Boston, the squadron operations officer—an air force lieutenant colonel and the number-two officer at the station—introduced a three-crew rotation with an air force officer in command of each team. This arrangement permitted round-the-clock staffing of the tracking station under constant and direct air force control. A satellite operations crew of sixty-two military and contractor personnel, almost evenly split between the two groups, conducted operations.[80]

Management's new ways caused a few ripples for contractors who did not move every two or three years and earned a decent wage for the most part. Contractors now backed up air force personnel on the consoles, assisting where necessary. For example, a staff sergeant usually worked at one operating position called the "17-inch scope readout." During a normal satellite support, the sergeant read the satellite's binary telemetry from the scope and confirmed that a command had been transmitted to the satellite and that the satellite had properly acknowledged it. The readout may also have indicated that further commands might be required, so the sergeant's report had to be accurate and timely. One sergeant took a particularly long time and frequently provided the wrong information, which forced the assistant shift supervisor, a contractor, to back him up from across the room while also running the tape recorders. The contractors strove for 100-percent error-free supports and came close most of the time. The air force eventually made the number of errors the basis for the contract award fee.[81]

Despite minor problems, operations went just as smoothly after the change as before. On August 18, 1960, *Discoverer 14* went into orbit as planned from its launch pad at Vandenberg AFB at 12:15 P.M. Pacific time. The 1,700-pound satellite with its 300-pound reentry capsule circled Earth every 94.5 minutes at 17,568 miles per hour with a perigee of 116 miles and an apogee of 502 miles.[82] At the windowless Satellite Test Center, Col. Alvin N. Moore, commander of the 6594th Test Wing (Satellite), along with high-ranking air force officers and Lockheed engineers, kept a close vigil on the vehicle. Information from the tracking stations at Vandenberg, Alaska, New Hampshire, and Hawaii and at sea from the USNS *Private Joe E. Mann* poured into the center by voice and teletype. Although depending on a supporting contractor, Colonel Moore's unit developed a real air force capability to operate any and all satellite systems whenever they become operational.[83]

The face of the new aerospace force—curious young scientists and engineers, both civilians and military—built the organization and instilled an ambitious focus. The leadership, a mix of seasoned officers, noncommissioned officers, and contractors, knew that experience gained through failure could be just as important as success.[84] Young technicians with stripes on their arms stood behind the officers and contractors with new knowledge and new tools, tuning and adjusting the systems. The satellite command and control system tolerated failures in those days; today it does not. National leaders, the press, the public, and so on placed a different premium on success because no one had ever launched satellites into space and used them to gather intelligence.

Today we talk about learning from failure; these inventors formalized that process in the early days, even if they did not call it "lessons learned." Said one former operator, "We just called it experience. But that's one thing we were doing, trying to go to school on each day, on each thing we did, on those things that would work, on those things that worked well, and on those things that didn't work so well."[85] As another veteran summarized the process, "Let's have a Coke, say hello to the wife and kids, then start over again."[86]

Managers, both contractors and military officers, began to replace the inventors of satellite command and control, who faded from the center of the air force's R&D activity. Some in the air force believed that the sole user of the WS-117L photos should be SAC, the nation's foremost nuclear command. What SAC leaders did not understand—or did not want to—was that other agencies in the U.S. government, particularly the CIA, also considered WS-117L's data necessary. People not privy to the decision makers at the highest levels often assumed that the air force should be the sole operator of WS-117L. The air force successfully argued that a service organization should be responsible for command and control of WS-117L, creating the 6594th Test Wing (Satellite) to perform that function, thus keeping the majority of space operations in the air force, even if the reconnaissance data went elsewhere. The 6594th displaced the inventors of satellite command and control with new management, bringing new opportunities to the Air Force Satellite Control Facility.

Summary

In their attempt to create satellite command and control from tried and true techniques, the Air Force Ballistic Missile Division and Lockheed tried to develop Subsystem H as much as possible. At the urging of the contractors and the air force, the structure began to expand. In addition, numerous players, attempting to win control of their own bit of the turf, prevented Lockheed and the air force from directing the entire system. By 1961, managers, both contractors and military officers, had begun to replace the inventors of satellite command and control, who moved from this important point of air force space activity to other satellite programs and challenges.

Furthermore, after successfully arguing that a service organization—not a combat unit—should be responsible for command and control of the WS-117L program, the air force created a more complex system consisting of service facilities. Thus the 6594th Test Wing (Satellite), which was established to service satellites, created the belief in satellite command and control as a critical air force function. The 6594th began to displace the inventors of satellite command and control with new management that had to face different challenges in the mid-1960s, including how to deal with the growth of the Air Force Satellite Control Facility. The air force had certainly managed to "get off of dead center," but as yet the new satellite command and control system still had only one customer: the Corona reconnaissance satellite.

4

Too Many Fingers in the Pie
Growing into a Satellite Control System

[There] was a different premium on success but, hey, folks were kind of stumbling around. They'd never done this [space operations] before. As my daddy would say, "This time and once more will make twice we did that."

—Lt. Gen. Forrest McCartney, USAF, Retired
Operator of Corona Flight 14

O N *DISCOVERER 14'S* seventeenth orbit, a controller at the Kodiak remote tracking station transmitted the eject command to the spacecraft. Three hundred miles above Earth, explosive bolts fired and separated the film-carrying reentry vehicle from the Agena vehicle, beginning the gold-plated bucket's fiery journey back to Earth. At 50,000 feet the capsule's parachute opened, and the capsule began transmitting its automatic radio beacon. As the capsule's descent slowed to 1,600 feet per second, air force Capt. Harold Mitchell and the crew of *Pelican Nine*, a recovery-equipped, C-119 *Flying Boxcar*, caught up with the descending capsule in plenty of time. Mitchell completed two passes over the parachute, closer to the water each time but unable to snag the reentry vehicle. On the third pass, a slight tug on the C-119's controls told Mitchell he would go down in air force history as the first pilot "to catch a falling star."[1]

By the time this highly significant event in aerospace history took place, the Air Force Satellite Control Facility was supporting three military satellite programs: Discoverer, the cover story for the Corona imaging satellite; Midas, America's first infrared missile warning satellite; and Samos, the ancestor of all modern reconnaissance satellites. Each system used a different combination of remote tracking stations with significantly different tracking equipment, personnel, performance quality, and methods of operation.[2] Engineers had not yet developed digital space computers and thus exercised technical creativity with the existing equipment. Tracking, orbit determination, telemetry

Catching a "Falling Star": U.S. Air Force Capt. Howard Mitchell's aerial recovery of Discoverer/Corona 14 *with a* C-119 Flying Boxcar, *August, 1960. Courtesy of the Air Force Space Command History Office collection.*

and data analysis, and command processing and generation all required extensive data processing using relatively simple and extremely bulky analog computers. In the early approach to satellite command and control, each tracking station analyzed, interpreted, and reduced most of a satellite's data. Controllers in Sunnyvale handled the operation of the payload, monitored the vehicle's general status, and controlled the satellite.

To perform the orbital calculations, the Air Force Satellite Control Facility (AFSCF) used several general-purpose computers, including two large CDC 1604 computers from Control Data Corporation. The CDC 1604, a fully transistorized, stored-program, general-purpose computer, had 32,768 48-bit words of core memory storage. In addition, Vandenberg and New Hampshire each had a single CDC 1604 computer for data analysis and control, making them essentially stand-alone command and control stations.[3] These rudimentary ground sites had simple antennas to track the satellite beacon, modified World War II-era SCR-584 radars for transmitting commands and receiving telemetry, and telemetry receivers and transmitters to reset the satellite's programming when necessary. Telephone and teletype circuits connected the ground sites to the Satellite Test Center in Sunnyvale.

Adequate communications made—and still make—orbiting satellites possible. An extensive computer system fed the control room of the Satellite Test Center at Sunnyvale, one of the world's most modern communications hubs. The test controller—the operator who sent commands to the satellite—and the test director—the expert on all on-board systems—had closed-circuit television screens, push-button communications panels, and two-way headsets all feeding them information. Other consoles recorded the communications. Twenty-six television cameras showed the plotting boards for the satellite and reentry capsule. Incoming and outgoing messages on the teletype systems and various combinations of voice conferences kept the test crews informed and up-to-date. Viewgraph screens showed current weather conditions over the recovery site, maps, plots, and everything else the operators needed to know.

Recovery crew of Discoverer/Corona 14 *with U.S. Air Force Lt. Gen. Bernard A. Schriever (center), August, 1960. Because they were not cleared for the Corona reconnaissance satellite program, the crew did not know it had just recovered more photos of the Soviet Union than in all the previous U-2 flights combined. Courtesy of the Air Force Space Command History Office collection.*

Time ticked off on three separate systems: local time (Pacific), Zulu Time (Greenwich Mean Time [GMT]), and system time (total elapsed seconds).[4] If anything, the operators had too much information, a problem even today.

This large technological system evolved in the early 1960s into a true satellite command and control network only by overcoming a variety of challenges. As the structure grew, problems developed as some components fell behind or out of phase with others. One major difficulty involved communications between the remote tracking stations and the Satellite Test Center. To accommodate a vehicle's requirements, the command center's network connected specific equipment, subsystems, and the remote tracking stations. At first, an antenna connected to a specific receiver interfaced with its own program-specific control, display, and command equipment, but the technology was unable to process the data as rapidly as the system engineers desired. The equipment at the remote tracking stations required hours or even days to configure and test each of the satellite programs on which the air force "experimented."

By the early 1960s, the air force satellite command and control system had evolved from a simple plan designed to support one program, Corona, into an increasingly cumbersome hodgepodge of equipment and procedures. Long satellite life exposed a number of problems that previous operations had not uncovered. For example, the early timing system simply counted the seconds after liftoff. Because early Corona flights lasted a maximum of only seventeen orbits, programmers limited the timing system's capacity to about 48 hours, or 172,800 mission-elapsed seconds. With more than one vehicle in orbit at the same time, engineers scrapped the system of counting mission-elapsed seconds in favor of using GMT. With one of the early vehicles in orbit over New Year's Day, a new dilemma arose: Because the programming could not handle the year change, the ephemeris computer refused to provide tracking predictions. When controllers gave the computer fictitious launch data, it started to generate the orbital data, affording a temporary solution.[5] Even then, on-orbit operations lasted only a few days.

Lack of engineering foresight was not the cause of every problem, however. In this complex technological system, the environment sometimes presented new challenges to overcome, such as what to do about new satellite programs on orbit. Furthermore, when experts could not correct a major problem within the context of the existing system, the solution gave rise to a new and competing system. As the AFSCF grew increasingly conservative, a radical command and control system was developed for the weather satellites; this competing program suggests that the AFSCF could have turned out quite differently.[6] By overcoming technical and operational challenges, AFSCF engineers created a network that was capable of supporting multiple reconnaissance satellites.

Technological Challenges

The earliest configuration of the Kodiak tracking station is a good example of the basic design of the first satellite command and control system. Two antennas—a VERLORT (Very Long Range Tracking), three-pulse tracking and commanding radar (an old bomb scoring radar that was modified to accommodate satellite orbital distances) and a trihelix, telemetry-receiving antenna—served Kodiak. The station communicated offsite by teletype or telephone. Encrypted teletype messages told Kodiak's controllers the launch and satellite support schedules; after each satellite support they sent the logs and telemetry readouts back by teletype, telephone, or mail. Controllers used real-time voice, transmitting in the clear, for every other operation.[7]

The simple design meant that technicians could easily overcome certain problems. In late 1961, a taper pin fell out of the elevation mechanism of the trihelix antenna during an early stage of a satellite support. The elevation axis fell to nearly zero, and the drive motor failed to raise the antenna. The azimuth axis continued to operate properly, however, and the sloppy beam pattern of the trihelix antenna—coupled with the powerful transmitter—meant that the support operation continued normally and collected all of the data even though the antenna probably never pointed directly at the satellite. The antenna motion followed along the horizon while the satellite passed nearly overhead.[8] The satellite's transmitter had more power than was needed, and the ground antenna had a higher gain than necessary, demonstrating how much the command and control community still had to refine, yet also how effectively it was already performing.

The inexperience in satellite command and control also meant that the tracking stations spent three or four weeks in operations rehearsals while gearing up to a maximum effort for a launch. The transmitter's oscillators required thirty minutes to tune, which necessitated a long time between satellite supports and was part of the reason for a lack of speed in satellite operations. In addition, the controllers had to tune the bore-sight transmitter and the tunable bandpass filter; as a result, they needed about forty-five minutes to change operating frequencies. Although the underdeveloped system required an extremely high level of maintenance, it nevertheless worked from the first launch, even if the boosters and satellites did not.

Information flow and data processing remained two of the most convoluted issues for the Air Force Satellite Control Facility in the late 1950s. The data flow involved in conveying a command plan to a tracking station required a separate, twenty-four-step procedure for each site. The process for transmitting an acquisition programmer tape to a remote tracking station began with verbal arrangements to verify readiness to transmit and receive by teletype.

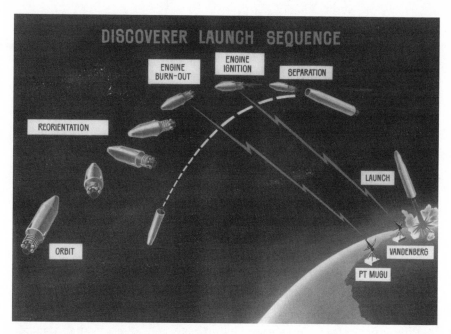

The Discoverer/Corona *launch sequence. Courtesy of the Air Force Historical Research Agency collection.*

The transmission had to be made at the acquisition of the satellite's signal minus thirty-five minutes in order to allow a preplot of the tape, verification of its validity, and any necessary adjustments to the equipment. Stations using computers linked through the Programmable Integrated Communications Equipment (PICE) experienced a shorter transmission period, but they, too, needed enough time to validate the program, print the data, and distribute the information to specified users.[9]

To make matters worse, the Air Force Satellite Control Facility also had two basic satellite tracking systems. First, the VERLORT radar system used frequencies in the S-band, normally operating in conjunction with an active beacon on the satellite. By supplying range and angles, the VERLORT enabled technicians to establish the orbital parameters (ephemeris). Second, the newer tracking system used the Doppler frequency shift of an active satellite (as it moved closer to or farther from the receiver) to determine range and thus orbital parameters. The basic system employed a transponder on the satellite, which returned the radio waves the ground station sent to it. Ground station computers compared the transmitted and received frequencies to derive the Doppler information. The vehicle transmitted its health and status through a telemetry link to the ground station, where controllers analyzed the data or sent the information to the satellite controllers in Sunnyvale. One telemetry system employed frequency-division multiplexing, which joined multiple channels of data (in this case up to eighteen) to one VHF radio transmission, with certain data multiplexed onto selected channels. The other telemetry system used time-division multiplexing, which linked multiple channels of data to one radio transmission by varying the time when the data were sent, a general-purpose and much more flexible system, but ultimately slower and carrying less data than frequency-division multiplexing. To control the vehicle in real time, rather than using commands stored on the vehicle exclusively, controllers in Sunnyvale used two basic commanding systems. One utilized digital modulation of VERLORT radar pulses while the other used analog modulation of radar transmissions, a much slower method.[10]

The technological constraints on the Air Force Satellite Control Facility affected the operators' ability to carry out tasks in real time. The significance of an operator's decision became one of the most important constraints because the time required to receive and analyze data, make decisions, and generate commands could be less than five minutes for a satellite with a 300-nautical-mile orbit. Because of the low orbits, it became nearly impossible—once an operator made a decision—to take corrective action, given the short satellite support times at the stations. Controllers "planned the flight and flew the plan." For near-Earth orbits, controllers used the "Six Second Rule: Two seconds to identify the problem, two seconds to decide what to do, and two seconds to do it."[11] When in doubt, they "safed" the vehicle to prevent a catastrophic failure. Because of the possibility of losing a satellite and its critical national security information, highly competent operators were essential.[12]

In April, 1959, the Air Force Satellite Control Facility lost a reconnaissance satellite. *Discoverer 2* successfully reached orbit in the correct orientation—tail first—and stabilized in all three axes, the first satellite ever three-axis stabilized. The test plan called for an automatic reentry, but the satellite orbited too low. As *Discoverer 2* passed over Kodiak, a controller entered the sequence to reset the timer on the automatic reentry counter. The console erroneously showed that he had sent the wrong command, so he reentered the command sequence. Then, under time pressure, he forgot to press the "Reset" button, and the new commands entered the vehicle, which added them to the old ones, locking out any further attempt to communicate. On April 14, one day after launch, the capsule ejected from the vehicle and came down not in the warm Hawaiian "ballpark" where C-119 pilots waited to snatch it from the sky but on snowy Spitzbergen Island, north of Norway, where Sergei Khrushchev, son of the Soviet premier, later confirmed that the Soviets had recovered it for Sergei Korolev's design bureau.[13]

Lockheed and Philco had built the satellite command and control system

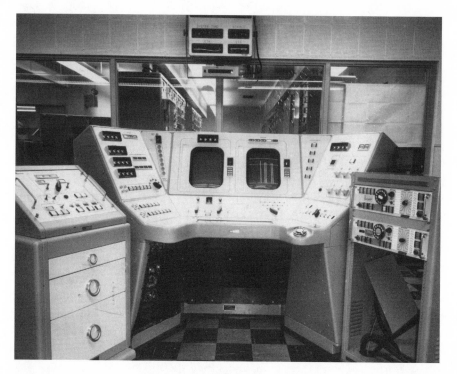

Payload control console at the Cooke (later Vandenberg) Air Force Base tracking station, 1960. Courtesy of the Air Force Historical Research Agency collection.

for a single satellite program, Corona, and included in the plan several ground stations and the control center, so they needed only a simple design. As other satellite programs matured, the air force and its contractors augmented the network with satellite-specific equipment for those programs, adding even more stations and equipment, in many cases just as a quick fix. Therefore, an important aspect of systems engineering became planning the future Air Force Satellite Control Facility's configuration and ensuring that it offered adequate support to all air force satellite programs. At the same time, the systems engineers tried to simplify operations and maintenance by making tradeoffs between simple subsystems with a minimum number of interconnections and complex subsystems with a great deal of automation.[14] As the national priority of space reconnaissance rose during the Cold War, the air force needed the AFSCF to handle multiple satellites in real time.

A future with multiple orbiting satellites complicated operations for the Air Force Satellite Control Facility. By 1961, planners understood that the AFSCF might reach a saturation point, for both personnel and equipment, because of the increasing number of satellites orbiting simultaneously. The factors that had led to the *Discoverer 2* failure would be exacerbated as the heavens filled with satellites. The proposed solutions included more equipment standardization, a unique operating frequency for each satellite, and augmentation of existing facilities.[15]

Just fulfilling operational requirements became difficult as the number of satellites in orbit increased and system requirement planning became too much for the AFSCF to handle. Col. Walter R. Headrick Jr., director of the air force satellite control project at Los Angeles Air Force Station, recognized the need for a separate office to direct the R&D in tracking station equipment configuration and procedures. Without standardized routines in every facility, the whole satellite command and control system could quickly degrade. To prevent saturation, the air force needed scientific and technical assistance in planning and evaluating new ideas, designing systems, evaluating contractors' proposals, and monitoring progress. As the system became increasingly complex, the actual R&D became more bureaucratized.

In 1961, Colonel Headrick asked Aerospace Corporation to establish a satellite control office to provide general systems engineering and technical direction support for the AFSCF. Aerospace had a senior engineering staff that possessed exceptional technical competence in instrumentation, computer applications, antennas, space communications, and data processing, which the air force lacked. Headrick appealed directly to Ivan Getting, Aerospace's president. Aerospace set up an office in the Palo Alto area under Ezra Kotcher to take charge of system engineering and technical direction. In October, Aerospace established a satellite control office under Stanley D. Crane at El Segundo, near Headrick's office. These civilian engineers helped the air force create a unified facility capable of rapidly and efficiently expanding its support of the swiftly increasing military space program.[16]

To achieve this new system concept, Aerospace's satellite control office conducted a series of engineering analyses. During its first nine months of operation, the satellite control office evaluated ideas about various subsystems to meet near-term support requirements. It also continued to assist current operations by identifying and solving immediate problems. Most important, the office developed a concept that was flexible enough to accommodate the support requirements of all satellite programs, present and future. To forecast future program requirements and instrumentation capabilities, the engineers extrapolated from the existing ones. They believed that a more sophisticated structure would result in increased data transmission rates and position measurement accuracy as well as longer satellite lifetimes.

In January, 1962, the air force contracted System Development Corporation (SDC) of Santa Monica, California, to review every aspect of the Air Force Satellite Control Facility in a series of studies. SDC, which evolved from the

Hawaii tracking station, 1961. Courtesy of the Air Force Historical Research Agency collection.

systems development division of the RAND Corporation, was established in 1955 to prepare Semiautomatic Ground Environment (SAGE) system-training programs for nuclear attack warning. They evaluated the capabilities and conditions of the existing systems and subsystems, existing and planned workloads, and expenditures and requirements. They assessed the AFSCF's ability to support the assigned load, and focused particular attention on the period from 1963 to 1965, when the air force planned to bring on line the Midas and Samos missile warning and observation programs. Their plan supported multiple satellite operations for extended periods by standardizing the configuration of station equipment and implementing system-oriented methods for data handling and control.[17]

SDC concentrated its new concept on multiple satellites and real-time supports, which required that the Satellite Test Center in Sunnyvale and all remote tracking station systems be simplified and standardized. Aerospace Corporation presented the detailed concept to the air force in early 1962. They had tried to ascertain the most cost-effective way to integrate new equipment, capabilities, and methods into existing ground systems and spacecraft. Aerospace documented its results and submitted them to Colonel Headrick for review. After acceptance, the Air Force Statement of Work comprised the Request for Proposal for the aerospace industry, forming the basis of the first major upgrade of the AFSCF, known as the Multiple Satellite Augmentation Program. Although its acronym was MSAP, most people called it simply "Augie." The air force approved MSAP in April, 1962, but, because of funding limitations, divided the program into two phases, MSAP-A and MSAP-B.[18]

Aerospace Corporation also planned a second upgrade program, called the "STC Interim Expansion." This program included the Advanced Data System project involving new software for the Air Force Satellite Control Facility and a new communications system called EXCELS. Aerospace Corporation saw the standardization of frequencies and satellite beacons as fundamental to these upgrades. The defense department's standard telemetry, command, and control system, called the Space-Ground Link Subsystem, grew out of the unified S-band system that Eberhardt Rechtin and others at NASA's Jet Propulsion Laboratory had developed between 1954 and 1964.[19] The air force implemented most of Aerospace Corporation's plans, resulting in vast numbers of hardware and software changes.

By the end of the MSAP upgrade, the Air Force Satellite Control Facility consisted of a central control station called the Satellite Test Center (STC) and six remote tracking stations, three of which could control two satellites at once. The STC had enough computers and operations areas to control six satellites simultaneously, dividing the data-processing subsystems into two main areas: The "bird buffer" complex had eight Control Data Corporation CDC 160A

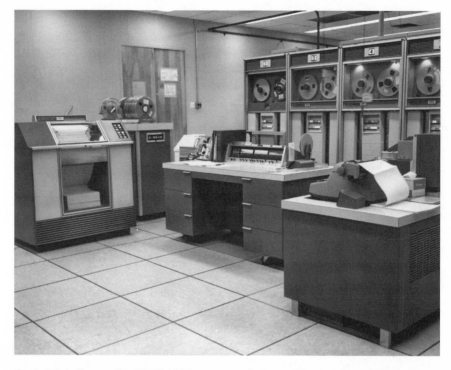

Control Data Corporation (CDC) 160A computers in the tracking and control area at the Cooke (later Vandenberg) Air Force Base tracking station, 1963. Courtesy of the Air Force Historical Research Agency collection.

computers, a fully transistorized, stored-program, general-purpose computer, each with a 32K core memory, individually assigned to an active satellite and acting as a data handler between the STC and the remote tracking stations; the other computer complex used four CDC 160A computers to do the main computational chores for the entire system. Computer-controlled switches connected the bird buffers with the CDC 160As on one side and the tracking station computers on the other. Each CDC 160A computer, "a flexible, multi-purpose computer constructed in a standard-size office desk," stored program data, processed, and converted them with high-speed, transistorized circuits.[20]

At the tracking stations, three main equipment groupings dominated. The antenna subsystems consisted of a 60-foot antenna and provided communications between the satellites and the ground. The data-processing subsystem included two CDC 160A computers, one for telemetry processing and one for tracking and commanding, handling data going both to and from Sunnyvale. The telemetry, tracking, and commanding subsystem passed data between the antennas and the data-processing computers. Manual patch

boards linked the three equipment groupings, adding flexibility to the tracking stations, but also creating many "opportunities" for manual errors.[21]

Unfortunately, the MSAP installation did not go smoothly throughout the
network. On July 17, 1963, a Western Development Laboratory (part of the
Philco Corporation) engineer under contract for the installation project attempted to balance the synchro cables from one building to another at New
Boston. When he reinserted the plugs, white smoke issued from the cable ter-
mination cabinet. Instead of connecting the plugs, he had short-circuited all
the leads to the junction box. The unit's historian recorded that a check revealed that an engineer had cross-connected a cabinet. Operations personnel
spent the next eight hours repairing the cable. The outage precluded the use
of the station for one operational support, risking the loss of a satellite. "Too
many fingers in the pie," wrote the historian.[22]

Despite the problems during installation, the MSAP created a new multiple satellite capability and, for the first time, a real satellite control network.
In late 1962, New Boston began continuously performing supports involving
as many as five different types of satellites at the same time, a far cry from the

*The Multiple Satellite Augmentation Program's FM-FM ground station at the Vandenberg
tracking station, 1964. Courtesy of the Air Force Historical Research Agency collection.*

one satellite in orbit every four or five weeks. The peak load consisted of four actual supports and one launch rehearsal. On eight-hour shifts around the clock, each of the three crews frequently tracked two satellites passing over the station simultaneously. As they did so, the available time to prepare for the next operation shrank, which required the crews to be increasingly proficient. In short, station activities grew during this period from assisting an occasional satellite to supporting several satellites constantly.[23]

In sum, the AFSCF overcame the technological challenge of supporting multiple, orbiting reconnaissance satellites by reengineering the command and control system to handle an increased load. From what had been individual remote command and control stations in a military organization, the MSAP tied the group together as a real network. Nevertheless, when the program presented obstacles the experts could not overcome within the context of the existing scheme, they created a new and competing system of satellite command and control.

Program II

The air force launched the first weather reconnaissance satellites in the early 1960s. Program II, as the National Reconnaissance Office initially called the system to mask its weather reconnaissance mission, depended for its first year of operation on the ground stations that Col. Thomas O. Haig, weather satellite program manager, had originally helped develop for Corona. Haig had to overcome the major difference between Corona and the weather satellite program: Corona vehicles orbited for only about three days and then returned their film, while the batteries on the remaining Agena booster died; the weather satellites, which did not return film but transmitted data, stayed operational and in orbit for months. The tracking stations spent three or four weeks in rehearsals to prepare for a maximum effort for a Corona launch but had only a few minutes to get ready for each support of a weather satellite. The system Lockheed initially built for Corona was unable to make rapid changes or to support multiple satellites.

After a Corona mission, successful or not, all of the tracking stations shut down, and everybody left. On average, Corona launched about once a month, and the early successful vehicles lasted for only about seventeen orbits of ninety minutes each. The weather vehicles, on the other hand, passed overhead two or three times a day at every tracking station, downloading weather telemetry each time, which meant the stations had to stay staffed and operating around the clock, which was not the way Lockheed had originally planned to operate the system. The weather program, despite its usefulness for prioritizing picture taking for Corona operators, disrupted the normal operations of the Lockheed-built tracking network. Additionally, Lockheed had no interest in the weather satellites because RCA had built them. The Lockheed-run tracking stations, to paraphrase Colonel Haig, gave the weather program terrible assistance. They supported only about half of the times the weather satellites were overhead and thus missed useful weather readouts. The weather satellite operators never knew for sure whether commands had actually gotten to the satellite until long afterward, when Lockheed reluctantly sent a message by teletype: "We got it" or "We didn't get it."[24] This inability to satisfactorily serve another program cost the AFSCF a potential customer. To solve the problem of intermittent support from the AFSCF, with significant implications for satellite systems, the weather satellite program simply built its own command and control network.

Colonel Haig, as Program II's manager for the National Reconnaissance Office, frequently traveled to Sunnyvale to berate people for the lack of support for his program, always starting with Lt. Col. Moose Mathison, the on-site commander. Together Haig and Mathison went to Lockheed and talked with the engineers and directors, who listened but ignored them. According to Haig, he got little response from them because the weather satellite program "annoyed" Lockheed. Eventually, Under Secretary of the Air Force Joseph Charyk, director of the NRO, issued an order that "Lockheed will support this program, period." Still, it took a long time for the order to affect the staff at the stations.[25]

Before the second year of operation began, Charyk told Haig to extend the weather satellite program. Haig went back to Lockheed to get an estimate of the cost for another year of command and control support. Using the Sult formula, Lockheed suggested a figure that would have consumed more than three-fourths of the total weather satellite budget, even before Haig had bought boosters and satellites. At that point Haig and his team spent two weeks of frantic effort designing their own ground stations and control center, using equipment components from the Eastern Test Range island of Eleuthera. They put together a proposal and then received Charyk's approval to go ahead. For about 20 percent of what Lockheed wanted to charge for one year's operation, Haig's team built and equipped the ground stations and the control center for the weather satellite program. Moreover, they did it all in under six months. Charyk later described his ideal program manager as a "kind of guy who, first of all, has a strong grasp of basic management principles, who has the energy and drive that goes with it, and [has] either the feel for the technical aspects of it, or [has] the good sense to know where to go to get it, that produces the best situation."[26] Charyk could have been talking about Tom Haig.

In case of a conflict between a Corona satellite and a weather satellite,

Lockheed and the AFSCF always paid attention to the Corona satellite, which Haig understood since his security clearance included access to Corona. The four hours the ground stations spent testing and configuring equipment before and after a Corona support exasperated the AFSCF's other potential customers. Those processes seemed wasteful and inflexible, but Lockheed insisted that this was "preparation time." For Haig, the contractors seemed very difficult to work with, even though the weather satellite program had no direct contract with Lockheed. Instead, Haig's program had to work through the AFBMD in Los Angeles. Fed up, Haig created a separate, two-station command and control network for the weather satellites.

Haig later moved to the NRO in the Pentagon, and there he made a recommendation to Alexander Flax, deputy NRO director, based on his experience with the weather satellite program, that began to separate the different, national satellite reconnaissance programs. Lockheed struggled with a great many technical difficulties, including conflicts between various satellites in orbit. In the early days of the Multiple Satellite Augmentation Program, Lockheed had still not learned how to support several satellites efficiently. Occasionally the satellites came by at the same time, so operators had to choose one or the other, which meant that one satellite did not get serviced, sometimes at a cost to national security, such as when not sending commands or receiving data resulted in lost data. Haig suggested that the NRO should separate, or "stovepipe," the satellites, that is, build a dedicated ground network for each system, rather than a consolidated one like the AFSCF. Flax recommended Haig's idea under his own signature, angering those in Los Angeles who feared an upset in the AFSCF empire.[27] Dedicated networks like those in Haig's proposal may even have hastened the "blue-suiting" of these programs. A simpler, dedicated ground environment seemed more sensible, and in fact some reconnaissance programs developed a dedicated system of some type. The long-term implications of this trend, though, proved wasteful and problematic as the AFSCF performed its mission more efficiently, budgets shrank, and the Cold War ended.

The weather program also developed its systems without a systems engineering contractor. From his experience with the tracking stations in Corona, Haig knew what a satellite ground station required. He also had in the program office one very smart, young air force officer, Capt. Lou Ricks. Because they had a small headquarters, just four officers and a secretary, they moved fast and made decisions quickly. In addition, Haig did not report to anybody but the NRO director. Once a month Haig created his word charts and jumped on an all-night flight from Los Angeles to Washington, D.C., where he reported to the NRO director, received instructions, went back to Los Angeles, and then reported to Brig. Gen. Robert M. Greer, the AFBMD deputy commander. Haig often went to Greer's office and gave him the same briefing he had given Charyk, plus all of the instructions Charyk had given him.[28]

For a while the weather satellite program operated smoothly and efficiently. According to Haig, Charyk and Brockway McMillan, Charyk's successor as NRO director, considered the program as "sort of a toy." They used it to "tweak Lockheed's tail and to do battle with [Space Technology Laboratories], too."[29] That the program succeeded extremely well with blue-suit operators "on fixed-price contracts without any Space Technology Laboratories involvement of any kind whatsoever was choked down Lockheed's throats many times." Said Haig, Aerospace Corporation chief "Ivan Getting considered me the biggest pain in the butt he'd ever had."[30] Every now and then, according to Flax, former NRO chief, someone in Congress or the Bureau of the Budget stumbled on the fact that the United States had two weather satellite programs: NASA's Tiros and NRO's Program II. Sometimes the air force program ran ahead of the NASA budget, sometimes the other way around. The two organizations did not have common cost-accounting systems, but the NRO, according to Flax, acquired its satellites "a hell of a lot cheaper than NASA's and they [NASA] said that was because we did our bookkeeping differently."[31] Even today government accounting is certainly a mystery, but the NRO did its accounting in the hidden world of the national intelligence program, while NASA's accounting occurred in the public eye, making comparisons tenuous at best.

The weather satellite program made direct contributions to ground station development. When he built the weather satellite ground stations, Colonel Haig, having learned from the Corona stations, overcame the need for a big bore-sight antenna calibration tower three to five miles away from the main antenna but within the receiving antenna's line of sight. The Corona bore-sight towers stood far enough away from the receivers to cancel out ground effects; thus the antenna operators were able to get a clear signal from a little transmitter at the top of the tower. The operators pointed the antenna at the bore sight to determine the electrical vector, the true pointing angle for the simulated satellite, and then used the little transmitter on the tower to calibrate the receiving loop all the way through the antenna down to the receiving equipment. The expensive bore-sight towers stood about 150 feet tall, requiring a significant amount of land. Haig's solution was much simpler. He suggested that they use the sun instead of using a bore-sight tower to determine the electrical axis of the satellite. The antenna technicians scanned across the sun in X and Y, both directions, noted the edge of the sun in each axis, took half of that, and, knowing their own latitude and longitude, used navigation tables to determine exactly where the antenna pointed at that time, thus calibrating the antenna. That method worked because the sun is a great emitter at all frequencies.

Haig also embedded a milliwatt transmitter in the base of the satellite
dish, pointed it at the feed, hermetically sealed it, and installed a splitter on it
so that half of the energy went to the antenna to be emitted and the other half
went to a Bird Corporation wattmeter. The antenna technicians took the output of the Bird wattmeter and displayed it on a dial on the control console,
thus telling the operator the precise strength of the signal and helping to calibrate the complete receiving system through to the data recorder. Radiation,
Incorporated, the contractor that had assembled the 46-foot dishes, liked this
idea so well that it immediately publicized the scheme to help sell its antennas. Radiation changed the system from a hermetically sealed can, which
proved not to be feasible, to one with a positive pressure inside by putting a
little dry nitrogen bottle in it that lasted for twenty years. Haig also eliminated
a requirement to evaluate the whole receiving link from the antenna feed
mechanism all the way through the preamplifiers, the amplifiers, and the
transmission lines. These innovations made it possible to eliminate the bore-
sight towers, reduce testing time, and save millions.[32]

The ground network Colonel Haig built for the weather satellite program
reveals in its differences that the AFSCF did not have to evolve in the way it
did. Colonel Haig built a dedicated satellite command and control network
for the program because he had a particular mission to accomplish and a
good deal of authority in the early days of his program. By the time the project reached a mature level for a space system, it operated in much the same
way as any other air force space program. The Air Force Satellite Control
Facility did not turn out the way it did because it was meant to; it turned out as
a network of satellite command and control because engineers built it. Sometimes, though, a system's environment also presents engineers with interesting challenges.

Environmental Challenges

Another important influence affecting the development of the Air Force
Satellite Control Facility in the early 1960s had to do with the location of the
tracking facilities. The initial plan called for only four tracking stations. This
implied that satellite operators had contact with a vehicle on the first and second orbits and then had no contact again until orbit seven or eight. Many
events could and did take place during the "dead" revolutions. Analysts found
it difficult to determine what went wrong and when because the satellites had
no onboard recorders. Until the air force encrypted space communications
in the late 1960s, a slight possibility existed that the Soviets could transmit to
a vehicle and command it. In addition, Vandenberg could not track or record
telemetry all the way to orbit insertion but only halfway to the burnout of the

Agena booster, so even if all of the onboard systems looked good at the initial loss of data, plenty of opportunities for trouble lay ahead.[33]

Adding the station at New Boston and putting a tracking ship downrange off the Pacific coast of Mexico partially closed some gaps in coverage, but a big hole remained in the entire Eastern Hemisphere. After extensive surveys in southern Africa and the Indian Ocean, including the French island of Mauritius and a visit to Johannesburg, South Africa, on board *Air Force 2*, the AFSCF put a new remote tracking station on the Indian Ocean island of Mahe, in the British colony of the Seychelles. The air force dispatched a ship with station components, housing modules, new receiving and transmitting equipment, and the tracking equipment. The ship arrived July 1, 1963, and the Seychellois who were hired to unload it unpacked an entire tracking station's worth of equipment in just five days. The temporary mess hall and housing area were outfitted ten days later; by the end of the month the antenna and station had also been erected. Station commander Maj. N. H. Beaulieu declared the station "conditionally operationally ready" on August 25. Teamwork, along with the leadership of Philco's program manager, French Harris, and Ted Green, manager of the installation and checkout group, made this remarkable effort possible.[34] Both the air force and Lockheed's leadership gave the people who were sent overseas to build the tracking stations a wide amount of latitude to accomplish their mission: building a first-world technological system in a third-world colony.

Travel to and from Mahe presented its own difficulties. Nearly 600 miles from land, the AFSCF operated the only airplane to Mahe until well after the Seychelles' independence from Great Britain in 1976. Beginning in September, 1963, a Pan American International Airways HU-16B *Albatross* flew regularly between Nairobi, Kenya, and Mahe. The plane came in handy in December, 1966, when Philco employee Martin Sheridan woke up unable to move his legs. After his admission to Victoria hospital in the island's capital, doctors determined that Sheridan had type 1 polio, the worst of the three categories (he had never received a vaccination). Station commander Maj. Donald E. Jensen and Philco manager Harris quickly evacuated Sheridan on the *Albatross* to the hospital for infectious diseases in Nairobi, where doctors put Sheridan in an iron lung. The *Albatross* pilots returned with a load of vaccine for the local Seychellois.[35] In 1969, when a Philco employee died after hitting a tree with his car, the station tried to return his body to the United States. Pan American, which had originally scheduled a flight to carry a critical spare part known as a klystron, rearranged its schedule on short notice to meet a flight in Kenya and flew the body back home.[36]

Isolation also worked to the air force's advantage. In 1969, following the *Apollo 11* moon landing, the Seychelles featured an artist's depiction of the tracking station on a postage stamp as part of a series showing the "standard, definitive . . . illustration of the Colony's history." The Seychellois expressed particular pride in their contribution to the moon mission. In the newspaper they quoted "American authorities," most likely the station commander, as saying that "all station personnel, American and Seychellois, performed duties of importance that contributed to the success of the mission and can truly believe that they were part of the first launch that put man on the Moon."[37] In fact, during the mission the station tracked the air force's VELA satellites, which detected the X rays and gamma rays from space-based nuclear explosions and served as a relay point for NASA's Advanced Range Instrumentation Aircraft (ARIA), which were flying over the Indian Ocean. The station's location and its unique relationship—which continued for more than thirty years—with the local population partly contributed to its continued success, and some of the original personnel were still there when the site closed in 1996.

Like the Seychelles, the Thule tracking station benefited from its location, this time in northern Greenland. Thule Air Base sits on territory leased from NATO ally Denmark and calls its Officers Club the Top of the World Club. To see the Northern Lights, residents have to look southward. When the AFSCF built the tracking station in 1961, SAC already had a sizeable presence there. More than ten thousand workers supported a B-52 bomber wing on airborne alert and a Ballistic Missile Early Warning System (BMEWS) radar site watching for Soviet ICBMs that might be bound for North America. Although they allowed information about the nuclear mission of the NATO ally's base, the Danes did not want it known that the AFSCF had a station at Thule that was supporting reconnaissance satellites for fear of repercussions in international public opinion in the 1960s. The state department assured Denmark that there would be no publicity about the satellite tracking station. Under orders from the assistant secretary of defense, the AFSCF classified the presence of its satellite command and control site as confidential. In all unclassified correspondence, the air force referred to the station as Operating Location Number 5 (OL-5) or by the station's call sign, POGO. The base commander did not even mention the station's presence in his mission briefing.[38] The location in Greenland meant the station served nearly every orbit of every polar-orbiting reconnaissance satellite, leading the air force to upgrade the station's equipment frequently and to add antennas there when needed. The big secret that the air force had a satellite command and control site at Thule did not remain undisclosed for long. On May 20, 1964, NBC's Huntley-Brinkley evening newscast mentioned the Thule site and even showed a picture. Later in 1964, the Army Corps of Engineers put out a call for bids on a project bearing the title "Thule AB, Tracking and Telemetry Station," and the base phone book listed the site as "Air Force Satellite Control Facility (OL-5)." The twelve

hundred Danish nationals, the four hundred monthly visitors to the base, and
the rest of the base population could not all be relied upon to keep the station or its mission a secret. By the mid-1960s the United States no longer con-
cealed its active reconnaissance satellite program. With the help of the state
department and the Danish Foreign Ministry, the AFSCF quietly declassified
its reconnaissance satellite operations at the Thule tracking station in 1969.[39]

Geography caused problems for the AFSCF that the air force overcame
with competent leadership and innovation. Distance and a lack of communications satellites meant the service had to use high-frequency, tropospheric
scatter radio links to connect the farthest stations with Sunnyvale. The Indian
Ocean station had a microwave link to Cape Canaveral through Ascension
Island in the South Atlantic. From stations equipped with only a microwave
link, such as INDI, on Mahe in the Seychelles, Sunnyvale could not get instant
receipt of telemetry data, which controllers needed to make split-second decisions about a satellite. If a controller wanted to talk to the stations, they
communicated either by teletype or telephone. For Thule, the tracking station "on top of the world," telephone connectivity to the United States over
the North Atlantic submarine cable worked only intermittently at best. Since
the activation of the circuit in February, 1962, on two separate occasions
something—or someone—had broken the submarine cable out of Thule.
The air force assumed that Russian trawlers had cut the cables, although another source suggested that icebergs might have been responsible. When the
cable went out, the station rerouted the circuit over the "tropo-scatter system,"
which used signals bounced off the troposphere, but this inherently unreli-
able circuit could not support the 1,200-bit data rate the station needed.[40]
Moreover, as the sun approached solar minimum in 1964 and the atmosphere
shrank, tropospheric scatter methods grew even less reliable.

The AFSCF brought these communications problem to the attention of
the Defense Communications Agency (DCA), which the U.S. Army controlled. Thule's communications priority rested right behind the Ballistic Missile Early Warning System in importance, but the DCA told the AFSCF that the
only real solution to the problem would be a satellite-based communications
circuit, which would not be available for at least a year, so the AFSCF was
forced to accept the situation. By 1964, the Thule to Cornerbrook, New-
foundland, submarine cable experienced six to eight breaks a year "caused by
icebergs or fishing trawlers." Each cable break required at least a week to re-
pair and became a part of routine operations for Thule until the army, which
was responsible for satellite communications channels because it adminis-
tered the DCA, established satellite communications links using the Initial
Defense Satellite Communications Program.[41]

The natural environment surrounding the AFSCF, a worldwide organization with twenty-four-hour operations, affected more than just the relaying of data to the customer. Two major events occurred at the Kodiak tracking station in 1964 that illustrate the effect the environment could have on technology: the earthquake and tidal waves on March 27 and the modification of the station to accommodate the Multiple Satellite Augmentation Program. The 1964 Alaskan earthquake, the largest in history, reached nearly 8.5 on the Richter scale and lasted more than two minutes. The quake's fault line ran only about two miles east of the Kodiak tracking station. During the six weeks following the quake, two hundred strong aftershocks ensued, some with a 6.4 magnitude, causing many people to leave Kodiak for the Lower 48. The three tidal waves, which occurred during the first few hours after the quake, caused most of the damage and deaths. A *williwaw,* a sudden, violent wind, arose two days after the quake and demolished the local fishing fleet because the quake and tidal waves had destroyed the sea wall around Kodiak's small harbor.

Lyle Burnham was in charge of Lockheed's operations at the site when the quake hit at about 5:30 P.M. on Good Friday. The controllers had just finished a satellite support and had no more scheduled for some time. Someone commented on the unusually beautiful and serene evening. When the quake struck, most of the "brown baggers," married personnel who lived in Kodiak, had already left the site and headed to town, so few people remained at the station. A broken diesel fuel line disrupted electricity to the station, shutting off communications with the outside world, but power was restored in about twenty minutes. The tracking station itself survived relatively undamaged, although the supply storeroom required several days to clean up.

The tracking station got off rather lightly, but the same could not be said for the nearby settlement of Chiniak. For several days after the quake, the site had only ham radio and citizens band (CB) radio to communicate with the village of Kodiak. Station maintenance personnel quickly restored the normal phone lines to the Satellite Test Center in Sunnyvale. The station handled several hundred phone and teletype messages from Kodiak's residents to their friends and relatives in the continental United States because the quake destroyed the phone lines out of Kodiak. Several local pilots who worked at the tracking station brought messages by plane from the surrounding villages out to the station, where teletype operators keyed the communiqués into the military circuits to Sunnyvale. Emergency messages also went out by Leroy Witlach's ham radio. Witlatch operated his radio continuously for several days until he was almost exhausted.

A month or so later some of the Chiniak crew formed four-wheel-drive-vehicle parties, usually with large, low-pressure tires. They made temporary road repairs in spots so they could travel back and forth to Kodiak at low tide.

Groups usually of three or more made the Kodiak trip at low tide until the road reopened for normal traffic in mid-December, 1964. To take advantage of the tides some of the road trips took place after midnight. Recalled Burnham, "The unique thing I found after the quake was how everyone worked together to get things accomplished. The brotherhood of man was highly demonstrated after the quake."[42]

The earthquake also affected the major system upgrade for the Kodiak station. The air force had awarded the MSAP modification contract with an estimated completion date of November 21, 1964, basing the date on road transportation from the town of Kodiak to the site, but the tidal wave after the earthquake wiped out the road. By July 1, 1964, it had become evident that sea and air transportation could not deliver construction equipment and materials to meet the completion date. Although the road became passable around the start of November, 1964, the installation schedule slipped; as a result, construction was not totally completed by the end of the year.

Not only did the lack of a road delay the construction program, but it also affected the station's primary functions: support and operation. While the road lay under water, the station depended on the navy—which did not always deliver promptly—for sea and air support. Once the station went without gasoline for three days; another time it got down to only one day's supply of meat. Throughout this period, the station's personnel relied on the local bush pilots to enable them to visit their families in town. On several occasions wind and poor visibility stranded personnel for two- and three-day periods. Finally, the station's accommodation of the construction and installation employees meant overcrowding in both the mess hall and the sleeping quarters. In addition, the support contractor added twelve to fifteen extra workers to support the station during construction and installation. Throughout all of this upheaval, morale at the station remained high, but everyone looked forward to going operational with the new MSAP system.[43]

Environmental problems also forced the Hawaii tracking station's personnel to adapt. Only one access road, Farrington Highway, led to the station, passing through the Makua Valley. Periodic heavy rainfall flooded portions of the road in the valley, but station personnel crossed these areas in an army truck. On the morning of December 23, 1964, the water remained so high and fast moving that even the army vehicle could not pass. A helicopter from Hickam AFB dropped emergency rations to the station personnel so they could eat. At 3:15 P.M., the swing shift finally relieved the night shift, which had arrived for work at 12:45 A.M.[44]

Clearly, the AFSCF was subject to a wide range of influences in the physical environment, as well as the economic, political, and bureaucratic setting.[45] Just

Farrington Highway to the Hawaii Tracking Station during the floods of 1968. Courtesy of the Air Force Space Command History Office collection.

as important as the technological and organizational challenges of the AFSCF's growth, the environmental challenges during construction and the early years of operation affected the entire satellite command and control system.

Summary

Challenges arise in technological systems—sometimes without warning. They can be organizational or technical or something entirely different and outside the system's control, such as its environment. Today, problems continue in the AFSCF as they do in all large technological systems, but none loom as large as the challenges of the early 1960s. The AFSCF managed to support multiple orbiting reconnaissance satellites by designing a system that could handle the increased demands. Known as the Multiple Satellite Augmentation Program, the new technology turned the AFSCF into a real network for the first time instead of a grouping of individual, remote command and control stations bound together in a military organization. Within MSAP, engineers overcame equipment interface problems, only to find still more trials lurking within the proposed solutions.

The AFSCF took an important step in its evolution into a satellite command and control system in this period, doing so in support of the rapidly evolving satellite reconnaissance programs. Engineers devised plans for the long-range implementation of a unified, general-purpose satellite control network, a strategy that changed the relatively simple Subsystem H of the Corona program into the multi-user AFSCF, which eventually supported most military space programs. Today the air force's satellite control network to some degree supports even those projects that have dedicated support facilities, such as the Defense Support Program. A complex team of air force officers and enlisted personnel, contractors, and government civilians undertook the project, which was designed to meet immediate requirements while simultaneously planning for the future.

5

Unbounded Faith
The Technological Style of the Air Force Satellite Control Facility

> *The pace is not set by technology, General Schriever declared, it is set by management. Brain power must replace manpower. And even the manpower available to [Air Research and Development Command] has shrunk, he said. It all added up to close cooperation of the military-industry team to win the technological war.*
>
> —The Airman, *February, 1961*

WHEN THE U.S. Air Force began studying satellite command and control, very few people had any idea how to track a satellite or predict an orbit. The mathematical model for calculating orbital parameters, known as an ephemeris, remained a matter of great mystery. One Lockheed programmer finally developed the computer software for taking antenna tracking angles, developing an ephemeris, and then pointing an antenna at a satellite. Retired air force Col. Thomas O. Haig called the program "the most monstrous pile of punched cards" he had ever seen. This engineer patched and repaired the software so many times the total number of cards sent through the computer amounted to "four or five times" the number actually needed. Although most of the cards patched and repaired the software, if the computer operator did not run all of them, the program would not work. Lockheed had only this one resource for giving directions to antennas and developing an ephemeris. Then, shortly before the first Corona flight in late 1959, the engineer resigned from Lockheed. Lockheed officials panicked and went after him, eventually hiring him back as a consultant at "three or four times" what they had paid him before as a Lockheed employee. According to Colonel Haig, the programmer now had only to load the cards in the proper order. "Then, when he was through running the program, he would squirrel the cards away and screw up the order so nobody else could do it."[1] No one should doubt the importance of a single human being in the development of new technologies.

Just as important as the role of people in technological systems' development, this particular event in the evolution of the Air Force Satellite Control Facility illustrates its early technological style: Engineers cobbled together a hodgepodge of systems, never doubting their ability to make it work. Technologists, like artists and architects, have creative latitude, and so did the developers of the AFSCF. No one best way existed to develop an ideal satellite control network, just as no one best way exists to paint *The Last Supper*, build the Taj Mahal, or write a computer program for calculating orbital elements. One look at the distinct and separate networks of the reconnaissance and the weather satellite programs dispels the notion that technologies developed in certain ways because they were "meant" to. When Colonel Haig cancelled Lockheed's plan to install a three-dimensional projection system in the Satellite Test Center, he thought the system would be "a useless display for decision making," an observation on the style of the AFSCF's technologists.[2] The technological style of the AFSCF is just as important to examine as the technology itself.

People Made It Work

In late 1960, while working with a 100-bit-per-second teletype circuit, a phone line, and a 60-bit-per-second secure teletype circuit, the controllers at the Satellite Test Center in Sunnyvale conducted operations in the interim control center because none of the target dates for the construction of the control center had been met.[3] At the core of satellite operations, leased commercial circuits linked the satellite control room to the tracking stations throughout the Pacific.[4]

To make all of the technology work as a system, the government and its contractors found a good working relationship essential. In the case of the air force's satellite command and control network, the prime contractors, Lockheed and Philco, competed with each other every step of the way. Complicating matters, the air force experienced an ambivalent relationship with its contractors because of its uncertainty about how much dependence to have on them. The 6594th Test Wing (Satellite) and a team of Lockheed contractors who actually operated the missions conducted each Discoverer mission under joint responsibility. In 1960, contractors outnumbered air force personnel by two to one, although the air force's goal of having every job performed by a military member, not a contractor, began a shift in that ratio. Major General Ritland spelled it out in the 6594th's mission statement:

> The 6594th Test Wing is directed to . . .
> d. At the earliest practical time, develop the capability to man and
> operate, with military personnel, the command, control, engineering

data processing and computing facilities associated with the Satellite Test Annex at Sunnyvale, California.

e. At the earliest practical time man, operate and support the following tracking and acquisition stations with military personnel:

(1) Vandenberg Air Force Base, California
(2) New Boston, New Hampshire
(3) Kaena Point, Hawaii
(4) Donnelly Flats, Alaska
(5) Other stations as may be designated[5]

If the organization realized this objective, the 6594th Test Wing would eventually number more than 2,000 military personnel.[6]

Lockheed personnel resisted integrating the arriving, uniformed, air force technical personnel because of "one major motivating factor—job security."[7] At the 6594th Launch Squadron at Vandenberg, contractors did not allow the military technicians to perform satellite checkout tasks before launch. When the contractors needed help, they used the military for menial tasks such as wire pulling. During two strikes—at Convair, maker of the Atlas missile, from June 6 to June 16, 1960, and at Lockheed, from June 15 to July 16, 1960—military technicians effectively checked out and launched satellites, demonstrating that the military personnel could take over from the contractors. When the strikes ended, the military personnel returned to their previous observer status.[8] Eventually the relationship between the military and the contractors smoothed out, and the air force technical personnel came under the direction of Lockheed's supervisors.

At the New Hampshire station, activated on October 1, 1959, to support Midas, the air force officers arbitrated disputes and "closely" monitored activities.[9] According to the contemporary unit history at the New Hampshire station, "positive Air Force management" stimulated improved effectiveness and performance of the satellite crew "beyond all expectation." Showing obvious bias, the air force historian concluded that this improvement "proved that Air Force management is far superior to contractor management."[10] The June, 1961, official history described the "mutual cooperation of contractor and military personnel."[11] Clearly, personalities made a significant difference.

Despite the differences in personalities, contractors simply had more experience with the equipment, which was the biggest distinction between them and the military staff. In some cases the on-console contractors had built the systems themselves and remained to operate them. On one occasion, for example, the operators at Kodiak waited for the first acquisition of a new satellite. When the vehicle came over the horizon on schedule, one of the technicians started the readouts. He announced the battery voltages, gas pressure,

The master control room at the Satellite Test Center, 1961. At the master console in the rear, Lockheed test director, Eugene Crowther, and air force test controller, Maj. Joseph P. O'Toole, confer during the final seconds before a launch. Other members of the integrated air force–contractor team are in the foreground. Courtesy of the Air Force Historical Research Agency collection.

and attitude and continued down the list. Then, as he watched, the values changed from those of a healthy, new vehicle to numbers that indicated a satellite out of fuel and on weak batteries. The Kodiak station had experienced angular coincidence with an older vehicle, and the antenna operator had simply followed the best signal strength. Using synchronous displays showing the predicted track, the antenna operator waved the antenna about slightly to obtain the strongest signal. In this case, the closer, older satellite had a stronger signal, so he followed it instead. The VHF trihelix had no autotrack capability, and because they used the older FM/FM modulation, it had no phase lock to keep it on the correct carrier. Catching the problem immediately, the decommutator operator quickly recognized the values as those of an older vehicle that Kodiak had tracked only an hour and a half earlier and knew he had a problem. When the information reached the back room, the control room team "launched their clipboards in panic" into the air. Precious seconds ticked by before they could get the antennas back onto the correct vehicle, and then all returned to normal.[12]

Each satellite's unique equipment configurations necessitated going slowly in satellite operations in order to get the system configurations right the first time. Even experience could not speed up a relatively slow process. If the trend continued, the AFSCF could end up with myriad receivers for myriad satellites, each with its own peculiar operating characteristics. To alleviate part of the problem, Philco, the subcontractor for the ground stations, proposed designing a generic receiver that would be capable of operating at multiple input frequencies, within which new satellite programs would have to operate if they wanted AFSCF support. Using modular plug-ins and adjustments to meet specific program needs, the ground stations could all have similar receivers, even though their overall missions might be different.[13] This solution promised to save not only money but also time.

The air force preferred to use its own personnel instead of contractors to operate and maintain the satellite command and control system. The service planned for officers with engineering degrees to launch and operate the satellites and for enlisted people with technical training to operate and maintain the ground equipment. In the April, 1960, edition of *Air Force/Space Digest,* General Terhune described the satellite operations in Sunnyvale. He related how the air force planned for enlisted technicians to perform telemetry, tracking, and control at the remote tracking stations, which the air force considered similar to having its own personnel service fighters, bombers, and cargo planes. Civilian engineers and scientists would continue to research and develop new programs, "but with operational systems, these jobs will belong to the men . . . and women . . . [sic] who wear Air Force blue."[14] To continue as the military space service, the air force planned to move ahead with a core of space operations and maintenance personnel, all wearing air force blue.

Lockheed had a different idea about the staff for the tracking stations. The facilities requirements report for the New Hampshire station that Lockheed managers R. Smelt and R. A. Proctor signed in 1959 stated clearly that Lockheed wanted the station "operated, maintained, and supported by contractor personnel." Although the air force had to provide some facilities, such as a building for the nonoperations staff and a dining hall, permanently assigned contractor personnel could "obtain support from the surrounding communities [Manchester and Nashua, New Hampshire], thereby reducing this cost to the government."[15] Even before the first successful Corona mission, the debate had already begun about who should operate the AFSCF: contractors or blue-suiters. The discussion over contractor or military staff would not be resolved quickly.

The air force had no uniformed expertise in operating and maintaining

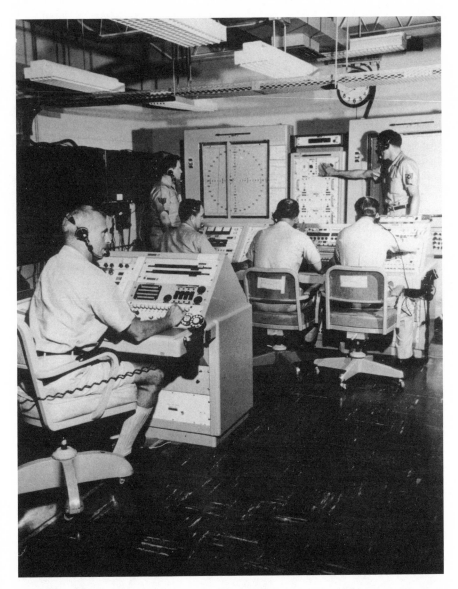

Blue-suit operators at the Hawaii tracking station, 1961. Courtesy of the Air Force Space Command History Office collection.

satellites, so the first air force officers joined the contractors already on console in 1959. Forrest S. McCartney, now a retired air force lieutenant general, joined the space program in 1960, with two other air force captains, Mel Lewin and Al Crews, shortly after *Discoverer 2*'s loss in Norway. The air force assigned the three space operations pioneers to work alongside Lockheed employees. To conceal the true nature of their mission from the public, these young captains wore civilian business attire as "somebody's idea of security." Recalled McCartney, "I kind of pushed back on it in the beginning, but it was at such an exciting time we didn't really have a big deal with [civilian clothes]."[16] Recalled Lewin, McCartney's carpool partner at the time and now a retired air force colonel, "I was so excited about what I was doing and enjoyed it a lot. It's not often you get in at the start of something."[17] People all over the Air Force Satellite Control Facility had that same feeling.

These officers paved the way for all air force satellite operators, using only their engineering background to get them going because no formal training program existed for any of the new satellite flyers, contractors or uniformed personnel. Three weeks after they arrived in Sunnyvale, that original group of captains had become the experts. Before actual flight testing began, the captains worked only in the back room on the displays, supporting the Lockheed engineers on the consoles. The officer-engineers drew with grease pencils on acetate, putting viewgraphs up on screens or on closed-circuit television for the satellite controllers to see. Nobody knew anything more than the Lockheed employees did. The officers' operational experience grew right along with that of the Lockheed employees. The captains did not have the technical expertise on the vehicle itself, but in terms of operational satellite control they essentially possessed as much expertise as the Lockheed people.[18]

To be fair, one could describe the early Corona reconnaissance satellite system as the Model T of the satellite business. When they arrived in 1959, McCartney and company did not have far to go on the learning curve of this rudimentary system. The first-generation Corona vehicles had only four commands: reset, increase, or decrease, and a "gray" command. Responding to a telephone call, a controller sent the order to a tracking station, which then sent the command to the satellite. The gray commands controlled the Corona camera, although the operators, not cleared for the Corona program, did not know this. Of course, not knowing did not keep the officers from discussing the possible uses for the gray commands until the CIA eventually cleared McCartney, Lewin, and Crews for Corona. According to McCartney, the trio speculated aloud too often, so the CIA briefed them to keep them quiet. Lewin recalled going to the Lockheed Advanced Projects Facility in Menlo Park, the so-called Northern Skunk Works, where they saw a Corona vehicle under construction. "We were very impressed with how important we were at that time," Lewin said. McCartney later "flew" *Discoverer 14* the night the Corona camera took the first picture recovered from space; today a copy hangs on the wall in his office.[19]

The first Corona vehicles required satellite controllers to have considerable situational awareness for a successful mission. A continuous, punched Mylar tape controlled systems on the vehicle, so the satellite controller had to know what point the tape had reached and what point the vehicle had reached in its orbit, all from hundreds of miles away. Controllers reset the tape and increased or decreased its speed to match whatever orbit the Thor-Agena combination happened to inject into, an imprecise feat at the time. In the early satellites, contractors put the tape together before launch because they knew what the targets would be. The Mylar tape had thirteen channels for the thirteen "fingers" that rode on top of the tape; when the contact went into one of the rectangular holes, it activated a relay and initiated a function. Using the tape, operators turned the receivers on or off, or the camera on and off, or the reset monitor, or whatever they needed to do. Adding to the challenge and emphasizing the importance of situational awareness, the operators also had to take into account errors on the tape. Although the CIA mostly preplanned each mission, the success of the operation relied on the operators on console to synchronize the timer so that the satellite would perform as needed.[20]

The CIA planned satellite reconnaissance missions weeks ahead of time but found that this was inefficient. Bad weather over the target area of the USSR or a vehicle anomaly could mean the camera took pictures of clouds or, worse, nothing of strategic value. The CIA officer in charge in Palo Alto, Charles Murphy, tried to convince Lockheed's engineers to build a command into the satellite to give control of the camera to the operators in the Satellite Control Facility. "We finally got one command for the camera system, which was kind of a simple-minded thing, too. You could tell it to ignore the next hole in the tape or use the next hole in the tape. That's the way we turned the camera on and off." To help preserve the most precious commodity on board the satellite (its twenty pounds of Kodak film), Lockheed gave the satellite operators some control over the payload by adding a few more commands.[21]

Nevertheless, a simple system did not necessarily mean it was an easy one to operate. To keep a single person from getting into too much trouble, controllers always worked in pairs: One acted as the primary controller, and the other functioned as support. At first, the air force officers always backed up the Lockheed controllers. Operations remained segregated until the young officers displayed their ability to control the satellites without the contractor's supervision. Lockheed was somewhat concerned, as the program office in Los Angeles probably was, too, because everyone easily tripped up during rehearsals and made mistakes. If someone made a mistake during a real event and a controller lost a vehicle, the implications could have been enormous, but no one ever did. The leadership quickly figured out that the military team learned quickly and worked as proficiently as the contractors. Slowly the military assumed the primary role for the satellite supports, rotating the senior position among the three officers. Eventually they were able to operate as an all-military crew, with one primary and another backup and then switching seats.[22]

Not surprisingly, the young officers and their contractor associates did not work together like fingers in a glove. McCartney, for example, had a problem working for Lockheed. In turn, the contractors looked upon the three officers "not as the customer so much as the competition." McCartney and company thought of themselves as more capable than the Lockheed people and did not make much secret of their opinion, which probably ruffled some Lockheed feathers. McCartney admitted:

> It was probably pretty cocky, too, you know, but we were good. . . . I call it friendly competition, but we were dead serious about making sure that we would be better than [the Lockheed controllers] were. And what is better is meaning that you can handle the [supports] smoother. You had better command, knew what the equipment was doing and not doing. You knew the capabilities of the crews. We used to practice endless hours with the crews at the stations, and we could work problems faster.[23]

To McCartney, relative skills as a satellite operator had nothing to do with education because everyone involved in the satellite reconnaissance business had a comparable engineering education. In McCartney's mind, the military officers' ability to think faster and maintain their composure under pressure made them better operators.[24]

Eventually the three young captains became full-fledged test controllers, and Lockheed scheduled them along with their own people. This small victory marked the beginning of the air force's brief transition to all-military space operations. McCartney and crew sat on console, pulling shifts, together with the Lockheed employees. Lewin confirmed McCartney's estimation of the air force's relationship with the contractor. "We were equals with the Lockheed guys, [and we] worked side by side with them." No differences separated a Lockheed employee and an air force satellite test controller. They worked with each other without distinction. They all had a great deal of pride in what they did, and the Lockheed people made them part of the team very quickly.[25] Recalling his days in the AFSCF, McCartney stated that no one had a feeling one way or another about transferring satellite operations to uniformed personnel: "We just always thought it would happen and took it for granted. We just believed that would happen. I mean, it was just a question of time. . . . I never questioned but that sooner or later it would transition to blue-suiters."[26] Col. Frederic Oder, head of the satellite program office in Los Angeles, had a transition to military in mind all along.[27]

The air force also grew increasingly convinced that it could handle operations and maintenance on its own, using officers to "fly" satellites and enlisted technicians in the same sorts of maintenance roles they performed in flying units. A May, 1962, human resources study submitted to the Space Systems Division in Los Angeles suggested turning over communications at the Satellite Test Center to air force personnel. In fact, "blue suiting" the entire satellite command and control operation could save the air force $400,000 annually, it pointed out.[28] After all, a technical sergeant (E-6) with ten years of service earned only $290 a month in 1963 (plus benefits such as commissary, base exchange, medical care, and so forth).[29] In 1958, a Philco employee at Annette, Alaska, earned $529 a month, plus free room and board, and Lockheed employees at Kodiak, Alaska, started at $400 a month, plus benefits.[30] The air force had an obvious financial advantage in blue-suiting operations and maintenance, but the resulting lack of experience imposed long-term consequences on the Air Force Satellite Control Facility.

The lack of training material challenged newly assigned blue-suiters the most. Second Lieutenant Lou Adams joined the AFSCF in 1966 after graduation from Radar Maintenance Officer School at Keesler AFB, Mississippi. Because the air force did not have a space operations career field for officers or enlisted personnel, it sent them to the schools that trained students in work that most closely resembled the job they would have in the AFSCF. Assigned to the New Boston tracking station as an operations controller, Adams almost immediately noticed the wide variety of people working there. In the control room contractors and officers of varied backgrounds, education, and experiences all did the same, basic everyday jobs. In the work centers, contractors and enlisted personnel worked alongside each other. Without a formal training program or written material to study, Adams faced no small challenge in learning to become an operations controller. Each satellite program published and distributed a Technical Operations Order (TOO), which described the requirements, operations concepts, and technical aspects of the satellites in a particular family, but nothing existed that put the information all together for a trainee. Instruction essentially followed the hit-and-miss process of over-the-shoulder observations, asking questions, and reading available pertinent material.[31] Into the mid-1960s, the air force still largely did on-the-job training, despite whatever technical training the service had provided beforehand.

Carl Malberg, who arrived in New Hampshire in 1962 as a second lieutenant fresh out of ground electronics officer training, recalled that in the early days enlisted members even worked on the console in the control room as tracking controllers and eventually as command controllers and even assistant operations controllers (AOCs). He did not recall an enlisted person ever sitting as an operations controller (OC), "but if they were certified as an AOC, they were certainly qualified to work as an OC." The various areas had assigned enlisted technicians, mostly instrumentation specialists, who pulled shifts right alongside the contractors. Once the staff—officers or enlisted personnel—became certified in their primary job, they still performed it under the watchful eye of a contractor. Before certification, the contractor performed the primary duty under the inquisitive eye of the blue-suiter.[32]

By late 1962, satellite crews at some sites consisted of equal numbers of contractors and air force members.[33] At the Hawaii tracking station, officers and enlisted persons worked with Lockheed personnel, all of whom performed their assigned tasks "with competence."[34] For example, Howie Althouse served at the New Boston tracking station as the area supervisor of the telemetry area from 1963 to 1964:

> I had 66 [Philco] TechReps working for me, [and I was] responsible for 2 telemetry areas and 3 shifts (24 hr. support). [I also] had a dozen or so airmen assigned, [but I] couldn't count on them much as you never knew when they would be there to work a shift. Between having to go to Grenier Field [New Hampshire] or Hanscom AFB [in Massachusetts, about an hour away] for medical, dental, records check, or whatever, they were unreliable for support. Anyhow, we [contractors] supported.[35]

These satellite command and control crews, a highly motivated group of contractors and military, cross-trained and became certified in several positions. They worked with innovative, state-of-the-art technology, functioning as a team, regardless of who their actual employer was. In Sunnyvale the contractors and military "welded into an effective technical organization completely dedicated" to their mission. Shift supervisors, uniformed or contractor, had full charge of all personnel, military or Lockheed, designated to work on their shifts. The shift supervisors, regardless of who their employer was, were "all professionals in engineering and science" and exhibited "professional job performance."[36] At the tracking stations a contractor regularly acted as the operations controller with an air force assistant on one support; then they often switched for the next satellite support. That way everyone stayed current in all of the procedures.

Because the air force had no satellite operations career field for officers or enlisted personnel until the 1980s, the AFSCF had to draw capable operators from a number of different air force career fields, including many that were already critically staffed, difficult to fill, and difficult to retain. The problem grew more critical as the United States expanded its role in Vietnam and as the aerospace industry expanded to meet the demands of the Cold War. Finally, the unique environment of the AFSCF entailed a large on-the-job training investment with a small return on outlay because of the low retention

The WS-117L ground station at the Cooke (later Vandenberg) Air Force Base tracking station, 1959.

probability and low experience levels. All of this amounted to chronic military personnel problems.

Another money and time-saver, the Multiple Satellite Augmentation Program, introduced new computers to some of the stations. At New Boston, two CDC 160A computers replaced the older CDC 1604s and analog computers. One CDC 160A formatted tracking data and handled commanding; the other formatted telemetry for real-time relay to Sunnyvale on a higher data-rate microwave link. These two computers interfaced with an identical one at the Satellite Test Center called the "bird buffer," which moved the data to where they needed to go. MSAP also replaced the VERLORT antenna at New Boston (it later became the nucleus of the Guam tracking station). In its place the station received a 60-foot, three-axis hydraulic antenna and a second control room and thus became a dual-sided station capable of simultaneously supporting two satellites. MSAP, although good for satellites, hurt morale because staffing did not increase to meet the new workload. In fact, personnel numbers decreased as the station went from four shifts to three with only every third weekend off.[37]

Former location of the WS-117L ground station, which was removed during the Multiple Satellite Augmentation Program upgrade at the Vandenberg Air Force Base tracking station, 1967. Courtesy of the Air Force Historical Research Agency collection.

Before long, a growing workload justified an increased number of personnel. Despite the MSAP installation, the remote tracking stations believed their staffing requirements should remain high because the number of supported satellites rose with each launch success. New Boston complained in early 1963 about operating under strength twenty-four hours a day, seven days a week, creating "a fatigue and potential morale problem." New Boston had supported just 77 passes in June, 1962, and a mere 46 in July, 1962, in comparison to their 1,399 passes between January and June, 1963, an average of more than 230 a month.[38] New Boston had a total assigned strength of 29 officers, 315 enlisted personnel, and 412 contractors; the three operations crews consisted of 54 percent military and 46 percent contractor employees.[39] MSAP clearly had an effect on the numbers of satellite supports, so understaffing remained a serious issue because of the steadily increasing support load.

Problems in the air force personnel system also had an effect on staff. The major area of concern at New Boston soon became the "staggering military attritional losses without replacement [*sic*]." In 1963, New Boston completed four years of continuous operation. The air force normally rotated personnel to their next duty station after three or four years at one base, but the contractor population seldom moved. From January through June, 1963, the station lost thirty-seven fully trained, highly skilled technicians

> compared to a replacement factor of five, low-ranking . . . technical school graduates. Contractor-wise, seventeen experienced Philco employees departed and nine new inputs were gained. A problem area has been losing qualified troops and gaining basic airmen. With contractor replacements, the situation has been more fortunate in that replacements are from Vandenberg AFB, Thule [Greenland] and Annette [Alaska, recently closed], thus a reduction in transition training requirements. The salient feature of the manpower crux is a bare minimum of three crews and a steadily increasing workload [sic].[40]

Personnel problems worsened before improving, not just at New Boston, but everywhere.

An ordered reduction in contractor personnel accompanied the MSAP upgrade. At New Boston, Philco, the station's prime contractor, planned an overall reduction of seventy employees, almost half the total staff. Because the phase-out of old equipment served as the basis for this reduction, the station supervisors grew increasingly alarmed as it became apparent that the air force would not phase out the old equipment on schedule. The station commander contacted his headquarters, but received no response.[41]

The personnel problem worsened when it turned out the military and contractor staffing arrangement was actually breaking the law. In 1965, the General Accounting Office announced that the government could contract for an end item but that the contractors working in the AFSCF alongside air force members were in fact performing illegal "personal services."[42] In response, the air force decided to staff the Vandenberg station with only military and to staff the other stations with only contractors. This compromise tested the feasibility of an all–blue-suit operation, provided a comparison for the contractor-operated stations, and preserved the illusion in the air force of the ability of military staff to command and control satellites. The air force sent selected military personnel from the other stations to staff Vandenberg. In reality, Vandenberg never achieved a truly all–blue-suit status. It always had a cadre of technical advisors assigned to each work center to assist with training and to provide technical assistance as needed. Then, once Vandenberg became the *only* station where the military performed satellite control and equipment maintenance functions, the personnel problem became acute because no other stations could rotate personnel to California. Moreover, the air force personnel system, already unable to satisfy the human resource needs of the unique AFSCF, viewed the organization as an R&D outfit rather than an operational or fighting unit and therefore as the lowest unit on the personnel totem pole. Many contractor technical advisors augmented the air force operations and maintenance teams because of turnover and chronically low experience levels. Once these issues became a nagging problem, the air force threw in the towel and transitioned Vandenberg to an all–contractor staff.[43]

Personnel problems remained a headache for the AFSCF leadership until the late 1960s. The air force constantly dealt with the conflict between wanting to operate with military technicians but not being able to because of a lack of trained workers. With the escalating demands of the Vietnam War drawing technical personnel away, the military began to run out of enlisted technicians, which made the air force's goal of providing satellite command and control with uniformed staff a harder one to meet. Filling in the gaps with either the contractor's employees or more technology to eliminate personnel

The computer complex for the Multiple Satellite Augmentation Program at the Vandenberg tracking station, 1966. Note the blue-suit operators. Courtesy of the Air Force Historical Research Agency collection.

Vandenberg tracking station, 1965. Courtesy of the Air Force Historical Research Agency collection.

seemed to be the only solutions. As the personnel available to Air Research and Development Command shrank, the military and the contractors had no option but to work together.

By 1964, an acute shortage of uniformed workers with the appropriate technical qualifications made it unlikely the air force could ever achieve an all–blue-suit operations and maintenance capability for space. By the end of the 1960s, the air force gave up on military space operations and maintenance and fell back, relying on contractors to perform that vital national service.[44] Although the air force continued to claim preeminence in space operations, no blue-suiters actually operated antennas in the Air Force Satellite Control Facility.

Operations Culture versus R&D Culture

The approach to operations competing for influence within the Air Force Satellite Control Facility is another interesting aspect of the system's technological style. Managers and technicians in the AFSCF preferred a concept of operations that resisted standardization in favor of the flexibility that is necessary in a test environment. The air force tried to overcome the momentum induced by the R&D culture and the special relationship between the AFSCF and the National Reconnaissance Office. Overcoming this concept proved difficult. To normalize space operations, the air force tried to "operationalize" the AFSCF, trying to make satellite command and control more like flying standardized fighter or tanker aircraft than specialized test planes. The air force struggled to standardize satellite command and control operations because no one had any real idea of how to control a satellite.

The air force considered a lack of formal training acceptable because of the test nature of the space operations environment. Trying to learn and understand orbital mechanics challenged the newest space operators, who learned without formal training or textbooks for satellite hardware, orbital mechanics, and vehicle commanding. These operators depended on Lockheed to help them with technical training such as understanding the Agena commands and what they did. Lockheed built the Agena right across the street from the satellite operations area in Building 104, so the operators often went there to see the equipment before it reached orbit. Life for new satellite operators thus included constant study and an internal class. They assembled and shared their own study materials.[45] Corona's status as the Discoverer test program allowed them to take their time.

In addition, the Air Force Satellite Control Facility rehearsed an on-orbit operation almost every day, regardless of whether a vehicle actually orbited, by taking tapes from previous flights and replaying the data. General McCartney recalled that sitting on console as a satellite operator felt like "a pressure cooker thing because in those early days that equipment was not very good to you. You . . . really had to think ahead, and you had to be able to . . . assess the situation, understand what was going on, think on your feet, figure out what to do, and do it. And you didn't have time for other people to do any real prompting of you."[46] Ultimately, all of the rehearsals yielded valuable returns.[47]

The lack of formal procedures caused some problems in the Corona program. In late January, 1968, for example, on mission 1045, Corona flight 123, the vehicle ran into some difficulties when the field test force director miscalculated the number of commands required to go from the acquisition command position to the fade command position, in part because of abnormal telemetry from the vehicle. The problem occurred because the other operators did not verify his calculations; the operations planner and test controller simply initialed the master command sheet, assuming that the director had gotten it right. The incident prompted an investigation, and Col. Charles Murphy, the investigating officer, relieved the field test force director of his position and issued letters of reprimand to the people on duty that day who had failed to verify the command calculations. Colonel Murphy also introduced a new procedure to prevent the event's recurrence, one that required each member of the control team to compute the number independently.[48]

In part, the air force stuck with the test culture because it functioned less rigidly than the culture of aircraft or missile operations. Before it separated from the AFSCF entirely, the weather satellite program had a five-person office, which meant that they had no bureaucracy to satisfy before they could move on a problem. Only the director of the National Reconnaissance Office (DNRO) could say no to weather satellite program boss Col. Tom Haig, and the DNRO usually said yes when Haig proposed something new. In addition, Haig achieved a high morale in the weather satellite office by making the officers responsible for the program and then letting their decisions stick. For example, Capt. Dick Geer, who ran the booster part of the weather satellite operation, figured out why the program was losing so many small NASA-built Scout boosters. The first launch failed because the third stage blew up after a bad ignition. The second launch succeeded when they got the satellite into an orbit satisfactory enough for the weather data. The third and fourth launches again failed, but each occasion looked like something other than an ignition failure. Geer solved the mystery: The range safety officer had shut down the transmitter that illuminated the booster when it flew out of the range boundaries. When he turned the transmitter off, the automatic gain control on the booster's receiver went to maximum and picked up random emissions from broadcast stations in Los Angeles. Geer claimed that Frank Sinatra's voice—singing in his high register—had triggered the destruct mechanism. More than likely the explosion had occurred when a spurious signal from a radio broadcast in the area set off the destruct mechanism. In a sense, the air force had destroyed its own boosters until Geer figured out that the range safety officer had to illuminate the receiver all the way into orbit. On Geer's suggestion, the range controllers changed their procedures, preventing further accidental Scout booster explosions. As Colonel Haig put it, Geer "had to be pretty sharp to figure that one out."[49] The test culture, which was nonexistent in the operational air force, provided Geer the latitude to solve the problem.

After it pulled out of the AFSCF, the weather satellite program achieved the first truly operational status of any space program. Because the weather satellites operated every day, staffing at the tracking stations and a control center was continually required, in contrast to the intermittent staffing needed for the Corona vehicles. In 1962, SAC took over the operations for the weather satellite program, making it the air force's first operational satellite mission. According to Colonel Haig, for the next six years the "SAC-umsized" operators never missed a satellite support, including the time that a nor'easter blew the inflated radome off the antenna at the station near Loring, Maine. As the

40-foot receiver dish vibrated wildly in the high winds, the maintenance workers scrambled outside in the stormy weather and held the edge of the dish
while it tracked the satellite for a weather data readout. The crew managed to
keep the dish from vibrating so that it could stay with the satellite and get a
clear signal. The operational, mission-oriented culture they had learned in
SAC encouraged them to exert this extraordinary effort, proving that another method for operating a satellite command and control system existed
other than that of the informal R&D culture.

For Colonel Haig, the whole experience with the all–blue-suit launch and
operations crews also confirmed his opinion that the air force could run a
satellite program much better than the contractors could. To his mind, the
difference included focus, dedication, basic intelligence, and competence.
Said Colonel Haig later, "My faith in blue-suiters is unbounded. There is no
one outside [the Air Force] who is smarter than those who serve on the inside."[50] Capt. Charlie Croft in the weather satellite program office found a
couple of abandoned army Nike missile stations, one in Washington state and
the other in Maine, that were about to become county parks and latched onto
them for two ground stations. The sites had old but serviceable wooden
buildings. When the director of the NRO gave him permission, Colonel Haig
briefed Air Force Chief of Staff General LeMay and SAC boss General Power,
and within a week crews at those two stations began repairing the buildings.
"[B]y golly, by the time we got the [weather satellite program] equipment up
there, they had 'Spic and Span'd' the buildings and grounds, and the morale
was so high you just couldn't stop them. They were great guys."[51] SAC interviewed and recruited good officers and enlisted technicians at the ground
stations and control centers, telling these space pioneers, "You're the first military crew to run a space program. You are the basis. You're the foundation
for the Air Force's mission in space." SAC drilled that fallacious idea into
them, from General Power on down, but they believed it and performed as
though it were true. SAC required its strict form of checklist discipline and
regular method of operations, and the weather satellite program went on to
become one of the great success stories of the air force's space history.

The weather satellite's role in space operations is a perfect counterpoint
for this story because it serves as an exception, not the rule. Until the 1980s,
the Air Force Satellite Control Facility remained in Air Force Systems Command, which was the air force's major command responsible for research and
development. The AFSCF remained an organization with a "make it up as you
go" attitude, even as operations grew significantly more standardized.

The introduction of the Mission Control Center in the mid-1960s standardized satellite operations procedures more than any checklist-driven culture could have. With Project Forecast in 1964, the air force looked ahead in

the same way Theodore von Kármán had made the service think about new roles, missions, and opportunities in *Toward New Horizons*. For this new project, however, uniformed engineers—not civilian scientists—led the study's panels. Headed by Air Force Systems Command leader General Schriever, whom Gen. Hap Arnold himself had profoundly influenced when stationed together in California before World War II, Project Forecast tried to take a long-range look at air force R&D in an attempt to predict the changes that might occur in the next ten years.[52] Best known for its endorsement of the doomed Manned Orbiting Laboratory, Project Forecast included an examination of command and control and a specific look at its importance for space. The Mission Control Center concept of operations emerged in the air force's attempt to redefine its role as the operator of the nation's military satellites.

Brig. Gen. Jewell C. Maxwell chaired the Space Support Panel. Annex E of Volume III, Space Command and Control, laid out a roadmap for developing future space test facilities and operational command and control networks. The logical path, the Maxwell panel argued, meant developing space operations the same way that air force personnel had developed their own operations for a generation—using the concept of centralized control and decentralized execution. To work as efficiently as it worked for airplanes, the concept first required decentralized mission control centers. In the new concept of space operations, mission control center commanders had complete operational control of their satellites, just as pilots had over their aircraft. Each mission control center was able to receive, analyze, and process payload data, generate its own orbital ephemeris, and issue commands. The Maxwell panel conceived of mission control centers as decentralized elements in the space mission, "mission-oriented control centers" capable of performing all of the special functions necessary for the satellite's mission, often reconnaissance of the Soviet bloc. As independent units plugging into the common-user Air Force Satellite Control Facility, mission control centers could be added to or deleted from the satellite command and control system without major disruption.[53] This concept took a step toward an operational space corps, one that was distinct from the flying air force.

The mission control center concept also increased the independence of the individual satellite programs. During a mission, satellite operators in a mission control center controlled the ground facilities of the AFSCF only for the period allotted by the schedule. After the mission time elapsed, another mission control center that had prearranged for the time could step in and assume control of the AFSCF's resources. Using the air traffic control system as an analogy, the report stressed that supporting satellites could be as simple as flying airplanes and scheduling commercial airliners. The mission control center concept also provided added security and isolation for the various satellite programs.[54] With satellite operations and planning contained in one unit behind a single entry door, satellite programs increased the level of secrecy of their missions, a further step toward independence for air force space operators.

The Aerospace Corporation included the idea of mission control centers in its suggestions for expanding the Sunnyvale operation. In that company's concept, all of the elements of satellite program control and operation occupied the same field, rather than remaining discrete, as in the older configuration of the Satellite Test Center. The test controller, now called a "mission commander," worked with key personnel in a single, secure, multiroom complex, keeping track of data as a computer displayed them on TV screens in a centralized operations room. The functions performed in the complex included orbit planning, data analysis, payload analysis, command generation, and direction of the tracking station assigned for support of the satellite. The new mission control console had seven television monitors on which the operators could select any one of twenty separate telemetry channels, all coming into the complex in real time, thanks to the space-ground link subsystem modification. The console also had two remote control units for 35-mm projectors, secure and nonsecure telephones, and time-display units. In Aerospace Corporation's opinion, the mission control center arrangement more effectively employed the "highly trained engineer and technician personnel" assigned to the Satellite Test Center.[55]

The air force used the mission control center concept to justify an increase in personnel for the Sunnyvale operation. The air force's 1966 decision to operate the Manned Orbiting Laboratory in Sunnyvale rather than at NASA's Manned Spaceflight Center in Houston prompted a major expansion of the Satellite Test Center, including an additional $1.2-million building with twelve new mission control centers.[56] The cost soon ballooned when the air force added four floors to the operations building and bought the land for it from Lockheed, which boosted the price to $8.2 million. When Congress learned that the air force planned to buy the land from Lockheed for $49,000 an acre, they balked at including it in the Military Construction Program for 1967.[57] Congress eventually relented and approved the new windowless building before the AFSCF outgrew its accommodations. Today they simply call it "the Blue Cube."

Each mission control center now had its own complete operations team, whereas the earlier satellite programs had shared some personnel. The centers took staff members from existing functional areas of the Satellite Test Center, introducing considerable duplication because each mission control center operated just one family of similar satellites. In mid-1965, those working at the central control center in Sunnyvale included 123 officers, 208 enlisted persons, 8 civilians, and 405 contractors, totaling 744 employees. The air force believed that an expansion of the Sunnyvale operations to twelve mission control complexes, even before Manned Orbiting Laboratory requirements, needed an additional 429 personnel authorizations, including 171 officers, 252 enlisted persons, and 6 civilians, plus 230 contractor spaces, a total of 659 new workers for Sunnyvale.[58] As justification for the huge increase in staff, the air force offered a brief history of satellite operations. From 1959, when the service activated the 6594th Test Wing operation at Sunnyvale, until 1961, staff numbers increased as rapidly as the number of satellites the test center supported—about 60 percent. With the longer life of satellites and the increasing number of satellites in space, on-orbit operations stood at 6,500 satellite supports in 1963; planners expected satellite supports to almost triple to 18,800 by 1965, without an increase in personnel. The STC absorbed the increased workload "by more efficient equipment, better organization, streamlined procedures, and excessive overtime by both military and contractor personnel."[59] In short, the Sunnyvale operation nearly doubled in size because of the new Manned Orbiting Laboratory assignment and the new mission control center concept.

Blue-suiting the air force's space operations remained a justification for increasing the number of personnel. The air force insisted it needed to maintain a military capability at the Satellite Test Center: "[W]e *highly desire* the authorization of these 429 military spaces, if the Air Force is to retain a significant capability in the command and control of satellite operations."[60] The request suggested that the air force could reduce its military requirements by replacing those positions "with higher cost contractor personnel." The AFSCF did not want to replace military workers with the contractors' employees "since it would reduce military control of space operations."[61] When Air Force Systems Command sent its authorization message, the AFSCF received 466 additional personnel authorizations, only about two-thirds of its request.[62] The AFSCF did not use the contractors to make up the difference, choosing to implement the mission control center idea anyway.

In May, 1966, crews in the first mission control center conducted a satellite support with the Hawaii tracking station using the new concept. The mission control center model thereafter became the standard for air force satellite command and control operations, and today every air force satellite operations squadron except one operates on this standard. In late 1966, several satellite programs moved their operations into mission control complexes. Satellite programs using this concept found "the complex to be very satisfactory." By the end of 1966, while operations continued in the central control room, the four mission control centers enabled the AFSCF to support ten different satellite programs at once.[63] Satellite operations increased dramatically in the period that followed. In the first six months of 1966, the AFSCF supported sixty-four vehicles during 3,776 supports, an increase of 56 percent over 1965.[64] Operations became standardized like any operational air force flying unit.

Later on, even more standardized procedures came into the AFSCF from air force regulations and inspection directives. In 1968, the evaluators of the AFSCF's standardization and evaluation branch concerned themselves with the quality of satellite supports. They uncovered a tendency in the control rooms to lose sight of the mission during long-duration satellite supports of high-altitude vehicles. In other instances, inadequate staffing, because of high personnel turnover at some stations, did not ensure optimum support or the ability to cope with various contingencies. Thule, for example, experienced a 38-percent turnover of the contractors' technical personnel in the first six months of 1965.[65] At other sites operators did not accomplish their training on new equipment such as the space-ground link subsystem; they often supported orbiting vehicles without it. The evaluators also found that the condition of the command transmitter equipment was generally "substandard." The maintenance personnel assigned to this equipment, usually new AFSCF personnel, did not receive adequate training in how to maintain the equipment properly. As they became qualified, they moved on to more complex equipment such as the space-ground link subsystem, thus adding to the shortage of experienced personnel. Critically, evaluators found FR-1600 telemetry recorders in bad operating condition or totally inoperable because of the poor training of maintenance workers, a lack of periodic maintenance, or a shortage of maintenance equipment for these important backup tools. They also noted deficiencies in training. By the end of 1968, Lockheed and Philco had many of these problems under control.[66]

To normalize and to make a stronger case for itself as the nation's provider of military satellite command and control, the air force tried to operationalize the Air Force Satellite Control Facility to make this system more like flying aircraft than specialized, individual satellites. The technological style of the R&D culture of Air Force Systems Command actually made the air force's method of satellite command and control more rigid than flexible. An introduction of the mission control center concept attempted to overcome institutional momentum, but, if anything, it simply created another kind of resistance by further isolating the satellite programs from one another.

Summary

By the end of the 1960s, the air force had given up on uniformed operations and maintenance, reluctantly giving in to having contractors perform the vital national service of satellite command and control. The engineers inside and outside the air force, whether contractors, civilians, or military, built the AFSCF because they had unbounded faith in each other that they could do the job and that they had the technology to make this national service work. In the middle of the Cold War they also had limitless trust in their country, knowing that the network they built supported the national space program, which was a source of international prestige for the United States. Those with special access worked with extra diligence because they knew that the AFSCF supported the National Reconnaissance Program, which was considered essential to the country's security in the dangerous days of the Cold War.

In the case of the Air Force Satellite Control Facility, an extraordinary player in the background continued to pulled strings. As the AFSCF grew in ability and importance for the overall national space effort, a struggle inside the air force ensued over the control of the military satellite command and control system, requiring the AFSCF to acquire a sponsor. This patron turned out to be the National Reconnaissance Office, which constantly looked after its own parochial interests.

6

The Pressure Cooker
Overcoming Momentum

You can't run an operation given a black [covert] status and not bring the operators in because then they don't know what the hell's going on.

—Gen. B. A. Schriever, USAF, Retired
Former Commander, Air Force Systems Command

WHEN BRIG. GEN. William G. King Jr. became the commander of the Air Force Satellite Control Facility in September, 1966, he introduced a system for the remote tracking stations to score their performance in supporting the National Reconnaissance Program. The senior members of his staff resisted the idea as "too complicated" and possibly even damaging to morale, but King implemented the system over their objections. He ordered the scores to be sent by teletype to all of the stations so they could compare themselves with each other. In his mind, the satellite programs that were using the AFSCF needed this performance information. Showing the stations their weaknesses also helped them improve their operations.[1]

Differences of opinion notwithstanding, everyone on King's staff and at the tracking stations scored their satellite supports professionally. Formally known as the Performance Management Evaluation System, the largely subjective scoring program gave the AFSCF commander a monthly operational performance and discrepancy summary from the stations. Field test force directors—the satellite program engineers in Sunnyvale—collected information on each support operation, including a complete analysis of discrepancies that occurred during the prepass, pass, or postpass phases.

Unfortunately, General King's adjutant created a mess when the first set of scores went out to the stations. In those days the air force classified as confidential the association of the call sign of a remote tracking station with its military designator; for example, saying POGO and Operating Location 5, or

Thule Air Base, Greenland, created classified information. King's adjutant did not have a security clearance and thus did not know which call signs went with which station, resulting in guesses that reversed some of the scores. COOK, the adjutant suspected, went with New Boston because it frequently won the award for the best dining hall in the air force; BOSS went with Vandenberg because the station could command satellites on the pad to verify everything before launch. Vandenberg actually scored the highest, and New Hampshire the lowest, but the official scores went out by teletype with Vandenberg as the worst station and New Hampshire as the best.[2]

When General King got back from one of his frequent trips to Washington, D.C., he found Col. Jerry Flicek, the Vandenberg tracking station commander, waiting in the outer office. Flicek wanted to talk about the scoring message, but King tried to put him off. Flicek said, "We're not that bad," but King brushed him off with "I know, you're a good station, but I really have to go see my boss now." Flicek left and went back to the real COOK—at Vandenberg AFB, the former Cooke AFB. When King came to work the next morning, he recalls, "Somebody had put the biggest goddamned rooster you have ever seen in my office and closed the door. . . . What he did to that office, you won't believe it. I know damn well it must have been Jerry, telling me I was 'chicken.'"[3] Over many objections, the scoring system stayed. Today the air force uses it to determine part of the award fee the satellite control network contractor earns.

System builders strive to increase the size of the system under their control, and this certainly took place in the Air Force Satellite Control Facility. The AFSCF grew from a small, single-user, regional network of satellite command and control stations to an enormous, multi-user, worldwide system. As it developed, the AFSCF built up a momentum that it used to keep out other satellite programs, beginning with the weather satellite program in the early 1960s. Chapter 4 presents evidence of this danger in the conflict between Lockheed and the weather satellite program, as well as in the challenges that the network overcame with technology. The large mass buildup in the AFSCF arose from the corporate and military organizations that were committed to it. Engineers, managers, technicians, civil servants, and politicians all had vested interests in the growth and durability of the AFSCF. The present chapter examines the development of the space-ground link subsystem (SGLS) and looks at the organizations that tried to claim control of the AFSCF.

Managers tried to increase the AFSCF's importance by introducing the space-ground link subsystem and making the AFSCF vital for every satellite program in the department of defense and valuable for some NASA programs as well. At the same time, SGLS helped the AFSCF overcome the momentum that was building up in the large numbers of personnel that were still required to operate the Multiple Satellite Augmentation Program (MSAP) by further reducing their numbers. SGLS, which was envisioned in 1962 but not introduced into the air force satellite command and control system until the late 1960s, made the AFSCF a common-user network that served every satellite program in development.

The AFSCF's institutional and technological momentum proved difficult for managers to overcome. For example, those who ran the AFSCF and the primary customers (who justified its existence)—the national reconnaissance community—built momentum into the system. The SGLS served both parties, advancing command and control technology while enabling the development of even more sophisticated satellites. The AFSCF prospered in its special relationship with the National Reconnaissance Office (NRO) because the system supported this patron, often at the expense of other important, national space priorities. The commitment of the engineers and managers to the AFSCF and of the corporations that were heavily invested in it, Lockheed and Philco, contributed to the network's driving force.[4]

Space-Ground Link Subsystem

In the military system of satellite command and control, technological momentum manifested itself in the development of the space-ground link subsystem. While trying to expand into the realm of NASA support, the Air Force Satellite Control Facility retained its position as the servant of the National Reconnaissance Office. The managers required SGLS to advance the AFSCF's capabilities well into the 1970s. They not only created a more capable system, especially as reconnaissance satellites increased in complexity and capability, but also made the AFSCF compatible with NASA's growing fleet of space vehicles.

Satellite systems development required the integration of payload, booster, satellite vehicle, control, and recovery subsystems. Their operational effectiveness and capability depended on the integration of the various subsystems and the technical trade-offs among them. This process of compromise continued throughout the research and development program as engineering contractors determined each subsystem's particular set of requirements and constraints. As with all of the subsystems, the one for command and control had constantly changing constraints, including political limitations and restrictions imposed by the location of the tracking stations, rapid technical advances in the security of communications links, or trade-offs between flight test performance and mission requirements. Trying to simplify as much as possible, while keeping the system maximally flexible, constantly challenged the network engineers.[5]

In 1962, the Aerospace Corporation's satellite control office and the air force's satellite systems office had suggested a standardized command and control system to support the multiple satellite environment expected after 1965. The new arrangement, called the space-ground link subsystem, integrated the separate tracking, telemetry, and commanding subsystems into a single array that used a single, self-tracking ground antenna and compatible vehicle equipment on board the satellite. Two separate structures had handled those tasks in the first two AFSCF designs. The new plan provided flexible communications channels between the ground and the vehicle, variable enough to satisfy a larger variety of requirements in command rate, telemetry rate, and tracking accuracy via a building-block concept of modular equipment for satellites. The program office planned for SGLS to transmit from ground to space in the 1.7–1.85-gigahertz frequency range and to receive at 2.2 to 2.4 GHz. (NASA claimed the 2.2–2.3 GHz part of the frequency spectrum for their own use, but the U.S. government's Interdepartmental Radio Advisory committee, which made all radio frequency assignments to government agencies, gave the air force the complete spectrum for SGLS.) In addition, the new system included encryption and decryption devices for both ground-to-space and space-to-ground communications, adding a layer of security and reducing the threat posed by the Russian trawlers.[6] The new communications method simplified matters while making air force satellite command and control much more flexible and secure.

The new technology provided voice, analog, and digital command services over a ground-to-space communication link and voice and telemetry over a space-to-ground link. Simultaneously the system measured range, range-rate, and position of the spacecraft with respect to the tracking station and did it all with only one antenna, thereby saving on maintenance costs and personnel. By multiplexing both the command and tracking data onto a single uplink and the tracking and telemetry data onto a single downlink, SGLS technology achieved much higher data-transfer rates. Some significant SGLS features included spacecraft equipment that was designed to meet the requirements of a variety of space programs and data rates and semiautomatic configuration control and test facilities to minimize operations and maintenance personnel needs. In addition, the essentials for SGLS included the ability to reconfigure the ground station for another satellite support operation, the so-called turn-around time, within five minutes, a significant advance over the hours it sometimes took.[7] Not only simpler, the new subsystem also saved personnel costs and satellite development time by standardizing all of the spacecraft communications equipment.

The air force went with a tried-and-true partner to develop the new communications proposal. In March, 1963, the air force awarded TRW's Space

Technology Laboratories (STL) a contract to define a detailed configuration capable of serving the air force well into the 1970s. STL suggested that the design meet the needs of a wide variety of air force satellite programs while remaining compatible with NASA's unified S-band communication system. STL also suggested that the new method be planned for further expansion, while simultaneously eliminating the multiple-satellite problems that had plagued the AFSCF in the past.[8] In November, 1964, the air force gave STL permission to proceed with the design and fabrication of two demonstration ground stations and eight sets of satellite equipment for four satellite flight tests to try out the system (each spacecraft had one redundant onboard system). In October, 1965, the contractor delivered the demonstration ground station to Vandenberg, where the flight demonstrations would take place. Shortly after the air force and STL signed the contract, an unidentified "potential user" asked for faster implementation of the basic SGLS system. Around the same time, the defense department stated its intention to abandon the VHF band of the radio spectrum for space operations by the end of 1969, so the AFSCF speeded up the SGLS implementation. Accelerating its schedule to meet the demands of the "potential user," STL completed the demonstration stations at Vandenberg and Thule by late February, 1966.[9]

The installation engineers ran into difficulties in the design of the digital telemetry multiplexer for the satellite portion of SGLS. Their problems resulted in a cost overrun on the contract of well over $4 million. The air force approved the extra funds, pushing the fiscal year 1966 SGLS budget into a 17-percent overrun.[10] Despite the problems, in October and November, 1966, the air force conducted two orbital SGLS tests with such a high degree of success that the satellite control program office in Los Angeles cancelled the remaining two tests. The two test ground stations, Vandenberg and Thule, transferred data to Sunnyvale for processing and display, thrilling the satellite operators who could now monitor satellites in real time. The cancellation of the last two test flights saved the air force $1.5 million and hastened the system's operational capability.[11] The air force's deputy chief of staff for R&D ordered the installation of the new equipment at all the AFSCF ground stations by the end of 1969.[12]

The air force began shipping equipment to the stations as fast as possible, which led to more problems. The testing for New Boston's SGLS equipment at the Developmental Test Facility in California ended on January 27, 1968, and Philco loaded the gear onto trucks. On the way to New Hampshire in February, the first of two cargo trucks had an accident, which damaged the signal-switching facility, two magnetic tape recorders, and the 10-kilowatt transmitter, a piece of equipment worth well over $20,000. Philco shipped the equipment back to Palo Alto immediately and sent the replacements the same day. To take the SGLS equipment to Kodiak, the air force arranged for the freighter *City of Alma,* but because of a lack of crew members, the ship did not leave San Francisco harbor. Lt. Col. Philip Porter and Capt. F. Boyle arranged to have the ship unloaded and the equipment airlifted to Kodiak from nearby Travis AFB. Other complications arose when the movers dropped the 10-kilowatt, radio-frequency unit in Hawaii. The damage totaled more than $20,000 on the RF unit alone, but the total damages during the rush to get SGLS to the stations exceeded $110,000.[13] Given the high-priority nature of the new communications system, the air force considered the losses acceptable. When the SGLS equipment finally arrived, Philco technicians quickly installed it. Testing at New Boston began on March 18, 1968, and ended on April 15, with the air force taking possession of the equipment almost right away. At New Boston, the contractors offered eight training courses on operating and maintaining the new SGLS equipment. It graduated 137 students, mostly personnel who had been at the station for a while and who would actually operate the new equipment.[14]

A major step for AFSCF managers and the National Reconnaissance Program's capabilities, the SGLS implementation at the AFSCF took a lot of the decision making out of the hands of the tracking stations and centralized it in the Sunnyvale operations center. The antennas at the tracking stations now acted only as conduits, passing data to or from the main control center in California; thus they lost their ability to make decisions on their own about satellite missions. After SGLS, the AFSCF made no other major technological upgrades until the advent of the Automated Remote Tracking System in the 1980s, a system that took advantage of the microcomputer revolution to scale back personnel at the tracking stations. SGLS technology successfully expanded the capability of the AFSCF, which became better able to serve its customers, of which the NRO was among the most important. So far we have seen the National Reconnaissance Office's influences on the development of the AFSCF. At this point, therefore, a discussion of the NRO's contribution to the AFSCF's organizational momentum is pertinent.

The NRO's Influence on Organizational Momentum

Technological challenges are certainly important, but large technological systems also face organizational difficulties. General Schriever assumed that "increased scientific and engineering competence" would not speed up the rate of technical progress unless the air force learned to administer its resources "more wisely and efficiently," which it tried to do with the introduction of SGLS.[15] The leadership in Los Angeles can be credited with getting the stations set up as quickly as they did and preparing them to support Corona and the programs that soon followed. As General King added later, the success of air force satellite command and control had as much to do with the management as it did with the money flowing in from the CIA.[16]

From the beginning, the AFSCF had a special relationship with the CIA, one beginning with the Corona program but evolving after the creation of the National Reconnaissance Office. President Eisenhower's approval for the reconnaissance satellite program forced the CIA and the Advanced Research Projects Agency (ARPA) to provide all of the funding for reconnaissance satellite research, development, and procurement, while General Schriever's Air Force Ballistic Missile Division (AFBMD) in Los Angeles acted as the executive agent for the program, running it from day to day in an air force weapon system program office. President Eisenhower wanted the CIA to have complete and exclusive control of all of the intelligence phases of the reconnaissance satellite operation but left the air force to manage the technical aspects of the program's development. ARPA exercised general supervision over the development of the vehicle, but AFBMD handled the details, especially the provision of necessary ground facilities. The CIA participated by supervising the development of the actual reconnaissance equipment and was responsible for its covert procurement.[17] In fact, the relationship perpetuated a similar one between the CIA and air force during the development of the U-2 reconnaissance airplane, including some of the same people. As in the U-2 program, Lockheed served as primary contractor. Only a handful of people knew anything about the true nature of the satellite program as a reconnaissance vehicle.[18]

Despite the president's preferences for security, the reconnaissance satellite program did not initially proceed in absolute secrecy. To increase its concealment, on August 31, 1960, Eisenhower ordered the Corona program placed under a civilian-directed office in the Department of the Air Force. Joseph V. Charyk had the unique opportunity to bypass the chain of command when he took over leadership of the secret Satellite Reconnaissance Program Office, located behind door 4C1000 on the Pentagon's fourth floor.[19] A small group of military officers and government civilians reported directly to Charyk, who in turn reported to the secretary of defense, bypassing even the secretary of the air force, under whom he nominally served. After the change of national leadership in early 1961, Charyk stayed on as director of the National Reconnaissance Office, leaving two years later to run the new Comsat Corporation.[20] In September, the CIA and DoD formally established the National Reconnaissance Program, consisting of all satellite and aerial reconnaissance programs, secretly creating the NRO and classifying its very existence. An accompanying agreement between the DoD and the CIA gave joint leadership responsibility to the director of the NRO (Charyk, who also served as the undersecretary of the air force) and the CIA's deputy director for plans (Richard M. Bissell Jr).[21]

A May, 1962, agreement between the director of the CIA, John A. McCone, and the defense secretary, which Deputy Defense Secretary Roswell L. Gilpatric signed, outlined a basic policy for the NRO. The CIA and DoD agreed that the NRO would directly respond "to, and only to, the photographic and [redacted] collection requirements," as determined by the U.S. Intelligence Board. The CIA and DoD also agreed that the reconnaissance mission schedule would be the NRO's sole responsibility and that the NRO would assign operational control for individual projects under the National Reconnaissance Program to the Department of Defense.[22] In March, 1964, CIA director William Raborn and Deputy Defense Secretary Cyrus Vance signed the current NRO charter, DoD directive TS-5105.23, the only one partially declassified. The two agencies agreed to make the NRO a separate agency within the DoD and also made it accountable for the management of the National Reconnaissance Program, not the operation of satellite programs. The directive gave the NRO director the responsibility "for consolidation of all DoD satellite and air vehicle overflight projects for intelligence into a single program defined as the National Reconnaissance Program, and for the complete management and conduct of this Program in accordance with policy guidance and decision of the Secretary of Defense."[23] TS-5105.23 did not give the NRO responsibility for operations, only for management of the National Reconnaissance Program. The NRO interpreted "conduct" to mean its charter also bestowed on it *operational* responsibility for reconnaissance satellites. In the following years the NRO and its contractor teammates designed, built, launched, *and* operated all of the nation's reconnaissance satellites.[24]

The NRO gradually expanded its control over satellite reconnaissance, while keeping a tight lid on security for the National Reconnaissance Program. In 1963, Eugene Kiefer, deputy NRO director, believed that the Corona program had regressed. After years of steady improvement, it experienced a string of failures, which indicated to him the need for major changes in program management. In one major change Col. Lee Battle, the air force officer who had been running the reconnaissance satellite program in Los Angeles for some time, moved to Schriever's headquarters in the Washington, D.C., area. Kiefer wanted to pick technically competent, responsible people, one from the CIA and one from the air force, to control the program as a team as it had been at the outset, when air force Col. Frederic C. E. Oder ran the weapon system program office and CIA officer Charlie Murphy (also an air force officer at the time) ran the CIA field detachment and controlled the missions.[25] Kiefer ignored the technically competent, responsible individuals who were already involved in the program, even at the lowest levels of operations, and did not hire any of them to replace Colonel Battle. Most of the operators did not have clearance for the Corona program, so they did not know the actual mission of the satellites they operated. This early cadre of experienced personnel could have offered their technical and operational expertise for the development of the system if NRO had allowed them to participate in the National Reconnaissance Program beyond their limited role as satellite operators.

Their expertise would also have been useful if the CIA's proposal for another command and control site had borne fruit. In an effort to devise a more effective means of exploiting the limited film supply available in Corona vehicles, the CIA discussed a plan to establish an additional satellite command and control facility at one of the tracking stations to give the field test force director, the actual reconnaissance mission commander, more selectivity in the areas that the camera photographed. Without the tracking station control center, the field test force director preprogrammed 30 percent of the film, including the camera's "on/off" decisions for the entire first five passes over the USSR, when the satellite orbited out of range of the U.S.-based tracking network. Increased selectivity would allow the limited film supply to be expended in areas of primary interest, areas of best weather, and areas not previously covered. With a tracking station-based control center, the mission commander committed only 10 percent of the film at once.[26] Most of the people who worked on the Corona program did not have a clearance for the photoreconnaissance mission, so significant problems developed down the line for the satellite operators.

By not clearing more people for the Corona program, the CIA made its job more difficult. As a rule, the CIA did not grant the level of access given to technical experts such as then Captains McCartney, Lewin, and Crews, the first air force officers to "fly" a reconnaissance satellite. The air force was accountable for the health and status of the vehicle, but the NRO and the CIA tightly controlled the payload operations and security access. The CIA provided the air force with the calibration data and telemetry charts from the Lockheed Advanced Projects (AP) facility in Menlo Park, California, where contractors assembled the reconnaissance satellites. "[H]ighly trained Lockheed technicians under Government contract" conducted diagnostic analysis of telemetry at AP all of the time. When a satellite problem arose, AP engineers immediately went to the Satellite Test Center to assist, but they provided so little help on a daily basis that air force operators accused the CIA of withholding information that they needed for launch and recovery. The CIA refused to provide payload data, believing the air force wanted to duplicate "a payload analysis that was already adequately covered by a Government-funded effort involving experienced and competent personnel at the CIA facility" in Menlo Park.[27]

Difficulties between the CIA, the NRO, and the air force grew out of a period when "less than vigorous top-level leadership on the CIA side of Corona" gave the air force, led by Air Force Undersecretary and therefore NRO chief Brockway McMillan, more of a leading role in the reconnaissance satellite business. The CIA accepted a freer air force hand as long as the Corona program suffered no major setbacks. In 1962, the air force successfully orbited seventeen payloads and retrieved fourteen of them, including 69 percent of the film. When operations went downhill in 1963 with a string of launch failures and a 50-percent dip in film recovery, McMillan proposed that the air force take over the Corona program completely. At that point the CIA stepped back up to the plate. Senior members in both the CIA and the White House did not intend to make the National Reconnaissance Program a strictly military responsibility, so the CIA held on to its role in satellite reconnaissance.[28] Satellite reconnaissance, the CIA reckoned, remained too important to leave to the generals.

Army Lieut. Gen. Marshall S. Carter, the CIA's deputy director, worried about NRO boss McMillan's making "a clear-cut effort to run the CIA out of the satellite business and mak[ing] this critical intelligence collection system a complete blue-suit operation." Carter believed that McMillan attempted to gain control of the reconnaissance program by using the desire to acquire as much knowledge as possible about the vehicle to cover his real intentions. McMillan suggested in a conversation with General Carter that air force operators needed to have not only telemetry on the vehicles' health and status but also calibration data for the Corona camera. General Carter refused to give the air force operators the calibration data, arguing that they would not know what to do with the information if they had it. He stated that he "had no intention of establishing or allowing to be established a separate diagnostic, analytical function by an agency not having responsibility for the payload." Carter ended the meeting with McMillan without giving any ground on the payload issue, certain that the bureaucratic sparring would "continue as long as McMillan, [redacted], [Paul] Worthman, [Frank] Buzard and [Charlie] Murphy are in the act."[29] Clearly, the CIA intended to stand in the way of the air force's efforts to regularize space operations.

In a 1965 memo titled "Examples of the Air Force Impacts on the Corona Program," the CIA tried to show how the NRO had "reached the heights of irresponsibility" by attempting to disable the Advanced Projects facility team and "inject into the program an inexperienced [redacted] element with an unprepared and inadequate systems [sic] of operation." For example, the

NRO's meddling in the smallest of details caused "undesirable duplication, increased cost[, and] unnecessary delays without contributing anything which, at least in the payload area, has proved beneficial." While acting as project engineer and reviewing all of the wiring changes, the NRO failed to use the available resources that made the program a success, while the CIA had to justify its existence in the Corona program through numerous meetings, especially design and specification reviews.[30] The CIA's memo further criticized air force operators for ignoring the CIA operations chief during mission 1013, which launched on November 2, 1964.[31] Shortly after launch, the test controllers and the field test force director discovered a problem with the vehicle. After studying the telemetry, the CIA's expert confidently reported normal payload operation and ordered the tracking station, through the field test force director, to command the payload "on." When bad telemetry came back again, the field test force director and the satellite program office in Los Angeles ordered the payload turned "off." The CIA's operations chief failed to remedy the situation before the vehicle went over the horizon and out of commanding range from the tracking station. The lack of communication resulted in the loss of important intelligence information.[32]

The CIA convinced itself that the air force, which made up the majority of the small NRO staff, controlled the NRO and that the reconnaissance satellite program badly needed the CIA's guidance. A 1965 memo condemned NRO's attempts to "undermine" the Advanced Projects facility community's confidence in the CIA's ability to guide the Corona program, providing a litany of examples of how the air force failed to support the CIA. Satellite program officer Captain Johnson directed Lockheed to cancel the proven environmental tests on three Corona missions, resulting in a buildup of static discharge on the film, known ironically as "the corona effect." The second of the three missions, Corona flight 75 in December, 1963, mission 9062, produced largely unusable pictures because of the corona effect.[33] When the CIA's technical representative forced the return of the third mission to the AP facility, retests of the equipment revealed that the film system also had a bad roller and would have produced bad pictures. The CIA saw this incident as proof that it needed to lead the Corona program.

The memo's anonymous author perceived NRO and air force satellite program office personnel as too removed from the intelligence mission and more interested in launch schedules and recoveries than in the quality of the pictures. For example, at a meeting in early 1965, a sharp exchange took place between Colonel Buzard of the NRO staff and an anonymous member of the CIA staff. Colonel Buzard apparently stated that the NRO had scheduled sixteen Corona launches for 1965 and that they intended to meet the schedule. "Mr. [Redacted] made it clear to Colonel Buzard that Corona was an intelligence reconnaissance program and that the missions would be flown in response to intelligence requirements, not in response to pre-established Air Force launch schedules."[34] Buzard says the memo's author took his comment out of context:

> I have absolutely no recollection of any such meeting or of making such a comment. I have read that comment in another document somewhere, but it was made at a much earlier date when it was [alleged] that the Air Force wanted to launch on a regular schedule to reduce overtime etc. All this was at a time when we in the Project Office were always launching just as often and as quickly as we could get the hardware ready to go.[35]

Naming the air force specifically, the memo criticized NRO's attempts to expand its control over Corona, something the CIA wanted to prevent.

NRO director McMillan did not give up on his quest for greater control of the satellite reconnaissance mission. On November 30, 1964, he directed the NRO to handle all premission, mission, and postmission Corona messages exclusively at their operations center in Washington, D.C., and at the Satellite Test Center on the West Coast. Further, he moved the mission command post to the STC and made changes to the operations manual. The next day the NRO added the STC to the list of organizations receiving Corona message traffic and deleted the CIA's Advanced Projects facility in Menlo Park. The CIA responded by saying that the Satellite Test Center could not provide adequate support without significant additional training, including two to four months of necessary software upgrades. CIA headquarters required field units to obey previous orders as if the November 30 memo from McMillan had never been issued. They perceived McMillan's message as "the climax of a power grab attempt within government circles. The actions taken were not only poorly staffed and technically unrealistic, but they demonstrated a much greater concern on the part of the D/NRO [McMillan] for the political management policies than for intelligence reconnaissance operations."[36] The CIA had guessed right: McMillan had again attempted to expand NRO's sphere of influence, a sphere that included the Air Force Satellite Control Facility. As former CIA officer Herbert Scoville put it later in an interview with Jeffrey T. Richelson, McMillan's most important talents included "empire-building."[37]

General Schriever felt that the NRO's attempt to expand its sphere of influence not only extended beyond its original mandate, but also did more harm than good by keeping the operators out of the loop. In effect, this separation kept them from developing an intimate knowledge of the technology about which they should have known the most. Schriever presented the U.S.

flag that had been on board *Discoverer 13* to President Eisenhower, but no one felt he had a need to know that *Discoverer 14* carried a camera. In fact, Schriever believes, satellite command and control suffered during the NRO's expansion. Furthermore, Schriever expressed in a 2001 interview with the author that the NRO should be a policy-making organization, not a hardware group. Making the NRO a bureaucracy with operational responsibilities "was the wrong move to take, because the operator was really taken out of the loop. If you look at all the 117L babies, they were practically all gobbled up by the NRO. That, plus the fact that you find people that are always trying to protect their rear ends—'what's been' instead of 'what we can get'—and that sure as hell happened in space." Schriever wanted to restrict the NRO's area of responsibility. Because about 90 percent of the NRO's staff came from the air force in the early days, the air force—if given a chance—could have done as good a job operationally as the NRO or, in Schriever's words, "maybe better."[38]

To be fair, in the early 1960s the NRO did not behave like the massive bureaucracy that typifies it today. In the early 1960s, most of the bureaucratic squabbles and jockeying for power went on at the highest levels of the government. The CIA officer in charge in Palo Alto, air force Lt. Col. Charles Murphy, says the NRO acted largely transparently to the satellite operators. The CIA and air force people involved in the program in California had an excellent relationship. They did not have to call back to Washington and ask permission to make decisions; they just made them, even if they were planning something for the first time. In fact, the program succeeded because the working people—wrench turners and engineers and those making decisions in the field—ignored the bureaucratic squabbles and did what they had to do to accomplish the mission—with the AFSCF caught in the middle.[39]

The NRO did reasonably well at gathering strategic intelligence while delaying the air force in normalizing space operations. Because the NRO had a specific charter to acquire strategic intelligence, it actively kept other organizations, particularly the air force, whose legal mandate included acquiring strategic reconnaissance, out of the satellite operations arena.[40] The AFSCF had no choice but to go along for the ride during the bureaucratic tugs-of-war. In the midst of the bureaucratic quarreling in Washington, the air force tried to take as much control over satellite operations as it could in California and throughout the network by standardizing procedures and operating the AFSCF much like any "normal" flying unit.

Overcoming Organizational Momentum

As they all scrambled for a piece of the new space reconnaissance pie, each of the major players tried to grab control of the Air Force Satellite Control Facility. For the AFSCF, the greatest challenge stemmed from the air force leadership's belief that it was the only organization that possessed the ability to carry out the military space mission, while other groups, just as eager for a piece of the space budget, tried to hold on to or expand what they had. To maintain its position as the preeminent service for space, the air force attempted to acquire complete authority for missile- and space-related management and the opportunities extending into satellite command and control as well.

On November 16, 1963, Secretary Robert S. McNamara informed the air force that he wanted significant and "mandatory" changes in the management of the Department of Defense's missile and space ranges.[41] He saw an "obvious need" for improvements in the administrative arrangement of the DoD ranges because "successful performance of assigned missions has occurred despite, rather than because of, the management structure." Noting that several agencies shared the responsibility for global tracking, McNamara sought to centralize all command and control functions into one agency to help resolve the "interface" problems between the Atlantic missile range, the Pacific missile range, and the AFSCF.[42] Thus, McNamara saw the need for a central organization that could preside over the operations and planning of military space and missile command and control. In the U.S. electric power generation industry, management created holding companies to facilitate operations. In this case, government managers simply invented a new echelon of command that was responsible for all space and missile command and control and called it the National Range Division (NRD).

The air force stood to benefit from McNamara's efficiency movement in the defense department when he ordered the consolidation of several major space and missile test ranges under air force management. The navy lost a shore installation when McNamara combined the naval missile facility at Point Arguello, California, and Vandenberg AFB, into a single air force base. The secretary also tried to "nationalize" the AFSCF by making it accountable for the "management and operation of a world-wide satellite tracking and control facility for all DoD programs." McNamara laid out his directions in a memo to the service secretaries. "The Air Force shall establish a central authority for the combined planning of ICBM and space vehicle launch area ranged instrumentation and satellite on-orbit control facilities to include Cape Canaveral and Point Arguello/Vandenberg launches, as well as remote tracking stations world-wide."[43] McNamara directed that the AFSCF come under the new authority no later than 1964.

The air force, therefore, prepared to assume control of the new National Range Division. On December 3, 1963, Air Force Chief of Staff Gen. Thomas D. White wrote General Schriever and SAC Commander in Chief Gen. Thomas Power, that the assignment of these responsibilities to the Air Force is predicated upon our establishment of a single manager capability to centrally plan for and manage the execution of test programs with optimum economy. . . . The several instrumentation networks, now being separately planned and managed by the Ranges and [Air Force] Satellite Control Facility, must be managed in the future as a group of test facilities and networks to most economically serve all DoD users.[44]

General White considered McNamara's decision a milestone in the "furtherance of Air Force objectives and mission in aerospace" because it virtually promised the air force the role of the defense department's executive agent for space, which guaranteed bigger budgets.

Maj. Gen. Leighton I. Davis, commander of the Air Force Missile Test Center at Patrick AFB, Florida, chaired the National Range Implementation Group, which was chartered to simplify the management of the military ranges. General Davis assumed that the defense department and air force directives required the establishment of a single, field-level organization to coordinate and integrate the Atlantic missile range, the Pacific missile range, and the AFSCF into one "National Range Division," which he assumed would be assigned to General Schriever's Air Force Systems Command.[45] Major General Davis was quickly made responsible for the Atlantic and Pacific missile test ranges.

The issue of the AFSCF did not go away quite so easily as the missile ranges. Following McNamara's direction, Lt. Gen. Howell M. Estes Jr. ordered Davis to take command of a provisional National Range Division with headquarters at Andrews AFB, where Schriever's Air Force Systems Command was also headquartered. In his order Estes did not include the AFSCF in the new NRD but left it as part of the Space Systems Division in Los Angeles. He asked Davis to study the "feasibility" of transferring the AFSCF to the NRD.[46] Air Force Secretary Eugene M. Zuckert wrote McNamara that the air force would study "the time-phasing for complete transfer" of the AFSCF into the NRD.[47]

McNamara took one look at the air force's plan for the implementation of the National Range Division proposal and, believing the service was stalling on the decision to move the AFSCF, offered a compromise. "We expect the Air Force to assign a single agency the responsibility for management and operations of world-wide satellite tracking and on-orbit control facilities for all DoD programs. . . . We anticipate that the current organization now responsible for the Satellite Control Facility will form the nucleus of that agency."[48] Zuckert followed orders and issued a directive to reorganize the AFSCF under the new management structure.[49] However, the Air Force Systems Command ignored his order, leaving the AFSCF outside the National Range Division.

The air force resisted McNamara because the service had organized the two major functions of satellite command and control separately. The command and control community performed two major activities: satellite command and control operations in response to program requirements and planning for the development and improvement of the command and control system. The 6594th Aerospace Test Wing in Sunnyvale handled satellite operations, while the Deputy for Space Test Operations at Space Systems Division in Los Angeles handled planning. Undersecretary of the Air Force and NRO chief Brockway McMillan ordered the combining of all operations and planning activities under a single organizational element, headed by a general officer, instead of the two separate but equal colonels. This new general officer position would be given the responsibility for the overall direction of operation of all of the remote tracking stations as well as for the planning and implementation of future actions for improvement or growth of the network.[50] Seeing a new way for the air force to get its managerial house in order while continuing to fight the idea of the NRD, the air force chief of staff concurred with McMillan.[51]

The air force also resisted McNamara, not in a bureaucratic grab for turf, but because of the influence of the AFSCF's primary customer, the National Reconnaissance Office. McMillan, who served not only as undersecretary of the air force but also as NRO director (although the DoD kept that title classified), refused to release the AFSCF to the new National Range Division. Once satellite "programs other than the specially classified ones" constituted the majority of AFSCF's support activities, McMillan said he would consider releasing the network to NRD.[52] McMillan, in effect, wanted to consolidate the AFSCF, which was the sole provider of satellite command and control for the defense department's space programs, with the CIA's Office of Special Projects—the CIA's agency for developing reconnaissance satellites—under one organization, preferably the air force's Space Systems Division in Los Angeles.[53] McMillan made a play much broader than simply managing space and missile command and control. His plan tried to take the entire reconnaissance satellite business for the air force and the NRO.

The new National Range Division and the established Space Systems Division (SSD) quickly began a paper war, bureaucratically throwing their opinions at each other. General Davis grew understandably upset at this violation of his mandate from McNamara. In a 1964 issue paper, he reiterated NRD's differences with SSD and cited the secretary of defense's memo as evidence that the NRD should have sole responsibility for planning authority.[54] The SSD's response was this: Engineers designed and wired on-orbit stations for operation as integrated units in support of unique or of very similar missions, not geographically for logistical support. The SSD believed, therefore, that the agency carrying out the mission had to have complete jurisdiction over mission, communications, logistics, and administration. The SSD disagreed with NRD's plan for division on a functional basis. Under NRD's proposal, the Air Force Satellite Control Facility would manage and operate all equipment for satellite command and control, but the stations would be grouped geographically for logistical and administrative help. Where NRD could assist administratively and logistically, as in the case of Mahe, Seychelles, which the eastern test range at Patrick could support, the NRD would administer the station. Otherwise, the AFSCF could manage and operate its own stations. General Davis thought the NRD had the most logical position and could fulfill the secretary of defense's directive to improve efficiency in the DoD.[55] A classic bureaucratic turf war raged inside the air force, which had organizational responsibility for both the AFSCF and the National Range Division, as well as coresponsibility with the CIA for the National Reconnaissance Office.

In the end, the influence of agencies outside the air force pushed the issue of control of the AFSCF to a final resolution. In 1964 the two sides arranged to settle the internal air force squabble with a memorandum of agreement, which Maj. Gen. Ben I. Funk, Space Systems Division commander, and General Davis, National Range Division commander, both signed. The agreement said in effect that the Space Systems Division retained command and overall technical and managerial control of the AFSCF and that the NRD would leave them alone.[56] The NRD remained responsible for the missile ranges for a time, but the air force disestablished it in the late 1960s and returned to the older methods of management.

The AFSCF had won a major battle to remain independent of any national range establishment. Now one stronger organization had responsibility for both planning and operations of air force satellite command and control, and a one-star general commanded it. The National Range Division's attempts to take over satellite command and control proved less powerful than the desires of the National Reconnaissance Office.

Summary

The air force overcame management challenges by emphasizing the Air Force Satellite Control Facility's unique place in the department of defense's space mission. The AFSCF did not use tracking range radars for IRBM and ICBM tests off the Atlantic or Pacific coasts. These ranges launched rockets and missiles but did not have the equipment to handle command and control and satellite troubleshooting. The AFSCF acted as a different kind of range, a concept that was lost on many. Once the air force convinced the DoD's leadership of this significant difference, the AFSCF held onto both its unique place in the service and to its special relationship with the users who existed outside the

DoD, in particular the NRO, whose partner, the CIA's Office of Special Projects, made it known that it patronized the AFSCF because its money made satellite command and control work.[57]

The managers who ran the AFSCF and the primary customers who justified its existence built momentum into the system. The space-ground link subsystem served both parties and advanced satellite command and control technology while enabling the development of even more sophisticated satellites. In its special relationship with the NRO, the AFSCF paid homage to its patron, often at the cost of supporting other important national space priorities such as the military's own weather satellites. In the pressure cooker of the 1960s' space program, internal, institutional momentum diverted well-meaning proposals into a move to isolate space operations from the rest of the air force operations community despite the presence of a common-user Air Force Satellite Control Facility.

Conclusion
Inveniemus Viam vel Faciemus

---

*The tracking and data-acquisition system serving "ETR," the eastern
test range, makes this miracle [spaceflight] possible. It is probably
even more complex than the space vehicle whose performance was
just announced [Mariner II].*

— Wernher von Braun
Director, George C. Marshall Space Flight Center

THIS STORY ENDS in 1969 because in that year the Air Force Satellite
Control Facility became a complete satellite command and control system. After 1969, the changes in the system became less qualitative, more
regular, and to some extent predictable.[1]

After 1969, changes in the AFSCF occurred in much smaller increments
than the dramatic improvements of the 1960s. Few organizational changes
took place. Although the AFSCF changed names a few times well into the
1990s, it continued to be the primary provider of satellite command and control services to the military and the National Reconnaissance Office. In addition, with the rise in the 1970s of new building codes and sensible thinking
about earthquake hazards (the Sunnyvale facilities sit right on the San An-
dreas fault) and with the advent of NASA's space shuttle in air force planning
in the early 1980s, the service built a newer and more secure satellite control
facility outside Colorado Springs. The air force did not pilot the space shuttle
as it had originally envisioned, but the Colorado Springs facility, first known
as the Consolidated Space Operations Center and now known as Schriever
Air Force Base in General Schriever's honor, eventually became the center of
all air force satellite command and control operations.

By the end of the decade, the air force had its system of satellite command
and control in place, having reached its goals using whatever available or appropriate means it could. The most dramatic changes included the introduction of new computer technology. The Advanced Remote Tracking Station

computers accomplished tasks that one hundred or more people had performed at the original tracking stations and reduced the number of personnel required to just two. In 2003, the Air Force Space Command had under consideration a proposal to eliminate all personnel at the tracking stations except for maintainers. This technical modification would automate the last of the operations functions, finally reducing the number of "antenna drivers" in the air force satellite command and control system to zero. Also in 2003, the air force considered a "lights out" plan that would involve a system similar to NASA's use of tracking and data relay satellites, which would all but eliminate the need for ground tracking stations worldwide.[2] Such a system raised space dependence questions, such as satellite vulnerability to enemy action.

This study uses a model of the social construction of technology that historian Thomas Parke Hughes articulates.[3] His model serves well in meaningfully describing the way human beings created a large technological system for satellite command and control. Another reason I use his model is to add something to it, further refining and possibly expanding it by adding a new perspective. This book is hardly the first comprehensive look at an artifact produced largely by the federal government,[4] but in its analysis of the evolution of a large technological system designed solely to meet governmental needs, this study follows the lines of Hughes's own examination of electrical power networks or Boston's Central Artery/Tunnel.[5] In addition, this research adds to the body of knowledge that shows that there is no need for a "Eureka!" moment in the evolution of technological systems, particularly when management plays a more important role than the engineers do, as the case of the Air Force Satellite Control Facility illustrates.

During the process of invention, scientists and engineers solved the critical problems associated with making satellite command and control work. No "Eureka!" moment sparked the birth of the AFSCF because teamwork in science and engineering built the system. The flying air force, uninterested in new, nonaircraft technological systems for reconnaissance, did not contribute to the development of this new technology, which threatened airplane-based reconnaissance. The normal weapons procurement system could not bring a spectacular new system online as quickly as the United States needed photoreconnaissance of the USSR in the early days of the Cold War.

The air force went outside, therefore, to a group of scientific advisors who represented the best minds in the nation and to the RAND Corporation to find answers to questions the air force could not answer alone. Gen. H. H. Arnold gave Theodore von Kármán room to maneuver, and *Toward New Horizons* became the blueprint for the U.S. Air Force for the rest of the twentieth century. Gen. Curtis LeMay gave Douglas Aircraft's Research and Development group broad authority to investigate the usefulness of satellites. RAND's series of reports on the utility of a "world-circling spaceship" eventually became the first technical studies in the history of satellite command and control. Just as important, General Schriever did not report through normal air force channels but instead—with the highest national priority—informed the secretary of the air force and the president of the United States directly. Schriever's wide latitude to develop the ICBM and the reconnaissance satellite independently helped achieve these feats far more quickly (although certainly not any less expensively). The air force purposely put the Western Development Division on the West Coast, not just to get it closer to the nation's airplane manufacturers, but also to get it out of Washington, D.C.

Engineers embodied in the AFSCF the economic, political, and social characteristics it needed to survive by turning ideas about satellite command and control into a comprehensive system. Then they instilled economic and social characteristics into the AFSCF to create an organization that fended off rivals. Finally, with development essentially over, the AFSCF expanded its role in the air force's space program to increase its indispensability.

By 1960, the product had come into use. The Subsystem H engineers, given a free hand, used state-of-the-art equipment and created a command and control system absolutely necessary for the early reconnaissance satellites, even before the first launch. Satellite-based reconnaissance, a radical idea, needed command and control support, essentially a conservative idea that implemented practices borrowed from the ICBM test environment. Meanwhile, at the urging of the contractors and the air force, the size of the system expanded. Those presiding over Subsystem H, the Air Force Ballistic Missile Division and Lockheed, developed satellite command and control as much as possible, while numerous players each attempted to add elements of their own control to the system until the air force finally won the day. By 1961, managers, both contractors and military officers, had replaced the inventors of satellite command and control. After successfully arguing that a service organization—not an operational nuclear command—should be responsible for command and control of the WS-117L reconnaissance satellite program, the air force created the 6594th Test Wing (Satellite) to perform that service, thus retaining command and control as a critical function for the air force test community to perform.

As the system expanded, problems developed, which Hughes refers to with the military term "reverse salient." The AFSCF overcame the technological reverse salient of supporting expanding numbers of satellites in orbit by designing an essentially new system that could handle the increased requirements. Known as the Multiple Satellite Augmentation Program (MSAP), it turned the AFSCF into a real network for the first time instead of a group of command and control stations loosely bound in a military organization. Within MSAP, problems occurred that required solutions, especially equipment interface problems. The space-ground link subsystem (SGLS) followed MSAP later as the air force tried to expand the capability and reach of the AFSCF. The ground network Colonel Haig built for the weather satellite program reveals in its differences alternate paths that the AFSCF could have followed. When the air force tried to streamline space operations to make them more like the checklist-driven operational missile and aircraft communities, institutional momentum diverted this well-meaning goal into further isolating satellite operations from the rest of the air force operations community, thus pushing it into the covert world of national security space programs. The implications for the future included increasingly incompatible and isolated space systems, while a common-user Air Force Satellite Control Facility stood off to the side.

As the AFSCF overcame each reverse salient, it built momentum for future growth that kept away customers such as the weather satellite program and later the navigational satellite program known as the Global Positioning System (GPS), an unusual choice for a large organization. The command and control system did not become autonomous but acquired momentum because of the managerial and technological mass that pushed it along. The driving force of the AFSCF arose from the corporate and military organizations that were committed to the system. Engineers, managers, owners, investors, civil servants, and politicians all had vested interests in the growth and stability of the AFSCF.

The space-ground link subsystem, conceived in 1962, made the AFSCF a common-user network with the ability to serve every satellite program in development, but its managers chose not to support them all, only "special programs," a euphemism for reconnaissance satellites. Aided by the personnel cutbacks in SGLS, by the end of the 1960s, the air force gave up on having the military perform operations and maintenance in the AFSCF and fell back on using contractors to oversee the vital national service of satellite command and control. Finally, just as important as the technological and organizational challenges facing the AFSCF, adapting to its environment required the AFSCF's managers to compromise and thus affected the technological style of the entire satellite command and control system. The SGLS advanced satellite command and control technology while enabling the development of even more sophisticated satellites.

The special relationship with the NRO continued as the AFSCF supported its patron by often acting detrimentally to other important, national space priorities. Discussion about where the AFSCF fit into the department of defense

Operations Control Crew — Tracking
Controller, Operations Controller,
and Command Controller

Members of the integrated air force–contractor team at the New Hampshire tracking station, 1963. Courtesy of the Air Force Historical Research Agency collection.

picture included its unique relationship with the users who existed outside the DoD, in particular, the Central Intelligence Agency and that unusual DoD bureau—the National Reconnaissance Office.

Obvious from the story is that people designed the technology used for satellite command and control; the machines did not design themselves. Each major program came about not because technology evolves organically, but because human beings make decisions to change technology. If the Corona reconnaissance system had failed to detect Soviet ICBM capabilities, or if President Eisenhower had cancelled the program before the extraordinary success of *Discoverer 14* (Corona), there would never have been a Multiple Satellite Augmentation Program or a space-ground link subsystem. Each major upgrade to the AFSCF significantly increased its usefulness to the national reconnaissance community because of the significant participation of people who continually refined their techniques of launching ever more sophisticated reconnaissance satellites and made the upgrades necessary.

This story also concentrates on the interaction of technology and politics. Because one can define politics to mean the activities or affairs of a government, the managers made political decisions about upgrading the technology, involving officials at a variety of levels inside and outside the U.S. government and the military. The AFSCF's engineers did not make arbitrary decisions about satellite command and control technology because they wanted to upgrade or enhance it; they made decisions with political reasons in mind. A particularly good example of the role of politics in the evolution of air force satellite command and control is the debate over whether uniformed technicians, so-called blue-suiters, should perform operations and maintenance in the AFSCF. The Air Force Satellite Control Facility is as much a political artifact of the space race as it is a military or a technological one.

The model of system formation and growth that organizes this study provides room for the development and coordination of a number of subthemes. These may prove relevant not only to space history but also to the history of technology and military history generally. The subthemes relate in most instances to questions often asked about technological systems and the history of technology in general. For instance, the nature of the air force's role in the National Reconnaissance Program and the role of invention by committee raises questions about the function of institutions as opposed to individuals in shaping the development of technological systems. Primarily, the air force used its space effort to enhance its traditional mission capabilities, particularly the strategic mission. The air force developed the Air Force Satellite Control Facility as the sole provider of satellite command and control to the military to boost its position as the national military space service, but without ever actually achieving that status. Nevertheless, the United States started the Corona reconnaissance satellite program for one single reason: to crack open the door that kept the nature of Soviet strategic nuclear forces a mystery. American leaders believed that by acquiring as much information as possible about Soviet capabilities, they could better protect U.S. interests.

Another significant issue this study addresses is the idea that as they mature, technological systems tend to become less adaptable. As momentum increased, the Air Force Satellite Control Facility prevented other satellite programs from taking advantage of its unique common-user features, thus driving up the cost of the military space plan when those satellite programs had to build their own control networks, such as that for weather satellites. By 1969, the United States owned or operated several satellite command and control networks, the largest and busiest of which were in the air force. The United States also had NASA's Manned Spaceflight Network, a major contributor to the successes of the Apollo program. The NRO then constructed other satellite command and control networks separate from the AFSCF, which the NRO used for its own satellites because the AFSCF could not or would not do so, or perhaps the NRO did not want it to. These separate networks included a missile warning network and a weather satellite network, the most important of which was centered at Offutt AFB, Nebraska.[6] Unclassified satellite command and control networks include the system of ground stations specifically designed to support only the Global Positioning System, which the air force operates and maintains. In the 1980s, the air force space systems engineers built the three GPS ground stations at Kwajalein, in the Marshall Islands, Diego Garcia, in the Indian Ocean, and Ascension, in the South Atlantic, to support the GPS network. These stations cannot support any other satellite programs besides GPS. The air force built this alternate, "stove-piped" tracking network for GPS because the AFSCF could not—or would not—support the twenty-four satellites in the semisynchronous GPS constellation. In effect, the great momentum in the AFSCF exerted a kind of soft determinism on the other space systems under development and forced them to go elsewhere for support.

Engineers faced difficult challenges when trying to change the direction of a large satellite command and control system—and perhaps that of large sociotechnical structures in general—but such systems are not autonomous. Those who seek to control and direct large technological networks must understand that these are socially constructed artifacts of human culture, not isolated technological systems. Attempts to alter them without taking into account their social, political, and economic environments (among others) are difficult at best. If engineers change only the technology, the structure may revert to its earlier style, affected more by its environment than actual technology. Therefore, these surroundings must also be attended to because certain values may need to be changed or institutions altered.

The people who designed the Air Force Satellite Control Facility had one goal in mind when they began: winning the Cold War. A higher power motivated them, not a supreme being, but visions of new worlds and ideals of rational order were just as important to them as to the cathedral builders of the Middle Ages.[7] These engineers and managers believed they could win the space race, and they did. They planned to create a new, safer world by providing access to information the U.S. government did not have, particularly about Soviet nuclear capabilities at a time when the vast USSR lurked behind the Iron Curtain. The goal ultimately became something entirely different, but just as powerfully motivating—preservation of the command and control network they had built.

A secondary objective of the air force's space effort included the development of space systems, techniques, and the organizational and operational experience necessary to support the traditional air force mission: to fly and fight. Here the air force significantly failed in its developmental goals, never developing anything in space alone, always relying on the expertise and good will of contractors, with the solitary exception of Tom Haig's maverick weather satellite program. Development of the AFSCF did support the new horizons of Arnold's and von Kármán's vision but without also building the engineering expertise in the air force to enable it to develop weapons systems on its own. In this period the air force also failed to develop a cadre of space operators who were trained in the methods of space operations and who were able to fly and fight like pilots fly airplanes; instead, they preferred to rely on contractors not only to design spacecraft but also to operate them. The original all–blue-suit operations vision simply did not pan out.

The use of contractors did not—and does not—necessarily constitute a mistake. In the 1960s, space played a supporting role on the battlefield, so no compelling need existed—or exists today—to have military people performing these roles and missions. There are no uniformed war fighters in the space business, only warriors who perform "combat support" missions using space-based assets. Until the day when the United States "weaponizes" space (the brief flight of an ICBM warhead through the upper reaches of the atmosphere does not truly constitute a space weapon), many of the air force's other missions, including, for example, airlift, will remain an indispensable support task for the pilots, soldiers, sailors, and marines who do the actual fighting.

Yet, just as important as the contributions the AFSCF made to the air force in the 1960s, is the fact that the air force could never act as it wanted with the AFSCF, which effectively belonged to and was obliged to the NRO. The air force wanted the satellite command and control mission because it increased budgets and supported the myth that the air force had become the "Aerospace Force," but the AFSCF actually functioned as the NRO's own satellite control range in this period. As the NRO developed its reconnaissance capabilities, the AFSCF had to respond with upgrades to satellite command and control technology or with additional tracking stations, one even as recently as 1992 (Diego Garcia), but within its own budgetary means and without other financial support. The NRO and the CIA devoted themselves to space hardware and got out of the business of supporting the AFSCF.

As discussions occurred about what the NRO wanted to do with the AFSCF, deliberations also took place about what the air force wanted to do with the AFSCF. The air force debated for some time about whether the AFSCF would be an operational unit placed under the authority of a combat authority such as the Strategic Air Command or a test and engineering unit that would be left inside the Air Force Systems Command. The dialogues had as much to do with whether the service could operate satellites like airplanes as they did with budgetary considerations and empire building. The air force eventually concluded that it could not make operating satellites like flying airplanes because of a lack of airmen in the AFSCF and because many senior military officers

simply did not understand the space business. When Gen. James V. Hartinger
took over the newly created Air Force Space Command in 1982, without the
AFSCF as part of his command, he made a point of educating his staff about
space, even to the point of conducting pop quizzes on mandatory reading assignments during staff meetings and then posting the scores by name.[8] One
senior flying general showed the extent of his ignorance about space when he
looked at a flat projection of an orbital plot and asked, "How many g's is the
satellite pulling at the bottom of the orbit?" Even embarrassing revelations
like that have not made the air force as aware as it should be of the role of
space in its day-to-day operations. To some extent, the air force still has not figured out what it wants to do with space.

The Air Force Satellite Control Facility embraced the important myth that
the air force could accomplish space operations with an entirely blue-suit
workforce. During the 1960s, the air force's system of satellite command and
control did not achieve important new capabilities for the air service. For two
important reasons blue-suiting never happened: the Cold War and the influence of the NRO. Vietnam siphoned off a large number of air force technical
personnel who could have assisted the AFSCF by instead sending them to
fight, reducing their time in the military, and even affecting their inclination
to volunteer for military service. Further, the dramatic growth of the aerospace industry in the 1960s drained off even more technical personnel as airmen who might have stayed in the air force longer left and moved on to other
space projects.

In the 1980s, the air force reversed its thinking and tried again to make
satellite command and control like flying airplanes. The AFSCF faced another major organizational challenge in the creation of Space Command, the
air force's next attempt to make space operations commonplace and to grab
a bigger piece of the space budget. For a short time after the creation of the
new space command, the AFSCF remained in the test community of Air Force
Systems Command. Eventually, however, over the objections of many, the air
force folded satellite command and control into the operational community,
a sign of the increasing importance of the space mission to the air force's institutional vision and a move that brings to mind shaving the corners off a
square peg to make it fit into a round hole.

Another point in this story is the importance of contractors not only in the
designing but also in the operating of air force weapon systems. The NRO
simply preferred to have contractors on console and performing maintenance
tasks because it perceived them as more experienced, stable, professional,
secure, and cost-effective than military personnel. Today this perception still
rules, even though "out-sourcing" is a relatively recent term. During the early
phases of the development of the AFSCF, the hardware and software contrac-

tors collaborated to design the systems to air force specifications. They offered suggestions to the service for improving the system, ideas the air force often accepted because these contractors had previous system design experience.

Later, as the AFSCF gathered momentum, contractor involvement diminished, and an antagonistic relationship between the air force and its former contractor partners gradually developed. General Schriever offers an important warning: The government should not keep operators uninformed the way the NRO tried to keep the AFSCF in the dark, or people end up planning for or providing support that they should not—because they do not understand the real needs, which leads to waste and failed missions. One former contractor said that the best officers he worked with in the late 1950s and early 1960s let the contractors work without micromanaging them, which he attributed to an "operations-oriented, 'can-do'" attitude.[9]

This study is not just an intellectual exercise in relating the evolution of a large technological system. This work demonstrates how important the development of satellite command and control was to the National Reconnaissance Program and to U.S. space programs in general. I hope that when historians write about the American space program in the future, they will not neglect the satellite command and control system, which made those space firsts possible. What stays on the ground is at least as worthy of study as what goes into space.

Glossary of Acronyms

AAF	Army Air Forces
ABMA	Army Ballistic Missile Agency
AFB	Air Force Base
AFBMD	Air Force Ballistic Missile Division
AFHRA	Air Force Historical Research Agency
AFSC	Air Force Systems Command
AFSCF	Air Force Satellite Control Facility
AFSCN	Air Force Satellite Control Network
AFSPC/HO	Air Force Space Command History Office
AMC	Air Materiel Command
ANNE	Annette Island, Alaska, tracking station, call sign
AOC	Assistant Operations Controller
AP	Advance Projects Facility (a division of Lockheed)
APL	Advanced Projects Laboratory (a division of Johns Hopkins University)
ARDC	Air Research and Development Command
ARPA	Advanced Research Projects Agency
ARS	Advanced Reconnaissance Satellite (also called Corona, Pied Piper, or WS-117L)
ARSIC	Advanced Reconnaissance Satellite Intelligence Center
BMD	Ballistic Missile Division
BMEWS	Ballistic Missile Early Warning System
BOSS	New Boston, New Hampshire, tracking station, call sign
BuAer	U.S. Navy Bureau of Aeronautics
C2	Command and Control
CDC	Control Data Corporation
CIA	Central Intelligence Agency
COMOR	Committee on Overhead Reconnaissance
COOK	Vandenberg (previously Cooke) Air Force Base, California, tracking station, call sign
Corona	Covert name for the reconnaissance satellite program run by the CIA and the NRO (also called Pied Piper or WS-117L)
CSOC	Consolidated Space Operations Center

DARPA	Defense Advanced Research Projects Agency
DCA	Defense Communications Agency
DCI	Director of Central Intelligence
DCS	Deputy Chief of Staff
DDR&E	Director of Defense Research and Engineering
DGS	Diego Garcia tracking station, British Indian Ocean territory
DICE	Satellite Test Center, Sunnyvale Air Force Station, California, call sign
Discoverer	Biomedical cover story for the covert reconnaissance satellite program (also called Corona, Pied Piper, and WS-117L)
DMSP	Defense Meteorological Satellite Program
DNRO	Director of the National Reconnaissance Office
DoD	Department of Defense
DSCS	Defense Communications Agency Satellite Communications System
DSP	Defense Support Program
DTIC	Defense Technical Information Center
EHF	Extremely High Frequency
ETR	Eastern Test Range
FY	Fiscal Year
GAO	General Accounting Office
GPS	Global Positioning System
GTS	Guam tracking station, Guam
GUAM	Guam tracking station, Guam, call sign
HTS	Hawaii tracking station, Kaena Point, Hawaii
HULA	Hawaii tracking station, call sign
ICBM	Intercontinental Ballistic Missile
IGY	International Geophysical Year
INDI	Indian Ocean tracking station, Mahe, Seychelles, call sign
IOS	Indian Ocean tracking station, Mahe, Seychelles
IRBM	Intermediate Range Ballistic Missile
JCS	Joint Chiefs of Staff
JPL	Jet Propulsion Laboratory
KHz	Kilohertz
KODI	Kodiak, Alaska, tracking station, call sign
KTS	Kodiak, Alaska, tracking station
MHz	Megahertz
MIDAS	Missile Detection and Alarm System
MOL	Manned Orbiting Laboratory
MOUSE	Minimum Orbital Unmanned Satellite of the Earth
MRBM	Medium Range Ballistic Missile

MSAP	Multiple Satellite Augmentation Program
NACA	National Advisory Committee for Aeronautics
NASA	National Aeronautics and Space Administration
NATO	North American Treaty Organization
NOAA	National Oceanic and Atmospheric Administration
NORAD	North American Aerospace Defense Command
NPIC	National Photo Interpretation Center
NRD	National Range Division
NRL	Naval Research Laboratory
NRO	National Reconnaissance Office
NRP	National Reconnaissance Program
NSA	National Security Agency
NSC	National Security Council
OC	Operations Controller
OL	Operating Location
OSD	Office of the Secretary of Defense
PICE	Programmable Integrated Communications Equipment
Pied Piper	Program name for the Advanced Reconnaissance Satellite (also called ARS, Corona, and WS-117L)
POGO	Thule tracking station, Greenland, call sign
PRELORT	Precision Long Range Tracking Radar
R&D	Research and Development
RADAR	Radio Detection and Ranging
RAND	Rand Corporation, originally the Research and Development group of Douglas Aircraft Corporation
REEF	Diego Garcia tracking station, British Indian Ocean territory, call sign
RTS	Remote Tracking Station
SAC	Strategic Air Command
Samos	Name of the former SENTRY satellite program, but not an acronym
SAMSO	Space and Missile Systems Organization
SCF	Satellite Control Facility
SD	Space Division
SE/TD	Systems Engineering and Technical Direction
SGLS	Space-Ground Link Subsystem
SHF	Super High Frequency
SLBM	Sea-Launched Ballistic Missile
SSD	Space Systems Division
STC	Satellite Test Center
STL	Space Technology Laboratories (a division of Philco)

TIROS	Television and Infrared Observing Satellite
TOO	Technical Operations Order
TRW	Thompson-Ramo-Wooldridge, Inc.
TT&C	Telemetry, Tracking, and Control
TTS	Thule tracking station, Greenland
UHF	Ultra High Frequency
USAF	United States Air Force
VERLORT	Very Long Range Tracking Radar
VHF	Very High Frequency
WADC	Wright Air Development Center, Ohio
WDD	Western Development Division
WDL	Western Development Laboratories (a division of TRW)
WS	Weapon System
WS-117L	Advanced Reconnaissance Satellite (also called Corona, Pied Piper, and WS-117L)
WTR	Western Test Range

Notes

PREFACE

1. Shirley Thomas, *Satellite Tracking Facilities: Their History and Operation;* Eloise Engle and Kenneth Drummond, *Sky Rangers: Satellite Tracking around the World.*

2. Constance McLaughlin Green and Milton Lomask, *Vanguard: A History.*

3. Lloyd S. Swenson Jr., James M. Grimwood, and Charles C. Alexander, *This New Ocean: A History of Project Mercury,* 214–15.

4. Douglas J. Mudgway, *Uplink/Downlink: A History of the Deep Space Network.* Also needed, though, is a history of the ARIA aircraft, which were essentially flying tracking stations that NASA first used for the Apollo program, but which the air force recently retired because of their cost (around $100,000 an hour to fly), replacing them with the NKC-135B Big Crow. ARIA is an acronym for Apollo Range Instrumentation Aircraft, developed in 1968 to receive, record, and retransmit telemetry data and voice communications between astronauts and the Houston Control Center. Later known as the Advanced Range Instrumentation Aircraft, the ARIA fleet consisted of eight, highly modified EC-135 and EC-18B/D aircraft maintained by the Air Force Material Command's 452d Flight Test Squadron. ARIA aircraft served as airborne tracking stations, often over water when ground tracking stations were beyond the range of a satellite's mission profile. A recent success came in 1996, when NASA used an ARIA aircraft to help the Mars Global Surveyor reach its planned trajectory by sending data through an antenna at the Diego Garcia tracking station, into the Air Force Satellite Control Network data stream, and out to NASA's Goddard Space Flight Center (source: "ARIA," http://www.edwards.af.mil/capabilities/, accessed Dec. 27, 2003; Leigh Anne Bierstine, "ARIA Makes Final Touchdown at Edwards," Aug. 27, 2001, http://www.af.mil/news/Aug2001/n20010827_1185.shtml, accessed Dec. 27, 2003).

5. James R. Hansen, *Spaceflight Revolution: NASA Langley Research Center from Sputnik to Apollo,* 67.

6. David N. Spires, *Beyond Horizons: A Half Century of Air Force Space Leadership,* 167–69.

INTRODUCTION

1. *Journal Ministère Russie Defense* 47, sec. 7 (1845): 25, and O. J. Bliss, "Electrical Transmission of Electrical Measurements," *Transactions of the American Institute of Electrical Engineers* 31 (1912): 1537–40, both in Wilfrid J. Mayo-Wells, "The Origins of Space Telemetry," *Technology and Culture* 4 (Oct., 1963): 500–501.

2. Aerospace Corp., *The Aerospace Corporation: Its Work, 1960–1980,* 123.

3. Swenson et al., *This New Ocean,* 428.

4. John T. Mengel, Mar., 1956, quoted in Green and Lomask, 147.

5. The AFSCN makes over 150,000 satellite contacts per year. Contact success rate is above 99 percent. "Astro News," http://www.losangeles.af.mil/SMC/PA/Astro-News/2000/Mar/31maroo.pdf, accessed Feb. 9, 2004.

6. For more on how the air force encouraged the development of the complete systems in this period, see Stephen B. Johnson, *The United States Air Force and the Culture of Innovation 1945–*

1965, and John Lonnquest, "The Face of Atlas: General Bernard Schriever and the Development of the Atlas Intercontinental Ballistic Missile, 1953–1960."

7. Frederic C. E. Oder, USAF (retired), interview by Herb Zolot, Colorado Springs, tape recording, 1993, Air Force Space Command History Office, Peterson AFB, Colorado Springs (hereafter AFSPC/HO).

8. A brief note about organizational names: The air force organization responsible for satellite command and control has been through a series of names in its history. For consistency, this book uses "Air Force Satellite Control Facility" to designate the military organization that provides satellite command and control services to agencies of the defense department.

9. M.Sgt. Roger A. Jernigan, *AFSCF Historical Brief and Chronology* (Sunnyvale, Calif.: Air Force Satellite Control Facility History Office, 1983), 19–20.

10. See William E. Burrows, *Deep Black: Space Espionage and National Security;* Dwayne A. Day, John M. Logsdon, and Brian Latell, eds., *Eye in the Sky: The Story of the Corona Satellites;* Curtis N. Peebles, *The Corona Project: America's First Spy Satellites;* and Jeffery T. Richelson, *America's Secret Eyes in Space: The U.S. Keyhole Spy Satellite System.*

11. See Lonnquest, "The Face of Atlas"; Jacob Neufeld, *The Development of Ballistic Missiles in the United States Air Force, 1945–1960;* Thomas Parke Hughes, *Rescuing Prometheus;* Johnson, *The United States Air Force and the Culture of Innovation;* Stephen B. Johnson, "Samuel Phillips and the Taming of Apollo," *Technology and Culture* 42 (Oct., 2001): 685–709; and Stephen B. Johnson, "Bernard Schriever and the Scientific Vision," *Air Power History* 49 (Spring, 2002): 30–45.

12. See Desmond Ball, *Pine Gap: Australia and the U.S. Geostationary Signals Intelligence Satellite Program;* Jeffery T. Richelson, *America's Space Sentinels: DSP Satellites and National Security;* Curtis Peebles, *Guardians: Strategic Reconnaissance Satellites;* and Burrows, *Deep Black.*

13. Theodore Von Kármán with Lee Edson, *The Wind and Beyond: Theodore von Kármán, Pioneer in Aviation and Pathfinder in Space.*

14. Project RAND, "Preliminary Design of an Experimental, World-Circling Spaceship," report no. SM-11827 (Santa Monica: Douglas Aircraft, May 2, 1946; reprint, Santa Monica: RAND, 1996).

15. Day et al., 1.

16. Maj. Gen. Bernard A. Schriever, "ICBM—A Step toward Space Conquest" (address presented to the Space Flight Symposium, San Diego, Feb. 19, 1957), provided by General Schriever to the author.

17. Bernard A. Schriever, interview by author, Washington, D.C., tape recording, June 27, 2001.

CHAPTER 1

1. For more on the development of the first modulators and demodulators used on telephone lines and the computers built to serve the military's needs, see Kent C. Redmond and Thomas M. Smith, *From Whirlwind to MITRE: The R&D Story of the SAGE Air Defense Computer.*

2. Marv Sumner, email to author, no subject, Jan. 11, 2000.

3. James W. Plummer, interview with Herbert M. Zolot, Oct. 6 and Oct. 12, 1993, tape recording, Colorado Springs, AFSPC/HO.

4. Secretary of the Air Force Daniel Roche, in 2nd Lt. André Kok, "SECAF Talks Command, Control during Hanscom Visit," http://www.af.mil/news/Sep2001/n20010906_1244.shtml, accessed Feb. 9, 2004.

5. For more on concurrency, see Hughes, *Rescuing Prometheus,* esp. 69–138; and Lonnquest, "The Face of Atlas."

6. Arnold to von Kármán, Nov. 7, 1944, in Dik A. Daso, *Architects of American Air Supremacy: Gen. Hap Arnold and Dr. Theodore von Kármán*, 319.

7. Ibid., 321–22,Von Kármán to Arnold, Dec. 15, 1945.

8. Ibid., xix. See also Michael H. Gorn, *Harnessing the Genie: Science and Technology Forecasting for the Air Force, 1944–1986.*

9. Lt. Cdr. Otis E. Lancaster and J. R. Moore, ADR report R-48, "Investigation on the Possibility of Establishing a Space Ship in an Orbit above the Surface of the Earth," provided to the author by Rick Sturdevant, AFSPC/HO. Lancaster and Moore may have read the Oct., 1945, Arthur C. Clarke article in *Wireless World Magazine* suggesting a geostationary orbit for communications satellites and then expanded on it.

10. Robert Salter, interview by Martin Collins and Joseph Tatarewicz, July 29, 1986, and July 7, 1987, transcript, p. 14, RAND Oral History Collection, National Air and Space Museum Archives, Suitland, Md. (hereafter RAND/NASM). Thrust-to-weight ratio is an efficiency factor for total propulsion. A rocket with a high thrust-to-weight ratio will experience high acceleration. To achieve orbit using a single-stage vehicle requires a high thrust-to-weight ratio, currently achievable only with small objects, not large, useful satellites. For more on RAND and the Air Force, see Martin J. Collins, *Cold War Laboratory: RAND, the Air Force, and the American State, 1945–1950.* For more on single-stage-to-orbit vehicles, see Andrew J. Butrica, *Single Stage to Orbit: Politics, Space Technology, and the Quest for Reusable Rocketry.*

11. "Proposal Submitted for Consideration by the Space-Missile Committee," Oct. 22, 1945, 1, JPL archives, 5-372b. Provided to the author by Rick Sturdevant, AFSPC/HO.

12. Robert Frank Futrell, *Basic Thinking in the United States Air Force, 1907–1960,* vol. 1 of *Ideas, Concepts, and Doctrine,* 196–200. Strategic aerial reconnaissance became an officially exclusive air force mission in the 1948 Key West interservice agreement, although the air force acted both during and after World War II as though strategic aerial reconnaissance was their private sphere.

13. Salter interview, 45–47.

14. "Preliminary Design of a World-Circling Spaceship," viii.

15. Ibid., 132.

16. Ibid., 218.

17. Ibid., 233; Clayton R. Koppes, *JPL and the American Space Program: A History of the Jet Propulsion Laboratory,* 63.

18. Merton Davies, interviewed by Joseph Tatarewicz, Dec. 12, 1985, transcript, 35, RAND/NASM.

19. Frederic C. E. Oder, telephone interview by author, tape recording, Oct. 10, 2001.

20. For more on aerial reconnaissance, see William E. Burrows, *By Any Means Necessary: America's Secret Air War in the Cold War* (New York: Farrar, Straus, and Giroux, 2001), and John T. Farquhar, "A Need to Know: The Role of Air Force Reconnaissance in War Planning, 1945–1953" (Ph.D. diss., Ohio State University, 1991).

21. Morgan interview, 32.

22. Thomas Parke Hughes, "The Evolution of Large Technological Systems," in *The Social Construction of Technological Systems: New Directions in the Sociology and History of Technology,* ed. Wiebe Bijker, Thomas P. Hughes, and Trevor Pinch, 58–59; Morgan interview; Bruno Augenstein, interview by Martin Collins and Joseph Tatarewicz, July 28, 1986, transcript, 28, RAND/NASM.

23. Maj. Gen. L. C. Craigie, air force director of research and development, subject: "Satellite Vehicles," Jan. 16, 1948, with incl. by Gen. H. S. Vandenberg, vice chief of staff of the air force, subject: "Statement of Policy for a Satellite Vehicle," Jan. 15, 1948, to Brig. Gen. A. R. Crawford, chief, engineering division, Air Materiel Command, in Joseph W. Angell Jr., *USAF Space Programs, 1945–1962,* Tab A.

24. L. J. Carter, ed., *The Artificial Satellite: Proceedings of the Second International Congress on Astronautics,* 52–55.

25. Ibid.

26. Davies interview, 36. This problem disappeared in the late 1950s with the introduction of ablative reentry vehicles, which were not only quite feasible but also very lightweight.

27. Salter interview, 47. The report included an artist's conception of a space vehicle that was, according to Salter, "almost a dead ringer for [Lockheed's] Agena" booster.

28. James S. Coolbaugh, "Genesis of the USAF's First Satellite Programme," 285.

29. J. E. Lipp et al., "The Utility of a Satellite Vehicle for Reconnaissance," 249.

30. Salter interview, 48.

31. J. E. Lipp et al., 250–55.

32. Coolbaugh, 286.

33. J. E. Lipp et al., 255–61.

34. Mayo-Wells, 499–509.

35. S. Fred Singer, "Studies of a Minimum Orbital Unmanned Satellite of the Earth (MOUSE)," presented to the American Rocket Society, Apr. 20, 1955, in Logsdon, *Exploring the Unknown,* vol. 1, 323–24.

36. James A. Marsh, "Survey of Communications Problems Associated with Space Travel," in *Vistas in Astronautics,* ed. Morton Alperin, Marvin Stern, and Harold Wooster, 85–87.

37. Max Fishman, "Satellite Tracking Techniques," in Alperin et al., *Vistas in Astronautics,* 67–70.

38. Green and Lomask, 148.

39. John T. Mengel and Paul Herget, "Tracking Satellites by Radio."

40. Green and Lomask, 146.

41. John P. Hagen, "The Viking and the Vanguard," 445.

42. Arthur Radford, chairman, Joint Chiefs of Staff, memorandum for the secretary of defense, "U.S. Scientific Satellite Program," May 24, 1955, in *National Security Council, Minutes of Meetings,* A:III:0403. "It is important to preserve the 'Freedom of Space' concept in order not to impair our freedom of action to launch. . . . Since the mere solicitation of prior consent from any nation over which the satellite might pass in its orbit might jeopardize the concept of 'Freedom of Space,' the proposed policy would preclude any action which would imply a requirement for such prior consent." See also Walter A. McDougall, *The Heavens and the Earth: A Political History of the Space Age,* esp. chapter 7.

43. Green and Lomask, 158–61.

44. Mengel and Herget, 27.

45. Hagen, 446.

46. Mengel and Herget, 28.

47. Neil H. McElroy, secretary of defense, and T. Keith Glennan, NASA administrator, "Agreement between NASA and DoD on Global Tracking, Data Acquisition, Communications, and Data Centers for Space Flight," Jan. 10, 1959, in *National Security Council, Minutes of Meetings,* 13, A:III:0403.

48. Koppes, *JPL and the American Space Program,* 80–91.

49. Ibid., 95.

50. Swenson et al., *This New Ocean,* 214–16; see also Hansen, *Spaceflight Revolution: NASA Langley Research Center from Sputnik to Apollo,* 67.

51. Swenson et al., *This New Ocean,* 217–20. The $41-million figure for the cost of the Mercury tracking network is about $258.9 million in 2003 dollars.

52. Ibid., 405–409.

53. Charles S. Sheldon II and Marcia S. Smith, *Space Activities of the United States, Soviet Union, and Other Launching Countries/Organizations: 1957–1981*, 51.

54. Michael J. Neufeld, *The Rocket and the Reich: Peenemünde and the Coming of the Ballistic Missile Era* (Cambridge: Harvard University Press, 1995).

55. A. Shternfel'd, *Artificial Satellites*, 299–300.

56. A. N. Nesmeyanov, quoted in F. J. Krieger, *Behind the Sputniks: A Survey of Soviet Space Science*, 3. The articles in Krieger's collection are for the most part concerned with the atmospheric effects on radio waves and therefore experiments to determine the state of the ionosphere, which satellites travel through. There is no speculation about satellite command and control, and the only information on tracking has to do with "radio amateurs" taking an active part in "the interesting work of observing radio signals from the satellite and thereby mak[ing] a valuable contribution to the development of scientific research" (p. 307).

57. G. I. Pokrovskii, "Artificial Earth Satellite Problems," *Izvestia*, Aug. 19, 1955, in Krieger, *Behind the Sputniks*, 243–45.

58. K. Stanyukovich, "Artificial Earth Satellite Principles," *Krasnaya Zvezda*, Aug. 7, 1955, in Krieger, *Behind the Sputniks*, 239.

59. Lt. Gen. Yuriy Alexandrovich Mozzhorin (retired), in John Rhea, ed., *Roads to Space: An Oral History of the Soviet Space Program*, trans. Peter Berlin (New York: Aviation Week Group, 1995), 409.

60. Ibid., 411.

61. Col. Fyodor Yegorovich Pushkin, former head of missile tracking at the Baikonur Cosmodrome, in Rhea, *Roads to Space*, 352–53.

62. Lt. Gen. Nikolai Fyodorovich Shlykov (retired) in Rhea, *Roads to Space*, 154.

63. Asif A. Siddiqi, *Challenge to Apollo: The Soviet Union and the Space Race, 1945–1974*, 162.

64. Ibid., 162, 262.

65. Ibid., 535.

66. Lt. Gen. Mozzhorin, in Rhea, *Roads to Space*, 409. For a memoir of life aboard the NASA tracking ship USNS *Vanguard*, see Dan Kovalchik, *Range Rats at Sea: Tracking Satellites, Sailing the Tropics, and Searching for the Sybaritic Life*.

67. Siddiqi, *Challenge to Apollo*, 534–35, 666, 703; Sheldon and Smith, *Space Activities of the United States*, 30–31. When the Soviets failed in their bid to send a piloted mission to the moon in Dec., 1968, the United States knew about the failure, even though the Soviet press characteristically did not announce it, because the "Soviet space tracking and recovery ships in the Indian Ocean . . . dispersed or returned to port."

68. Siddiqi, *Challenge to Apollo*, 536. For those interested in the development of the Soviet ground communications network, Siddiqi recommends *Kosmos nechinayetsya na zemlye (Space Begins from the Earth)* (Moscow: Patriot, 1996), which is written by B. A. Pokrovskiy, one of the major players in the network's creation. There have been many memoirs published on the creation of the Baykonour Cosmodrome. Perhaps the best one is *Nezabyvayemyy Baykonour (Unforgettable Baykonour)* (Moscow: Interregional Council of Veterans of the Baykonour Cosmodrome, 1998), which among other things contains a blow-by-blow, detailed chronology of the launch range from 1957 to 1961.

CHAPTER 2

1. Thomas O. Haig, telephone interview by author, tape recording, Oct. 16, 2000. Later, the Air Force Satellite Control Facility mounted 60-foot antennas on surplus, navy 5-inch, twin gun mounts, based on modification instructions that the Massachusetts Institute of Technology provided under a DoD contract (*History of the Air Force Satellite Control Facility*, July 1, 1966–Dec. 31, 1966, attch. 7, 3, AFSPC/HO, Box 3-3-2, Folder JD-66).

2. Hughes, "Evolution of Large Systems," 59–64.

3. J. E. Lipp and Robert M Salter, "Project Feed Back Summary Report," RAND Corp., report R-262, Mar. 1, 1954, Defense Technical Information Center, Ft. Belvoir, Va. (hereafter DTIC), AD354297.

4. Air Force Space Command History Office, "Brigadier General William G. King, Jr.," *Air Force Space and Missile Pioneers* (Colorado Springs: Air Force Space Command, 2000), 11. Topeka native William G. King Jr. received an ROTC commission at Kansas State University, entered active duty during World War II, and served as an antiaircraft artillery officer in the Pacific theater. After the war, this early architect—if such a term should even apply to individuals—of the air force's Advanced Reconnaissance System returned to Kansas State and completed his B.S. in 1946. He later received a master's degree from the University of Chicago in business administration, with an emphasis on the management of research and development. General King retired from the air force in April, 1971, and then began an eighteen-year career with Aerojet General Corp., where he served as both vice president and general manger of the space surveillance division of the electronics systems division and as director of the Defense Support Program, the nation's ballistic missile early warning satellites.

5. Brig. Gen. William G. King Jr., USAF (retired), telephone interview by author, tape recording, Oct. 25, 2000. When King returned to Ohio, his boss, Lt. Gen. Howell M. Estes Jr., a LeMay protégé, gave King a stern talking-to. King's "sales trips," however, continued.

6. See Fred I. Greenstein, *The Hidden Hand Presidency: Eisenhower as Leader,* especially 129–31.

7. National Security Council, NSC 5520, "Draft Statement of Policy on U.S. Scientific Satellite Program," May 20, 1955, in *Exploring the Unknown,* vol. 1, 308–309.

8. Ibid., 310.

9. Ibid., 311.

10. Salter interview, 48–49.

11. Ibid., 49; Davies interview, 31.

12. Augenstein interview, 33; Air Force Space Command History Office, "James W. Plummer," *Space and Missile Pioneers,* 16.

13. Salter interview, 49.

14. Ibid.; Coolbaugh, "Genesis of the USAF's First Satellite Programme," 293; Oder, email to author, subject: "Early 117L," Jan. 28, 2000.

15. Maj. Gen. Bernard A. Schriever, commander, Air Force Ballistic Missile Division, Apr. 24, 1958, in *Hearings before the Select Committee on Astronautics and Space Exploration,* 677.

16. Bernard A. Schriever, interview by Edgar F. Puryear Jr. on June 20, 1977, transcript, 8, AFHRA, K239.0512-1492. As a comparison, $4 million in 1957 is the equivalent of about $26 million in 2003.

17. James H. Douglas Jr., interview by Hugh H. Ahmann, June 13–14, 1979, Chicago, transcript, 126, AFHRA, K239.0512-1126; Osmond J. Ritland, interview by Lyn R. Officer, Mar. 19–21, 1974, Solano Beach, Calif., transcript, 231–35, AFHRA, K239.0512-722.

18. Western Development Division, *WS-117L Advanced Reconnaissance System Development Plan,* Apr. 2, 1956, AFHRA, K243.8636-39. In 1956, $153 million was the equivalent of slightly more than $1 billion in 2003.

19. Oder interview by author.

20. Gen. Thomas D. White, "At the Dawn of the Space Age," 17. This article is a reprint of a speech he gave to the National Press Club on Nov. 29, 1957.

21. U.S. Air Force, *Air Force Manual 1-2,* and *United States Air Force Basic Doctrine,* Dec. 1, 1959, 1–2, quoted in Robert Frank Futrell, *Basic Thinking in the United States Air Force, 1961–1984,* vol. 2 of *Ideas, Concepts, Doctrine,* 714–15.

22. Scott J. King, interview by Martin Collins and Joseph Tatarewicz, July 22, 1987, transcript, 14, RAND/NASM.

23. Schriever interview by author.

24. "Report of the Scientific Advisory Board Reconnaissance Panel on Reconnaissance from Satellite Vehicles," May 28, 1956, Carl F. J. Overhage, chair, AFHRA, K243.012-34.

25. Memo, J. H. Doolittle to USAF chief of staff, Dec. 9, 1957, 3, AFHRA, K168.8636-10.

26. Trevor Gardner, "Foreseeable Scientific and Technological Trends as They Apply to Military Technology and Strategy," May 28, 1957, 10, AFHRA, 168.7171-232.

27. Ritland interview, 238a.

28. *Report of the Secretary of the Air Force Management Study Committee,* Clark B. Millikan, director, Jan. 29, 1960, 1–3, AFHRA, K168.8636-26. For a more detailed look at how General Schriever and his team arrived at the decision to use systems engineering and technical direction contractors, see Hughes, *Rescuing Prometheus,* and Lonnquest, "The Face of Atlas." For a highly critical view, see Edward N. Hall, *The Art of Destructive Management: What Hath Man Wrought?;* Col. Edward N. Hall, "Epitaph," Aug. 29, 1958, Ballistic Missiles Division, ARDC, AFHRA, K243.0122-7; Col. Edward N. Hall, interview by Jack Neufeld, Washington, D.C., July 11, 1989, transcript, AFHRA, K239.0512-1820; Thomas O. Haig, "Systems Engineering and Technical Direction as a Management Concept," student research report no. 67 (Washington, D.C.: Industrial College of the Armed Forces, 1966), provided by Colonel Haig to author; and Haig interview by author.

29. *Report of the Secretary of the Air Force Management Study Committee,* 3; "Brief History of Aerospace Corporation," in U.S. Congress, House, Committee on Government Operations, Military Operations Subcommittee, *Systems Development and Management,* 86th Cong., 1st sess., 1958, 1129–34; Ritland interview, 253–54.

30. Oder interview by author.

31. My experience with systems engineering and technical direction has shown me that the concept works for the AFSCF. While stationed at the Diego Garcia tracking station between Apr., 1996, and Apr., 1997, in my role as the quality assurance specialist, I spent a lot of time with the site's systems engineering and technical direction contractor, Lenny Carter. Carter's many years of experience on Diego and in the satellite control network was invaluable for the smooth operation of the station, especially when it came to integrating new equipment. With the 1996 closure of the Indian Ocean station in the Seychelles, Diego Garcia became the only station in the unclassified American system of satellite control between the United Kingdom and Guam. Therefore, when NASA wanted to transfer its quad-helix UHF antenna from the Seychelles to Diego, the government–contractor team had a major challenge on our hands—how to integrate the 1960s' vintage NASA equipment with the 1990s' air force system. NASA used the quad-helix antenna to relay data from the ARIA aircraft (essentially flying tracking stations) to the ground. NASA engineers and Lockheed contractors on Diego Garcia, with Carter's help, merged the ARIA data stream with the regular Diego Garcia data stream and shipped the data back to the NASA controllers at NASA Goddard in Maryland. The first success in 1996 was the Mars Global Surveyor satellite, NASA's Mars-orbiting and -mapping satellite. The transient lifestyle of the air force officers who rotated through Diego Garcia every twelve months could not match the experience of someone who had lived on Diego Garcia for years.

32. Bernard A. Schriever, interview by Maj. Lyn R. Officer and James C. Hasdorff, June 20, 1973, transcript, 40–41, AFHRA, K239.0512-676.

33. See Johnson, *The United States Air Force and the Culture of Innovation, 1945–1965,* particularly chapter 2.

34. Simon Ramo, interview by Martin Collins, June 27, 1988, Los Angeles, http://www.nasm.edu/nasm/dsh/transcpt/ramo1.htm, accessed Feb. 9, 2004.

35. Ibid.

36. Schriever interview by Officer and Hasdorff, 41.

37. Ramo interview.

38. House, *Brief History of Aerospace Corporation,* 1132.

39. Ritland interview, 255–56.

40. Howard Althouse, email to author, subject: "NBTS," Dec. 12, 2000.

41. Col. Melvin Lewin, USAF (retired), telephone interview by author, tape recording, Dec. 21, 2000.

42. McCartney interview by author.

43. Haig interview by author.

44. Ibid.

45. Thomas O. Haig, "Interview with Colonel Thomas O. Haig," interview by Maj. David Arnold, *Quest: The History of Spaceflight Quarterly,* 55 (hereafter *Quest* interview).

46. For more on the early military weather satellite program, see R. Cargill Hall, *A History of the Military Polar Orbiting Meteorological Satellite Program.*

47. Haig interview by author.

48. Ritland interview.

49. Haig interview by author.

50. Haig, *Quest* interview, 55.

51. Hall interview, 1.

52. Hall, "Epitaph"; Hall interview, 5.

53. Frederic C. E. Oder, email to author, subject: "Early 117L," Nov. 10, 1999.

54. Marv Sumner, email to author, subject: "AFSCF," Dec. 15, 1999.

55. U.S. Congress, Senate, Committee on Armed Services, Subcommittee on the Air Force, *Present and Planned Strength of the United States Air Force,* June 20, 1956, 2207–14.

56. Haig interview by author.

57. Howard Althouse, email to author, subject: "BOSS," Dec. 18, 2000.

58. Ibid.

59. Ibid.

60. Ibid.; Walter B. LaBerge, telephone interview by author, tape recording, Oct. 11, 2001.

61. A. Stormy Sult, telephone interview by author, tape recording, Sept. 8, 2001.

62. Ibid., email to author, subject: "Contractors," Aug. 29, 2001.

63. Lockheed's Corona program chief James Plummer said in an email to the author that Philco outbid Lockheed "largely because of overhead rates," certainly likely given Lockheed's tendency to use professional engineers and Philco's use of electronics technicians, who were paid far less (James W. Plummer, email to author, subject: "Fw: dissertation," Sept. 4, 2001); LaBerge agreed in a telephone interview that giving the Air Force Satellite Control Facility its own contract was most likely a cost-saving move by the air force. For more on personnel issues, see chapter 5.

64. Haig interview by author.

65. King interview by author.

66. Maj. Gen. Bernard A. Schriever, "Foreword," in Western Development Division, *Weapon System 117L Preliminary Development Plan (Initial Test Phase),* Jan. 14, 1956, i, AFHRA, K243.8636-39.

67. Ibid., 9.

68. Joe Schraml, email to author, subject: "Re: New Guestbook Entry!" Aug. 20, 2001; Alexander Czernysz, email to author, subject: "New Boston Tracking Station," Aug. 24, 2001.

69. N. N. Berger, N. E. Tabor, and L. Lutzker, *WS-117L Criteria for Geographical Configuration of Data-Acquisition Stations,* Aug. 12, 1957, Table III and Appendix A, DTIC, AD370463.

70. Ibid.; Sult interview by author.

71. Lockheed, *WS-117L Facilities Master Plan of 15 Mar 1957, Revision of 30 Sep 1957*, Sept. 30, 1957, III-1, DTIC, AD370425; Marv Sumner, email to author, subject: "AFSCN History," Dec. 15, 1999.

72. Frederic C. E. Oder, email to author, subject: "Re: Early 117L," Nov. 5, 1999. These sites also proved invaluable to the recovery of space capsules. The tracking station in Alaska sent the command to eject the film capsule, and aircraft then recovered the capsule over the Pacific Ocean in the area near Hawaii known as the "ballpark."

73. Lockheed, *WS-117L Facilities Master Plan of 15 Mar 1957, Revision of 30 Sep 1957*, III-8; National Reconnaissance Office, *A History of Satellite Reconnaissance*, vol. 2, Sept. 30, 1957, 251–52, AFSPC/HO.

74. Berger, Tabor, and Lutzker, *WS-117L Criteria*, Appendices C, E, and G.

75. Lockheed, *WS-117L Facilities Master Plan of 15 Mar 1957, Revision of 30 Sep 1957*, Table II. In 1957, $112.7 million was the equivalent of about $737.16 million in 2003. In 1968, well after the Air Force Satellite Control Facility was operational, the General Accounting Office (GAO) concluded that the air force rushed the network into operation using the concurrency method, wasting millions of dollars by "prematurely procuring" the sixty-foot antenna and other tracking systems. In particular, the GAO pointed out that the construction, teardown, and reconstruction of the Annette Island tracking station cost the government an extra $1.7 million. The air force agreed with the GAO and altered satellite program planning to allow for changes in launch schedules (GAO, "Opportunities for Savings in Space Program by Reevaluating Needs before Buying Facilities: Department of the Air Force," B-164027).

76. Marv Sumner, email to author, subject: "AFSCF," Dec. 15, 1999. Robert M. Siptrott, another Alaska veteran, confirmed in a telephone interview by the author on May 29, 2001, that the Russian trawlers sometimes left before a launch. When that happened, Siptrott picked up the phone and called the Vandenberg launch control center to ask whether engineers had cancelled the launch. "How did you know?" the launch controllers often asked. Siptrott replied, "Our Russian fishing trawler just left."

77. Col. Charles Murphy, USAF (retired), telephone interview by author, tape recording, Sept. 26, 2001.

CHAPTER 3

1. Coolbaugh, "Genesis of the USAF's First Satellite Programme," 299. The air force refurbished and reused the Thor on a subsequent mission.

2. Day et al., 52–53; Peebles, *Corona*, 66–67.

3. Dwayne A. Day, "The Development and Improvement of the Satellite," in Day et al., 52–62. *Discoverer 13*, a diagnostic mission, did not carry a camera, but the water-recovered capsule carried an American flag.

4. James W. Plummer, telephone interview by author, tape recording, Sept. 8, 2001.

5. Hughes, "Evolution of Large Systems," 64–66.

6. Memo, Lt. Col. V. T. Ford, office of the special assistant to the secretary of defense for guided missiles, subject: "Military Personnel News Letter," Sept. 14, 1956, 6, AFHRA, 168.7171-157.

7. To blur the command lines and eliminate military protocols, such as when captains in Sunnyvale gave directions to majors at tracking stations, the use of call signs came into practice. According to Keith R. Smith in an email to the author (subject: "Re: AFSCF," Nov. 16, 2000), the test controller at Sunnyvale became DICE, a corruption of IDCC, Interim Development Control Center; COOK worked for the California tracking station (originally Cooke AFB until the air force renamed it in 1958 in honor of the air force's second chief of staff, Hoyt S. Vandenberg, who died

from cancer in 1954, very shortly after leaving office); BOSS became the call sign for the New Hampshire station, located at New Boston Air Station; HULA obviously served the Hawaii tracking station, among many others. As already mentioned, the sites at Kodiak Island and Annette Island in Alaska, were KODI and ANNE, respectively. Today the Air Force Satellite Control Facility includes HAWK (the Schriever AFB control facility, formerly Falcon AFS) and DICE; PIKE (the Colorado tracking station at Schriever AFB and in the shadow of Pikes Peak); REEF (the Diego Garcia tracking station on a coral atoll in the Indian Ocean); GUAM (at Anderson AFB, Guam); LION (at RAF Oakhanger, United Kingdom); POGO (at Thule Air Base in northern Greenland); BOSS; and HULA.

8. Memo, Maj. Gen. James H. Walsh, asst. chief of staff, intelligence, subject: "Samos," to Secretary of the Air Force Dudley C. Sharp Jr., June 24, 1960, AFHRA, K243.012-33.

9. *Weapon System 117L Preliminary Development Plan (Initial Test Phase)*, Jan. 14, 1956, 1, AFHRA, K243.8636-38.

10. Col. O. J. Ritland, draft of "Preliminary Operational Concept of 117L," July 28, 1958, 5, AFHRA, K243.012-33.

11. Lockheed Aircraft Corp., missile systems division, *Pied Piper Development Plan*, vol. 2, *Subsystem Plan, J. Vehicle Intercept and Control, Ground Station* (Van Nuys, Calif.), Mar. 1, 1956, i, DTIC, AD370776.

12. *WS-117L Advanced Reconnaissance System Development Plan*, Apr. 2, 1956, B-10, AFHRA, K243.8636-39.

13. Ibid., F-2.

14. Ibid., G-1. This figure is $500 million in 2003 dollars.

15. McDougall, Appendix, "R&D Expenditures, 1927–1980: Data Points," 463.

16. Stares, *The Militarization of Space*, Table 1, "Space Activities of the U.S. Government, 1959–1984," 255.

17. *Weapon System 117L Preliminary Development Plan (Initial Test Phase)*, 3–1.

18. Neufeld, ed., *Reflections on Research and Development in the United States Air Force*, 88; that figure is about $65.4 million in 2003 dollars. The source for total money spent on governmental R&D is McDougall, Appendix.

19. Memo, Allen W. Dulles, CIA director, to the CIA comptroller, subject: "Project Corona," Apr. 25, 1958, Corona/Argon/Lanyard Collection, National Reconnaissance Office Freedom of Information Act Office, Chantilly, Va. (hereafter NRO) 1/A/0001; memo, Richard M. Bissell Jr., special assistant to the [CIA] director for planning and development, to ARPA director and asst. sec. of the air force (R&D), subject: "Financing of Project Corona," June 25, 1958, NRO 1/A/0003; memo, Geo. F. Kucera, authorized DPD-DD/P requester, subject: "Program Approval," to Richard M. Bissell Jr., deputy CIA director, and Allen W. Dulles, CIA director, Feb. 18, 1959, NRO, 1/B/0087. Marked with Dulles's initials are the words "Exact amount of overrun item to be subject to later approval."

20. Plummer interview by author.

21. *WS-117L Advanced Reconnaissance System Development Plan*, Nov. 1, 1956, vol. 2, *Subsystem Plans, J. Ground Support and Training*, 18.

22. M. E. Davies, A. H. Katz, et al., "A Family of Recoverable Reconnaissance Satellites," RAND research memorandum RM-2012, Nov. 12, 1957; Davies interview, 36; Augenstein interview, 32–33; Katz interview, 41.

23. R. T. Gabler, Appendix G, "Tracking," in "A Family of Recoverable Satellites," Nov. 12, 1957, 99–101.

24. "Introduction," *Weapon System 117L Development Plan for Program Acceleration*, Jan. 5, 1958, AFHRA, K243.8636-41; memo, Col. F. C. E. Oder, assistant for WS-117L, to Colonel Terhune,

Western Development Division deputy commander for weapon systems, subject: "R-W [Ramo-Wooldridge] participation in WS-117L," Feb. 14, 1958, AFHRA, K243.012-36.

25. *Weapon System 117L Development Plan for Program Acceleration,* Jan. 5, 1958, para 1.3.1, AFHRA, K243.8636-41.

26. Ibid., para. 2.4.

27. Ibid., para. 1.3.

28. *Weapon System 117L Program Status Report,* June 10, 1958, AFHRA K243.012-36; Howie Althouse, email to author, subject: "Re: AFSCF," Nov. 18, 2000; Oder interview by author.

29. Letter, Roy Johnson, ARPA director, to Richard Bissell, CIA, no subject, Aug. 13, 1958, NRO, 1/A/0004.

30. *Weapon System 117L Program Status Report,* July 8, 1958, AFHRA, K243.012-36.

31. Ibid., Apr. 23, 1958, AFHRA, K243.012-36.

32. Memo, Roy Johnson, ARPA director, to Secretary of the Air Force Douglas, subject: "WS-117L Program," Dec. 4, 1958, NRO, 1/A/0012.

33. *Sentry Program Status Report,* Dec. 10, 1958, AFHRA, K243.012-36.

34. Roy W. Johnson, director, Advanced Research Projects Agency, in *Hearings before the Select Committee on Astronautics and Space Exploration,* 85th Cong., 2d sess., 1171.

35. B. W. Augenstein, "Evolution of the U.S. Military Space Program, 1945–1960: Some Key Events in Study, Planning, and Program Development" (Santa Monica: RAND Corp., P-6814, 1982), 13.

36. Spires, *Beyond Horizons,* 56–95.

37. Augenstein, "Evolution of the U.S. Military Space Program," 15.

38. Cyrus Vance, deputy secretary of defense, department of defense directive number TS 5105.23, "National Reconnaissance Office," Mar. 27, 1964, in *Exploring the Unknown,* vol. 1, 373–74. With the exception of this directive, the defense department prohibited the use of the terms "National Reconnaissance Office," "National Reconnaissance Program," or "NRO" in any document. Any reference to NRO had to use the phrase "Matters under the purview of DoD TS-5105.23."

39. John L. McLucas, "The U.S. Space Program since 1961: A Personal Assessment," in R. Cargill Hall and Jacob Neufeld, eds., *The U.S. Air Force in Space: 1945 to the Twenty-First Century,* 85–87.

40. Memo, Col. William A. Sheppard, subject: "Status of Scientific Advisory Committee for Reconnaissance Satellites," to General Schriever, Nov. 17, 1958, AFHRA, K243.012-36.

41. Message, General Schriever, commander, AFBMD, to Secretary of the Air Force Douglas, no subject, Feb. 28, 1959, AFHRA, K243.012-36; message, Secretary of the Air Force Douglas to General Schriever, no subject, Feb. 27, 1960, AFHRA, K243.012-36. This initial $136 million figure is $844.5 million in 2003 dollars. The DoD's budget that year was nearly $48 billion ($298.1 billion in 2003).

42. *Sentry Program Status Report,* Dec. 10, 1958, AFHRA, K243.012-36.

43. Memo, subject: "Facts concerning the Pro's and Con's of Air Force Control over Project Corona," May 15, 1959, NRO, 1/C/0002.

44. Message, Secretary of the Air Force Douglas to General Schriever, no subject, Feb. 5, 1959, AFHRA, K243.012-36.

45. Memo, Roy Johnson, director of ARPA, to Secretary of the Air Force Douglas, subject: "Classification of Information on WS-117L," May 19, 1959, AFHRA, K243.012-36.

46. See, for example, Edison T. Blair, "From Saddles to Satellites," pp.7–19; Larry Booda, "First Capsule Recovered from Satellite," 41–43; Frank J. Clifford, "Discoverer: Trailblazer to Space," 12–19; John Nammack, "C-119's Third Pass Snares Discoverer"; Clarke Newlon, "Air

Force Satellite Program Gets New Boss"; Bernard A. Schriever, "The Operational Urgency of R&D"; Charles H. Terhune Jr., "In the 'Soaring Sixties' Man Is on His Way—Up"; Thomas D. White, "At the Dawn of the Space Age"; Joseph Kaplan, "How Man-Made Satellites Can Affect Our Lives," *National Geographic* 132 (Dec., 1957): 791–808.

47. Solis Horowitz, advisor to the president, oral history, John F. Kennedy Library, in Stares, *The Militarization of Space,* 64; see also George C. Wilson, "Is U.S. Formulating New Space Policy?" *Aviation Week and Space Technology* (June 18, 1962): 26–27.

48. For published newspaper accounts of the mission success, see, for example, Richard Witkin, "Washington to Hail Retrieved Capsule in Ceremony Today," *New York Times,* Aug. 13, 1960; "Air Force Shows Prize Capsule," *New York Times,* Aug. 14, 1960; Felix Belair Jr., "Eisenhower Is Given Flag That Orbited the Earth," *New York Times,* Aug. 16, 1960.

49. Schriever interview by author. Schriever was commander of Air Research and Development Command at the time.

50. NASA and the U.S. Department of Defense, "A National Program to Meet Satellite and Space Vehicle Tracking and Surveillance Requirements for FY 1959 and 1960," NSCA memo no. 1859, Jan. 19, 1959, in *Minutes of Meetings of the National Security Council,* A:III:0403.

51. National Security Council 6021, Dec. 14, 1960, "Missiles and Military Space Programs," in *Minutes of Meetings of the National Security Council,* B:V:0211.

52. Message, Col. O. J. Ritland, no subject, to Gen. Thomas D. White, chief of staff, July 23, 1958, AFHRA, K243.012-36.

53. Col. O. J. Ritland, draft of "Preliminary Operational Concept of 117L," July 28, 1958, 1–2, AFHRA, K243.012-36.

54. Ibid., 3–4.

55. Ibid., 6.

56. General Schriever, "The Operational Urgency of R&D," 235.

57. Col. O. J. Ritland, draft of "Preliminary Operational Concept of 117L," 6.

58. "Proposed Initial Press Release," Nov. 6, 1958, NRO, 2/A/0078.

59. Message, Secretary of the Air Force Douglas to General Schriever, no subject, June 6, 1959, AFHRA, K243.012-36; memo, Roy Johnson, director, ARPA, to Secretary of the Air Force Douglas, subject: "Reconnaissance Satellites and Manned Space Exploration," Feb. 23, 1958, AFHRA, K243.012-36.

60. *WS-117L Advanced Reconnaissance System Development Plan,* Nov. 1, 1956, vol. 2, *Subsystem Plans, J. Ground Support and Training,* 12, AFHRA, K243.8636-37.

61. Report, Major Weinberg, subject: "Intelligence Data Handling System Support for WS-117L," Feb. 20, 1957, AFHRA, K243.012-36.

62. Memo, Maj. Gen. C. M. McCorkle, asst. chief of staff of the air force for guided missiles, subject: "Conflicting Interests in Astronautics Projects," to Secretary of the Air Force Douglas, June 30, 1958, AFHRA, K243.012-36.

63. Memo, Col. C. H. Terhune, deputy commander for weapon systems, subject: "Status of ARSIC Planning," to Gen. O. J. Ritland, vice commander, Western Development Division, Feb. 26, 1958, AFHRA, K243.012-36.

64. Message, General Power, CINCSAC, no subject, to General Schriever and General Ritland, Dec. 30, 1959, AFHRA, K243.012-36.

65. Letter, General Power, no subject, to General White, chief of staff, June 16, 1960, AFHRA, K243.012-36.

66. Memo, General White, no subject, to General Power, June 29, 1960, AFHRA, K243.012-36.

67. Memo, R. F. Mettler, subject: "Operating Concepts for Military Satellite Systems," to General Ritland, Nov. 2, 1959, AFHRA, K243.012-36.

NOTES TO PAGES 83-91

68. Memo, Maj. Gen. O. J. Ritland, subject: "Operational Concept for Military Satellite Systems," to Mettler, Dec. 4, 1959, AFHRA, K243.012-36.

69. Memo, Herbert York, asst. secretary of the air force for R&D, subject: "Intelligence System Samos," to Secretary of the Air Force Dudley C. Sharp, Dec. 7, 1959, AFHRA, K243.012-36.

70. Memo, Gen. Curtis LeMay, air force vice chief of staff, subject: "Assignment of Operational Planning Responsibility," to commander, ARDC, and commander-in-chief, SAC, Aug. 5, 1959, AFHRA, K243.012-36.

71. Message, SecAF to General Schriever, no subject, Feb. 5, 1959; message, General Schriever, no subject, to Colonel Curtin, AFBMD, Oct. 1, 1958, AFHRA. The 6593d Test Squadron (Special), which caught returning satellites, would be transferred to the Air Rescue Service, and the Vandenberg tracking station would remain in ARDC for follow-on R&D.

72. General Ritland, "Mission Statement for 6594th Test Wing," Oct. 26, 1959, AFHRA, K243.012-36. Emphasis added.

73. Charles H. Terhune Jr., "In the 'Soaring Sixties,'" 71; "Samos 1 Fact Sheet," Oct. 11, 1960, AFHRA, K243.012-36.

74. General Ritland, "Mission Statement for 6594th Test Wing," Dec. 29, 1960, AFHRA, K243.012-36.

75. History of the 6594 Test Wing (Satellite), July 1–Dec. 31, 1960, 1, 15, AFSPC/HO, Box 3-3-1; 6594 Aerospace Test Wing, Satellite Control Facilities Capabilities Manual, appended to History of the 6594 Test Wing (Satellite). According to Ed McMahon, in an email to the author, PICE was originally called the Lockheed Integrated Control Equipment until someone high up realized what the acronym for that name would be.

76. History of the 6594 Test Wing (Satellite), July 1–Dec. 31, 1960, Appendix, 2, 5.

77. Ibid., Jan. 1–June 30, 1961, 31, AFSPC/HO, Box 3-3-1.

78. Robert S. McNamara, "Department of Defense Directive 5160.32," Mar. 6, 1961, in Richard I. Wolf, The United States Air Force Basic Documents on Roles and Missions, 363–64; Futrell, Ideas, Concepts and Doctrine, vol. 1, 292–95, 386–87. The policy was reversed again in 1970.

79. Satellite Control Facilities Capabilities Manual, B-1.

80. History of the 6594 Test Wing (Satellite), July 1–Dec. 31, 1961, Appendix, 3, 7, AFSPC/HO, Box 3-3-1.

81. Howard Althouse, email to author, subject: "BOSS," Nov. 29, 2000.

82. Sputnik 1 (Oct. 4, 1957) weighed almost 184 pounds and orbited at a maximum altitude of 586 miles. Sputnik 2 (Nov. 3, 1957), carrying the dog Laika, weighed more than 1,100 pounds and reached an altitude of more than 1,100 miles. Sputnik 3 (May 15, 1958) weighed more than 3,000 pounds and orbited at up to 1,000 miles. The U.S. satellites Explorer 1 (Jan. 31, 1958) and Vanguard 1 (Mar. 17, 1958) weighed 30 pounds and 3.5 pounds, respectively. They orbited at maximum altitudes of more than 1,412 miles and 1,679 miles, respectively (source: J. K. Davies, Space Exploration [Edinburgh, UK: Chambers, 1992], 221–22).

83. Blair, "From Saddles to Satellites," 9; Clifford, "Discoverer," 12–19.

84. Blair, "From Saddles to Satellites," 13.

85. McCartney interview by author.

86. Capt. Rob Roy, in Blair, "From Saddles to Satellites," 17.

CHAPTER 4

1. John Nammack, "C-119's Third Pass Snares Discoverer"; Clifford, "Discoverer," 16–19; Robert A. Flavell, "To Catch a Falling Star: Aerial Recovery of Space Objects."

2. Don Stevenson, untitled history of the AFSCF (Sunnyvale, Calif.: Aerospace Corp., n.d.). Provided to the author by Stevenson.

3. See 1st Lt. Joseph H. Binsack, "Satellite Control Facility Capabilities," 135–37.

4. Blair, "From Saddles to Satellites," 16.

5. Keith R. Smith, email to author, subject: "Your Letter," Nov. 16, 2000.

6. Hughes, "Evolution of Large Systems," 73–75.

7. Marv Sumner, email to author, subject: "AFSCN History," Dec. 15, 1999.

8. Ibid., Jan. 5, 2000.

9. Philco Corp., *Multiple Satellite Control Facility Study,* Jan. 5, 1962, DTIC, AD452208.

10. S. Weems, *Augmented Satellite Control Facility Description,* System Development Corp., Apr. 1, 1963, 23, DTIC, AD404800.

11. Patrick O'Toole, email to author, subject: "Answers to Your Questions," Sept. 11, 2001.

12. Lt. Col. A. W. Dill, USAF, and Niall E. Tabor, Lockheed Missiles and Space Corp., "Requirements Cycle for USAF Satellite Control Facilities," 43–45.

13. Richard Sweeny, "*Discoverer 2* Orbital Attitude Controlled"; Day et al., 52–53; Peebles, *Corona,* 66–67. According to Peebles, this mission was the source for Alistair McLean's novel *Ice Station Zebra,* in which Americans and Soviets raced to recover a Soviet reconnaissance satellite that came down in the Arctic carrying film of American missile silos. For more on the Soviet space program, see Asif A. Siddiqi, *Challenge to Apollo: The Soviet Union and the Space Race, 1945–1974.*

14. Richard G. Stephenson and R. C. Hansen, "Aerospace Corporation and Satellite Control Engineering," 50.

15. Dill and Tabor, "Requirements Cycle," 45–46.

16. Aerospace Corp., *Aerospace Corporation: Its Work, 1960–1980,* 124.

17. H. H. Jensen and R. G. Kramer, *Air Force Satellite Control Facility History,* 2, report no. TOR-0066(5110-01-)3, AFSPC/HO, Box 7-2-1.

18. *Aerospace Corporation,* 124.

19. Ibid., 125.

20. Weems, *Augmented Satellite Control Facility Description,* 1–2, 17.

21. Ibid., 17, 23.

22. *History of the 6594 Aerospace Test Wing,* July 1–Dec. 31, 1962, Appendix, 3, 8, AFSPC/HO, Box 3-3-2.

23. Ibid., Appendix, 7, 2.

24. Haig, *Quest* interview, 55.

25. Ibid.

26. Joseph V. Charyk, interview by James C. Hasdorf, Jan. 15 and Apr. 24, 1974, Washington, D.C., 78, AFHRA, K239.0512-728.

27. Haig, *Quest* interview, 57. Flax also served as chief scientist of the U.S. Air Force, assistant secretary of the U.S. Air Force for R&D, and as NRO director.

28. Haig interview by author.

29. Ibid.

30. Ibid.

31. Alexander Flax, interview by J. C. Hasdorff and Jacob Neufeld, Nov. 27–29, 1973, Washington, D.C., transcript, 132, AFHRA, K239.0512-691.

32. Haig, *Quest* interview, 59.

33. Frank Buzard, email to author, subject: "AFSCF History," Nov. 12, 2000.

34. *History of the 6594 Aerospace Test Wing,* July 1–Dec. 31, 1963, 8, AFSPC/HO, Box 3-3-1; A. Stormy Sult, email to author, subject: "AFSCF History," Sept. 4, 2001.

35. Maj. Donald E. Jensen, commander, "Indian Ocean Station, Historical Report," 3, in *Air Force Satellite Control Facility History,* July 1–Dec. 31, 1965, AFSPC/HO, Box 3-3-2, Folder JD65.

36. *Space and Missile Systems Organization History,* July 1–Dec. 31, 1969, attch. 2, 6, AFSPC/ HO, Box 3-3-1, Folder JD69.

37. Ibid., 8. The station even appeared on two Seychelles postage stamps over the years, including one celebrating the *Apollo 11* moon landing.

38. F. Robert Naka, interview by author, Colorado Springs, June 16, 1999.

39. Collection of documents on the Thule classification debate from 1964 to 1967, AFSPC/ HO, Box 3-5-2. All correspondence after 1969 refers to the station as the Thule tracking station.

40. *History of the 6594 Aerospace Test Wing,* Jan. 1–June 30, 1962, 5, AFSPC/HO Box 3-3-1.

41. Ibid., July 1–Dec. 31, 1964, 2–3, AFSPC/HO, Box 3-3-2. To make matters worse, the Syncom communications satellite program fell behind schedule and did not meet its initial operational capability until late in 1964 (Donald H. Martin, *Communications Satellites, 1958–1992* [El Segundo, Calif.: Aerospace Corp., 1991], 12–14).

42. Lyle Burnham, http://209.165.152.119/af_track/guest.html, accessed Feb. 9, 2004.

43. *History of the 6594 Aerospace Test Wing,* July 1–Dec. 31, 1964, 93, AFSPC/HO Box 3-3-2.

44. Ibid., 168.

45. Thomas Parke Hughes, *Networks of Power: Electrification in Western Society, 1880–1930,* 6.

CHAPTER 5

1. Haig interview by author.

2. Ibid.

3. *History of the 6594 Test Wing (Satellite),* July 1–Dec. 31, 1960, 1–7.

4. Ibid., 22.

5. Maj. Gen. Osmond J. Ritland, "Mission Statement," 6594th Test Wing, Dec. 29, 1960, AFHRA, K243.012-36.

6. Russell Hawkes, "USAF's Satellite Test Center Grows," 57.

7. *History of the 6594 Test Wing (Satellite),* July 1–Dec. 31, 1960, Appendix, 2, 5.

8. Ibid., 7, 11.

9. Ibid., Jan. 1–June 30, 1961, Appendix, 2, 8, AFSPC/HO, Box 3-3-1.

10. Ibid., 7, 2.

11. Ibid., 5, 7.

12. Marv Sumner, email to author, subject: "Re: AFSCN History," Jan. 5, 2000. "Several years later I was at the STC in Sunnyvale telling this story, and one of my listeners had been the System Controller on that pass. He clarified that they knew of the angular coincidence, but thought the older vehicle would have been passive." The same sort of event happened to the author while sitting on console for a DSP satellite support. A weather satellite, using the same downlink channel but orbiting at a far lower altitude (several hundred nautical miles versus DSP at 22,500 nautical miles) passed under my DSP satellite, and the antenna "walked off" to follow the DMSP vehicle. Immediately on my direction, the antenna operator at the tracking station broke track on the DMSP satellite and reacquired the DSP satellite.

13. Philco Corp., *Multiple Satellite Control Facility Study,* Jan. 5, 1962, DTIC, AD452208.

14. Terhune, "In the 'Soaring Sixties,'" 71.

15. R. Smelt and R. A. Proctor, "Base Support Facilities Requirements for the Northeast Development Operational Tracking Station," Apr. 17, 1959, DTIC, AD802012.

16. McCartney interview by author.

17. Lewin interview by author.

18. Ibid. By contrast, the author went to school for four months before joining his operational Defense Support Program squadron, and then it was another month before he could run a satellite support without supervision.

19. Maj. Gen. Robert A. Rosenberg, USAF (retired), telephone interview by author, tape recording, Dec. 21, 2000; Lewin interview by author; McCartney interview by author; memo, [name redacted], colonel, USAF, acting chief, DPD-DD/P, to deputy [CIA] director (Plans), subject: "Ground Controlled Commands Available in Corona Prime Vehicles," Aug. 17, 1960, NRO, 2/E/0047.

20. Lewin interview by author; McCartney interview by author.

21. Murphy interview by author.

22. McCartney interview by author.

23. Ibid.

24. Ibid.

25. Lewin interview by author.

26. McCartney interview by author.

27. Oder interview by author.

28. *History of 6594 Aerospace Test Wing,* Jan. 1–June 30, 1962, 14.

29. This was $3,480/year plus a $110/month housing allowance, for a total of $4,800/year (roughly equivalent to $28,831 dollars in 2003). Source: "Monthly Basic Pay and Allowances table, effective 1 October 1963," http://www.dfas.mil/milpay/priorpay, accessed Feb. 9, 2004.

30. Howard Althouse, email to author, subject: "Early Kodi," Nov. 18, 2000. Said Althouse, "Being single, no girlfriend, 25 years old, I said, 'I'll go!' The free room and board were the clinchers!" Said Bob Siptrott, "This included three great meals. An old movie once a night, access to our own bar. We paid for the booze. Decent rooms, clean sheets daily, and blankets changed every other week" (Siptrott interview by author).

31. Louis Adams, email to author, subject: "AFSCF History," Dec. 14, 2000.

32. Carl Malberg, email to author, subject: "BOSS," July 15, 2000.

33. *History of the 6594 Aerospace Test Wing,* July 1–Dec. 31, 1962, Appendix, 7, 2.

34. Ibid., Appendix, 5, 3.

35. Howard Althouse, email to author, subject: "BOSS," Dec 12, 2000.

36. *History of the 6594 Aerospace Test Wing,* Jan. 1–June 30, 1964, attch. 1, 4, AFSPC/HO, Box 3-3-2.

37. Malberg, "NHS 1962–1966," 8.

38. *History of the 6594 Test Wing (Satellite),* Jan. 1–June 30, 1961, Appendix, 5, 3.

39. Ibid., 1963, 15–16, AFSPC/HO, Box 3-3-1.

40. Ibid., 9.

41. Ibid., 2–3.

42. U.S. Congress, House, *Decision of the Comptroller General of the United States regarding Contractor Technical Service,* 5.

43. Louis Adams, email to author, subject: "Re: AFSCF History," Dec. 12, 2000; W. Warren Pearce, telephone interview by author, tape recording, Nov. 12, 2000.

44. "Report on the Manpower History of the Air Force Satellite Control Facility, Jan. 31, 1959–Oct. 6, 1967," in *History of the Air Force Satellite Control Facility,* July 1–Dec. 31, 1967, attch. 4, AFSPC/HO, Box 3-5-1, Folder JD67.

45. McCartney interview by author.

46. Ibid.

47. Ibid.

48. Message, Col. Charles Murphy, no subject, Feb. 2, 1968, NRO, 5/B/0065.

49. Haig, *Quest* interview, 56.

50. Haig, comments during the Air Force Space and Missile Pioneers Roundtable, Sept. 21,

2000, Colorado Springs. This event was one of several surrounding the induction of Colonel Haig into the Air Force Space and Missile Hall of Fame.

51. Haig, *Quest* interview, 55.

52. Bernard C. Nalty, ed., *Winged Shield, Winged Sword: A History of the United States Air Force,* vol. 2, *1950–1997,* 357; Spires, *Beyond Horizons,* 131; Schriever interview by author.

53. Brig. Gen. Jewell C. Maxwell, chair, Space Support Panel, Annex E of vol. 3, Space Command and Control, *Project Forecast,* Jan., 1964, E-2-E-3, AFHRA, 168.7171-218.

54. "History of the Test Control Branch," in *History of 6594 Aerospace Test Wing,* Jan. 1–June 30, 1965, AFSPC/HO, Box 3-3-2.

55. "Justification of Increased Manpower Requirements, FY 1968–1970," in *History of the Air Force Satellite Control Facility,* July 1–Dec. 31, 1965, AFSPC/HO, Box 3-3-2, Folder JD65.

56. Gerald T. Cantwell, *The Air Force in Space, Fiscal Year 1966* (Washington, D.C.: USAF Historical Division Liaison Office, 1968), 67, AFSPC/HO.

57. Cantwell, *The Air Force in Space, Fiscal Year 1967,* 61, AFSPC/HO.

58. *History of the 6594 Aerospace Test Wing,* Jan. 1–June 30, 1965; "Justification of Increased Manpower Requirements, FY 1968–1970," in *History of the Air Force Satellite Control Facility,* July 1–Dec. 31, 1965, AFSPC/HO, Box 3-3-2, Folder JD65.

59. "Justification of Increased Manpower Requirements, FY 1968–1970," in *History of the Air Force Satellite Control Facility,* July 1–Dec. 31, 1965.

60. Ibid. Emphasis in the original.

61. Ibid.

62. Message, Air Force Systems Command, subject: "Manpower Authorizations for the AF Satellite Control Facility," to Space Systems Division, Jan. 7, 1966, in *History of the Air Force Satellite Control Facility,* Jan. 1–June 30, 1966, AFSPC/HO, Box 3-5-1, Folder JJ66.

63. "Historical Report," Test Control Branch, n.d., in *History of the Air Force Satellite Control Facility,* July 1–Dec. 31, 1966, AFSPC/HO, Box 3-3-2, Folder JD66.

64. "Historical Report," Test Control Branch, July 21, 1966, in *History of the Air Force Satellite Control Facility,* Jan. 1–June 30, 1966, AFSPC/HO, Box 3-5-1, Folder JJ66.

65. "Historical Report," Operating Location 5 [Thule tracking station], in *History of the 6594 Aerospace Test Wing,* Jan. 1–June 30, 1965, AFSPC/HO, Box 3-3-2. Thule's turnover still remains higher than that of any other tracking station in the network.

66. "AFSCF Operations Capability Evaluation Summary for Calendar Year 1968," in *Air Force Satellite Control Facility History,* July 1–Dec. 31, 1968, attch. 1, 1–13, AFSPC/HO, Box 3-4-1, Folder JD68.

CHAPTER 6

1. *History of the Air Force Satellite Control Facility,* Jan. 1–June 30, 1968, attch. 12, Vandenberg tracking station, 39, AFSPC/HO, Box 3-4-1, Folder JJ68.

2. King interview by author. King recalled often thinking, "Thank God for Thule" because New Hampshire did not often get the commands to the vehicle on a northbound orbit.

3. Ibid.

4. Thomas Parke Hughes, "Technological Momentum in History: Hydrogenation in Germany, 1898–1933," 131.

5. Capt. Malcolm McMullen, engineering division, space vehicle office, subject: "Historical Report, 1 Jul 1962–31 Dec 1962," to Colonel Appold, Jan. 22, 1963, *Space and Missile Systems Organization Historical Report,* July 1–Dec. 31, 1962, AFSPC/HO, Box 3-3-1.

6. Captain Schorsch, systems engineering division, subject: "Historical Report, 1 Jul 1963–

31 Dec 1963," to SSEH, Jan. 30, 1964, *Space and Missile Systems Organization Historical Report,* July 1–Dec. 31, 1963, AFSPC/HO, Box 3-3-1.

7. P. Marshall Fitzgerald and Jackson Witherspoon, Philco-Ford Corp., *Space-Ground Link Subsystem Ground Station System Analysis Summary Report,* vol. 1, "System Design Analysis," Nov. 15, 1968, p. v, 1-1, DTIC, AD853122; P. Marshall Fitzgerald and Jackson Witherspoon, Philco-Ford Corp., *General Specification for Performance and Design Requirements for the Space-Ground Link Subsystem Ground Station,* Feb. 12, 1969, para. 3.1.1.1, DTIC, AD853946.

8. Space Technology Laboratories (STL), *Final Design Report: Space-Ground Link Subsystem,* vol. 1, Feb. 1, 1967, pp. 1–2, 1–3, DTIC, AD813154.

9. Cantwell, *The Air Force in Space, Fiscal Year 1966* (Washington, D.C.: USAF Historical Division Liaison Office, 1968), 67–68, AFSPC/HO.

10. Lt. Col. Robert S. Redpath, chief, equipment development branch, development engineering office, subject: "SSOND-2 History, 1 July 1965–31 Dec 1965," Jan. 26, 1966, 3; Maj. Henry L. Steven Jr., chief, budgeting and funding office, subject: "Historical Report 1 July 1965–31 Dec 1965," in *History of the Air Force Satellite Control Facility,* July 1–Dec. 31, 1965; Captain Sadovsky, subject: "SSOND History, 1 July 1966–31 Dec 1966," Dec. 22, 1966, 8, in *History of the Air Force Satellite Control Facility,* July 1–Dec. 31, 1966, AFSPC/HO, Box 3-3-2, Folder JD66.

11. Captain Sadovsky, subject: "SSOND History, 1 July 1966–31 Dec 1966," Dec. 22, 1966, 8–10, AFSPC/HO, Box 3-3-2, Folder JD66; Cantwell, *The Air Force in Space, Fiscal Year 1967,* part 1, 59–60, AFSPC/HO.

12. STL, *Final Design Report: Space-Ground Link Subsystem,* vol. 1, Feb. 1, 1967, iii–v, DTIC, AD813154. Then, almost as soon as they had successfully demonstrated SGLS's capability, the AF-SCF engineers began planning for the next generation, called the advanced space-ground link subsystem, which would extend the data rate to twenty megabits per second, which was especially important for satellites at geosynchronous altitudes. The air force estimated the cost of the new program at $3.4 million over nineteen months.

13. *History of the Air Force Satellite Control Facility,* Jan. 1–June 30, 1968, attch. 5, 2; attch. 11, 2, AFSPC/HO, Box 3-4-1, Folder JJ68; *History of the Air Force Satellite Control Facility,* July 1–Dec. 31, 1968, data hardware branch, 2, AFSPC/HO, Box 3-4-1, Folder JD68. In 1969, the train carrying the radome panels for Vandenberg's antennas derailed near Buffalo, New York, causing a one-month delay in radome construction and forcing double shifts for the workers who were constructing them (Lt. Col. Daniel S. Barnes, chief, equipment development branch, directorate for development, "Historical Report," *Space and Missile Systems Organization History,* Jan. 1–July 31, 1969, 6, AFSPC/HO, Box 3-3-1, Folder JJ69).

14. *History of the Air Force Satellite Control Facility,* July 1–Dec. 31, 1968, attch. 5, 2; attch. 11, 2, AFSPC/HO, Box 3-4-1, Folder JD68.

15. "Air Force Systems Command," *Air Force and Space Digest* (Sept., 1962): 165.

16. King interview by author.

17. Memo, Richard Bissell, CIA, to Maj. Gen. Jacob E. Smart, asst. vice chief of staff, USAF, subject: "Distribution of Responsibilities for Corona," Nov. 25, 1958, NRO, 1/A/0008.

18. Memo for the record, Gen. A. J. Goodpaster, Apr. 21, 1958, NRO, 2/A/0043; memo of conference with the president on Feb. 7, 1958; Gen. A. J. Goodpaster, Feb. 10, 1958, NRO, 2/A/0040. Present at the conference besides Eisenhower and Goodpaster were James Killian, the president's science advisor, and Edwin "Din" Land, president of Polaroid and the person responsible for the development of the Corona camera.

19. NRO's main Pentagon office, in rooms behind door 4C1000, earned them the somewhat pejorative and medieval nickname "Forcey One Thousand."

20. For a brief overview, see David J. Whalen, "Billion Dollar Technology: A Short Historical

Overview of Origins of Communications Satellite Technology, 1945–1965," especially 110–14, in Andrew J. Butrica, *Beyond the Ionosphere: Fifty Years of Satellite Communication*.

21. R. Cargill Hall, *The NRO at Forty: Ensuring Global Information Supremacy*, 2–3; Cyrus Vance, deputy secretary of defense, department of defense directive no. TS 5105.23, "National Reconnaissance Office," Mar. 27, 1964, in *Exploring the Unknown*, vol. 1, 373–74.

22. John A. McCone, director of the CIA, and Roswell L. Gilpatric, deputy secretary of defense, "Agreement between Secretary of Defense and the Director of Central Intelligence on Responsibilities of the National Reconnaissance Office," May 2, 1962, NRO, 2/A/0036.

23. DoD directive TS-5105.23, in Logsdon, *Exploring the Unknown*, vol. 1, 373–75.

24. Hall, *The NRO at Forty*, 4.

25. Memo, Eugene P. Kiefer, deputy NRO director, to Lt. Gen. Marshall S. Carter, deputy CIA director, subject: "Technical Management of Corona Program," July 9, 1963, NRO, 1/A/0039.

26. Memo, Colonel [name redacted], acting chief, DPD-DD/P, subject: "[Redacted] Tracking Station for Corona," June 15, 1960, NRO, 1/C/0019.

27. Memo for the record, Lt. Gen. Carter, deputy CIA director, subject: "Meeting with Mr. Vance and Dr. McMillan on Thursday, 25 March [1965]," Mar. 26, 1965, 1–2, NRO, 1/A/0096; memo for the record [name redacted], chief, special projects staff, subject: "Fact Sheet regarding the Allegation That since August 1964 CIA Has Been Withholding Payload Data from the Air Force in the Corona Program," Mar. 25, 1965, NRO, 1/C/0099.

28. CIA Office of Special Projects, *History*, June 1, 1973, NRO, 2/A/0075.

29. Memo for the record, Lt. Gen. Marshall S. Carter, deputy CIA director, subject: "Meeting with Mr. Vance and Dr. McMillan on Thursday, 25 March [1965]," 3–4.

30. "Examples of the Air Force Impacts on the Corona Program," Mar. 31, 1965, 1–4, NRO, 1/C/0100.

31. For details of every Corona mission, see Peebles, *Corona*, Appendix, 1.

32. "Examples of the Air Force Impacts on the Corona Program," 9–10. According to Peebles (Appendix 1), both cameras failed on orbit 52, though the air force recovered both reentry vehicles.

33. See Day et al., esp. 69–70.

34. "Examples of the Air Force Impacts on the Corona Program," 6.

35. Frank Buzard, email to author, subject: "Feb., 1965 Mtg.," Aug. 28, 2001. According to Buzard, "I just checked the record and we did launch 14 in 1965 (one may have been a non Corona mission which was destroyed by Range Safety because they thought it was going off course)."

36. "Examples of the Air Force Impacts on the Corona Program," 7–9.

37. Jeffrey T. Richelson, "Undercover in Outer Space: The Creation and Evolution of the NRO, 1960–1963," 335.

38. Schriever interview by author.

39. Murphy interview by author.

40. Schriever interview by author.

41. Memo, R. S. McNamara, subject: "Management and Organization of DoD Ranges and Flight Test Facilities," to the secretaries of the army, navy, and air force, Nov. 16, 1963, 1, AFSPC/HO, Box 7-2-1. See also Cantwell, *The Air Force in Space: Fiscal Year 1964*, 13–14, AFSPC/HO; press release, "Major Management Reorganization for Ballistic Missile and Space Test Range Facilities Announced by Department of Defense, for Release 10:00 PST," Nov. 20, 1963, AFSPC/HO, Box 7-2-1.

42. Memo, R. S. McNamara, subject: "Management and Organization of DoD Ranges and Flight Test Facilities," to the secretaries of the army, navy, and air force, Nov. 16, 1963, 2–3.

43. Ibid., 3–4.

44. Letter, General White, subject: "Management and Organization of DoD Ranges and Flight Test Facilities," to General Power and General Schriever, Dec. 3, 1963, AFSPC/HO, Box 7-2-1.

45. "Task Group Charter," National Range Implementation Group, Nov. 13, 1963, AFSPC/ HO, Box 7-2-1.

46. Letter, General Estes, subject: "Management and Organization of the National Range," to General Davis, Jan. 1, 1964, AFSPC/HO, Box 7-2-1.

47. Letter, secretary of the air force, subject: "Management and Organization of DoD Ranges and Flight Test Facilities," to the secretary of defense, Apr. 3, 1964, AFSPC/HO, Box 7-2-1.

48. Letter, secretary of defense, subject: "Management and Organization of DoD Ranges and Flight Test Facilities," to the secretary of the air force, Apr. 25, 1964, AFSPC/HO, Box 7-2-1.

49. Letter, undersecretary of the air force, subject: "Air Force Satellite Control Range," to the vice chief of staff, Aug. 14, 1964, AFSPC/HO, Box 7-2-1.

50. Ibid. Brig. Gen. King was the first to hold the combined position.

51. Letter, assistant vice chief of staff, subject: "Organization of Satellite Control Resources of the NRD and the SSD Satellite Control Range," to Air Force Systems Command, May 27, 1964, AFSPC/HO, Box 7-2-1.

52. Letter, undersecretary of the air force, subject: "Organization of Satellite Control Resources," to the director of defense research and engineering, Aug. 14, 1964, AFSPC/HO, Box 7-2-1; King interview by author.

53. Cantwell, *The Air Force in Space: Fiscal Year 1965*, 3–4.

54. Draft issue paper, "NRD/SSD Support Planning Relationships," n.d., MT 64-85104, 1–2, AFSPC/HO, Box 7-2-1.

55. Ibid., 3–16.

56. Memorandum of agreement between the commanders of the Space Systems Division and the National Range Division (Provisional) of the Air Force Systems Command, signed Feb. and Mar., 1964, AFSPC/HO, Box 7-2-1.

57. King interview by author.

CONCLUSION

1. The title of this chapter is the motto of the Air Force Satellite Control Facility: "We will either find a way or make one." For a detailed list of important dates in AFSCF's history, see Roger A. Jernigan, *Air Force Satellite Control Facility: Historical Brief and Chronology, 1954–Present.*

2. Warren Pearce, email to author, subject: "RE: New DoD Space Policy Letter," May 10, 2001.

3. For a short explanation of the model, see Hughes, "The Evolution of Large Technological Systems," 51–82.

4. See especially Glenn Bugos, *Engineering the F-4 Phantom II: Parts into Systems.*

5. See Hughes, *Networks of Power,* and Hughes, *Rescuing Prometheus,* 197–254.

6. Desmond Ball, *A Base for Debate: The U.S. Satellite Station at Nurrungar;* National Reconnaissance Office, *A History of Satellite Reconnaissance,* vol. 2 [redacted], n.d. (Washington, D.C.: NRO), 203–304, AFSPC/HO.

7. Arnold Pacey, *The Maze of Ingenuity: Ideas and Idealism in the Development of Technology* (Cambridge: MIT Press, 1974), vii.

8. James V. Hartinger, *From One Stripe to Four Stars: The Personal Recollections of General James V. Hartinger, USAF, Retired,* 251–52.

9. Joseph Weitzell, email to author, subject: "Re: IOS," Nov. 22, 2001.

Bibliography

MANUSCRIPT COLLECTIONS

Papers
Maxwell Air Force Base, Montgomery, Ala.
    Air Force Historical Research Agency (AFHRA).
        Gen. Bernard A. Schriever Papers, Classified Papers.
        Gen. Bernard A. Schriever Papers, Unclassified Papers.
        Air Force Ballistic Missile Division documents.
        Air Force Satellite Control Facility documents.
National Reconnaissance Office, Chantilly, Va.
    Freedom of Information Act Office.
        Corona, Argon, Lanyard Collection.
Peterson Air Force Base, Colorado Springs, Colo.
    Air Force Space Command History Office.
        Air Force Satellite Control Facility official histories 1959–Present.
        Air Force Satellite Control Facility documents.

Microfilm
Defense Technical Information Service, Fort Belvoir, Va.
    Contractor-produced technical reports.
Kesaris, Paul, ed., *Minutes of Meetings of the National Security Council,* Second Supplement. Frederick, Md.: University Publications of America, 1989. Microform.

ORAL INTERVIEWS

U.S. Air Force Oral Interview Transcripts
Air Force Historical Research Agency.
    James H. Douglas Jr.
    Howell M. Estes Jr.
    Edward N. Hall
    Thomas W. Morgan
    Osmond J. Ritland
    Harry J. Sands Jr.
    Bernard A. Schriever
    Dudley C. Sharp

Author's Oral Interviews (in person or by telephone)
    Thomas O. Haig. A portion appeared as "An Interview with Colonel Thomas O. Haig." *Quest: The History of Spaceflight Quarterly* 9 (January, 2002): 53–61.

Keith Kincade
William G. King Jr.
Walter B. LaBerge
Mel Lewin
Forrest S. McCartney
Charles Murphy
F. Robert Naka
Frederic C. E. Oder
W. Warren Pearce
James W. Plummer
Robert A. Rosenberg
Bernard A. Schriever
Robert M. Siptrott
A. "Stormy" Sult

National Air and Space Museum RAND Oral Interview Transcripts
NASM Archives, Suitland, Md.
Bruno Augenstein
Merton Davies
Amrom Katz
Scott J. King
Robert Salter

Electronic Mail to the Author
Louis Adams
Howard Althouse
Frank Buzard
Bill Clark
William Hubbard
Carl Malberg
Ed A. McMahon
Frederic C. E. Oder
W. Warren Pearce
Keith Ramsey
Randy Randazzo
Robert M. Siptrott
A. "Stormy" Sult
Joseph Weitzel

PUBLIC RECORDS AND DOCUMENTS

Adams, John R. "Ground Support Systems for Spaceflight: A Single Manager Concept." Maxwell AFB, Montgomery, Ala.: Air Command and Staff College, 1969.

Augenstein, Bruno W. *Evolution of the U.S. Military Space Program, 1945–1960: Some Key Events in Study, Planning, and Program Development.* Santa Monica: RAND Corporation, 1982.

Buchheim, Robert W. *Space Handbook: Astronautics and Its Applications.* RM-2289-RC. Santa Monica: RAND Corporation, 1958.

Decision of the Comptroller General of the United States regarding Contractor Technical Service. 89th Cong., 2d sess. H. Rep. 188. Washington, D.C.: Government Printing Office, 1965.

Davies, M. E., A. H. Katz, et al. *A Family of Recoverable Reconnaissance Satellites.* RM-2012. Santa Monica: RAND Corporation, November 12, 1957.

Davies, Merton E., and William R. Harris. *RAND's Role in the Evolution of Balloon and Satellite Observation Systems and Related U.S. Space Technology.* R-3692-RC. Santa Monica: RAND Corporation, 1988.

Douglas Aircraft Company, Inc. *Preliminary Design of an Experimental World-Circling Spaceship.* SM-11827. May 2, 1946. Reprint, Santa Monica: RAND Corporation, 2000.

Haig, Thomas O. "Systems Engineering and Technical Direction as a Management Concept." Student research report no. 67. Washington, D.C.: Industrial College of the Armed Forces, 1966.

Hearings before the Select Committee on Astronautics and Space Exploration. 85th Cong., 2d sess. Washington, D.C.: Government Printing Office, 1958.

Hungerford, John B. "Organization for Military Space: A Historical Perspective." Maxwell AFB, Montgomery, Ala.: Air Command and Staff College, 1982.

Katz, Amrom. *Some Ramblings and Musings on Tactical Reconnaissance.* Santa Monica: RAND Corporation, March, 1963.

Kirby, Donna Scott. *Fundamentals of Satellite Acquisition Ephemeredes.* P-1738. Santa Monica: RAND Corporation, June 26, 1959.

Lancaster, Lt. Cdr. Otis E., and J. R. Moore. "Investigation on the Possibility of Establishing a Space Ship in an Orbit above the Surface of the Earth." November, 1945. ADR report R-48, Jet Propulsion Laboratory Archives, file number 5-492.

Lipp, J. E., R. M. Salter Jr., R. S. Wehner, R. R. Carhart, and C. R. Culp. "The Utility of a Satellite Vehicle for Reconnaissance." R-217 (Santa Monica: RAND Corporation, April, 1951), in John M. Logsdon, ed., *Organizing for Exploration,* vol. 1, *Exploring the Unknown: Selected Documents in the History U.S. Civil Space Program.* Washington, D.C.: NASA, SP-4407, 1995.

Lipp, J. E., and Robert M. Salter. "Project Feed Back Summary Report." R-262. Santa Monica: RAND Corporation, March 1, 1954.

Myers, Harold A. "Space Tracking and Data Acquisition: The Relation between Military and Civilian Networks." Maxwell AFB, Montgomery, Ala.: Air War College, April, 1965.

Office of Naval Research. *Problems of Satellites and Space Operations.* Washington, D.C.: U.S. Department of Commerce Office of Technical Services, 1958.

"Proposal Submitted for Consideration by the Space-Missile Committee." October 22, 1945. JPL Archives, file number 5-372b.

Rand Corporation. *Space Handbook: Astronautics and Its Applications.* Staff report of the Select Committee on Astronautics and Space Exploration. Washington, D.C.: Government Printing Office, 1959.

Reynolds, James W. "A Management Analysis of Missile and Space Ground Support Operations." Maxwell AFB, Montgomery, Ala.: Air Command and Staff College, 1969.

Senate Committee on Armed Services. Subcommittee on the United States Air Force.

Sheldon, Charles S., II, and Marcia S. Smith. *Space Activities of the United States, Soviet Union and Other Launching Countries/Organizations: 1957–1981.* Subcommittee on Space Science and Applications, Committee on Science and Technology. 97th Cong., 2d sess. Serial Y. Washington, D.C.: Government Printing Office, 1982.

Shternfel'd, A. *Artificial Satellites,* 2d rev. and extended ed. Moscow: State Publishing House for Technical and Theoretical Literature, 1958. Prepared by the Technical Documents Liaison Office, Wright-Patterson AFB, Ohio. Report #F_TS-9570/V.

U.S. Congress. House. Conference reports.

Von Kármán, Theodore. *Toward New Horizons: Science, the Key to Air Supremacy.* In *Architects of Amer-*

ican Air Supremacy: Gen. Hap Arnold and Dr. Theodore von Kármán, ed. Dik A. Daso. Maxwell
     AFB, Montgomery, Ala.: Air University Press, 1997.

BOOKS, ARTICLES, PROCEEDINGS, AND DISSERTATIONS

Aerospace Corporation. *The Aerospace Corporation: Its Work, 1960–1980.* El Segundo, Calif.: Aero-
     space Corp, 1980.
Alperin, Morton, Marvin Stern, and Harold Wooster, eds. *Vistas in Astronautics.* International Se-
     ries of Monographs on Aeronautical Sciences and Space Flight. New York: Pergamon Press,
     1958.
Angell, Joseph W., Jr. *USAF Space Programs, 1945–1962.* Air Force in Space Studies. Washington,
     D.C.: USAF Historical Division Liaison Office, 1960.
Arnold, Henry H. *Global Mission.* New York: Harper and Brothers, 1949.
Ball, Desmond. *A Base for Debate: The U.S. Satellite Station at Nurrungar.* Sydney: Allen & Unwin,
     1987.
Benson, Charles D. *Moonport: A History of Apollo Launch Facilities and Operations.* Washington, D.C.:
     Government Printing Office, NASA, SP-4204, 1978.
Berger, Carl. *The Air Force in Space, Fiscal Year* 1961. Vol. SHO-S-66/142. Washington, D.C.: USAF
     Historical Division Liaison Office, 1966.
———. *The Air Force in Space, Fiscal Year* 1962. Vol. SHO-S-66/198. Washington, D.C.: USAF His-
     torical Division Liaison Office, 1966.
Binsack, Joseph H., 1st Lt. "Satellite Control Facility Capabilities." In *Proceedings of the IAS National
     Tracking and Command of Aerospace Vehicles Symposium,* pp. 135–37. February 19–21. New
     York: Institute of Aerospace Sciences, 1962.
Blair, Edison T. "From Saddles to Satellites." *The Airman* (February, 1961): 7–19.
Blanchard, William N. "The Evolution of Air Force Space Mission Command, Control and
     Communications." Colorado Springs: Ford Aerospace and Communications Corporation,
     1982.
Booda, Larry. "First Capsule Recovered from Satellite." *Space Technology* 3 (October, 1960):
     41–43.
Bowen, Lee. *The Threshold of Space: The Air Force in the National Space Program, 1945–1969.* Wash-
     ington, D.C.: USAF Historical Division Liaison Office, 1960.
Bugos, Glenn. *Engineering the F-4 Phantom II: Parts into Systems.* Annapolis: Naval Institute Press,
     1996.
Builder, Carl H. *The Icarus Syndrome: The Role of Air Power Theory in the Evolution and Fate of the U.S.
     Air Force.* New Brunswick, N.J.: Transaction Publishers, 1996.
Burrows, William E. *Deep Black: Space Espionage and National Security.* New York: Random House,
     1986.
Butrica, Andrew J, ed. *Beyond the Ionosphere: Fifty Years of Satellite Communication.* Washington, D.C.:
     Government Printing Office, NASA, SP-4217, 1997.
———. *Single Stage to Orbit: Politics, Space Technology, and the Quest for Reusable Rocketry.* Baltimore:
     Johns Hopkins Univeristy Press, 2004.
Cantwell, Gerald T. *The Air Force in Space, Fiscal Year* 1964. Vol. SHO-S-67/52/142. Washington,
     D.C.: USAF Historical Division Liaison Office, 1967.
———. *The Air Force in Space, Fiscal Year* 1965. Vol. SHO-S-68/52/186. Washington, D.C.: USAF
     Historical Division Liaison Office, 1968.
———. *The Air Force in Space, Fiscal Year* 1967. Part I. Washington, D.C.: USAF Historical Division
     Liaison Office, 1970.

Carter, L. J., ed. *The Artificial Satellite: Proceedings of the Second International Congress on Astronautics.* London: British Interplanetary Society, 1951.

"Chronology of Early Air Force Man-in-Space Activity, 1955–1960." Air Force Systems Command Historical Publications Series 65-21-1.

Clifford, Frank J. "Discoverer: Trailblazer to Space." *The Airman* (June, 1961): 12–19.

Collins, Martin J. *Cold War Laboratory: RAND, the Air Force, and the American State, 1945–1950.* Washington, D.C.: Smithsonian Institution Press, 2002.

Compton, William D. *Where No Man Has Gone Before: A History of Apollo Lunar Exploration Missions.* Washington, D.C.: Government Printing Office, NASA, SP-4214, 1989.

Conference on Artificial Satellites. Part C. Blacksburg: Virginia Polytechnic Institute, August, 1963.

Coolbaugh, James S. "Genesis of the USAF's First Satellite Programme." *Journal of the British Interplanetary Society* 51 (August, 1998): 283–300.

Daso, Dik A. *Architects of American Air Supremacy: Gen. Hap Arnold and Dr. Theodore von Kármán.* Maxwell AFB, Montgomery, Ala.: Air University Press, 1997.

Day, Dwayne A. "Corona: America's First Spy Satellite Program, Part I." *Quest, the History of Spaceflight Quarterly* 4 (Summer, 1995): 4–21.

———. "Corona: America's First Spy Satellite Program, Part II." *Quest, the History of Spaceflight Quarterly* 4 (Fall, 1995): 28–36.

———. "Taking the 'Special Relationship' to New Heights." *Journal of the British Interplanetary Society* 52 (November/December, 1999): 417–18.

Day, Dwayne A., John M. Logsdon, and Brian Latell, eds. *Eye in the Sky: The Story of the Corona Satellites.* Washington, D.C.: Smithsonian Institution Press, 1998.

Dill, Lt. Col. A. W. (USAF), and Niall E. Tabor, Lockheed Missiles and Space Corporation, "Requirements Cycle for USAF Satellite Control Facilities." In *Proceedings of the IAS National Tracking and Command of Aerospace Vehicles Symposium.* San Francisco, February 19–21. New York: Institute of the Aerospace Sciences, 1962.

Emme, Eugene M, ed. *The History of Rocket Technology: Essays on Research, Development, and Utility.* Detroit: Wayne State University Press, 1964.

Engle, Eloise, and Kenneth Drummond. *Sky Rangers: Satellite Tracking around the World.* New York: John Day, 1965.

Flavell, Robert A. "Catch a Falling Star: Aerial Recovery of Space Objects." *Air Power History* (Fall, 1994): 24–26.

Foley, Theresa. "Corona Comes In from the Cold." *Air Force Magazine* 78 (September, 1995): 82–87.

Futrell, Robert F. *Ideas, Concepts, and Doctrine.* Vol. 1, *Basic Thinking in the United States Air Force, 1907–1960.* Maxwell AFB, Montgomery, Ala.: Air University Press, 1989.

———. *Ideas, Concepts, and Doctrine.* Vol. 2, *Basic Thinking in the United States Air Force, 1961–1984.* Maxwell AFB, Montgomery, Ala.: Air University Press, 1989.

Gavaghan, Helen. *Something New under the Sun: Satellites and the Beginning of the Space Age.* New York: Copernicus Books, 1998.

Gorn, Michael H. *Harnessing the Genie: Science and Technology Forecasting for the Air Force, 1944–1986.* Washington, D.C.: Office of Air Force History, 1988.

Green, Constance McLaughlin, and Milton Lomask. *Vanguard: A History.* Washington, D.C.: Government Printing Office, NASA, SP-4202, 1970.

Greenstein, Fred I. *The Hidden Hand Presidency: Eisenhower as Leader.* New York: Basic Books, 1982.

Greer, Kenneth E. "Corona." *Studies in Intelligence,* Supplement 17 (Spring, 1973): 6. Reprinted in *Corona: America's First Satellite Program,* ed. Kevin C. Ruffner. Center for the Study of Intelligence. Washington, D.C.: CIA History Staff, 1995.

Grissom, Virgil I. "Gus." *Gemini: A Personal Account of Man's Venture into Space.* New York: Macmillan, 1968.

Hagen, John P. "The Viking and the Vanguard." *Technology and Culture* 4 (Fall, 1963): 435–51.

Hall, Edward N. *The Art of Destructive Management: What Hath Man Wrought?* New York: Vantage Press, 1984.

Hall, R. Cargill. "Early U.S. Satellite Proposals." In *The History of Rocket Technology: Essays on Research, Development, and Utility,* ed. Eugene M. Emme. Detroit: Wayne State University Press, 1964.

———. "The Eisenhower Administration and the Cold War: Framing American Astronautics to Serve National Security." *Prologue* 27 (Spring, 1995): 59–72.

———. *A History of Satellite Reconnaissance.* Vol. II, *Weather Satellite Program.* Washington, D.C.: National Reconnaissance Office, n.d., declassified 1996.

———. *The NRO at Forty: Ensuring Global Information Supremacy.* Chantilly, Va.: National Reconnaissance Office, 2000.

———. *A History of the Military Polar Orbiting Meteorological Satellite Program.* Chantilly, Va.: National Reconnaissance Office, 2001.

———, and Jacob Neufeld, eds. *The U.S. Air Force in Space: 1945 to the Twenty-First Century.* Washington, D.C.: USAF History and Museums Program, 1998.

Hansen, James R. *Spaceflight Revolution: NASA Langley Research Center from Sputnik to Apollo.* Washington, D.C.: Government Printing Office, NASA, SP-4308, 1995.

Hartinger, James V. *From One Stripe to Four Stars: The Personal Recollections of General James V. Hartinger, USAF, Retired.* Colorado Springs: Phantom Press, 1997.

Hawkes, Russell. "USAF's Satellite Test Center Grows." *Aviation Week* (May 30, 1960): 57–63.

Hayes, E. Nelson, ed. *Trackers of the Skies: The Smithsonian Astrophysical Laboratory's Tracking Network.* Cambridge: Howard A. Doyle, 1968.

Hughes, Thomas Parke. "Technological Momentum in History: Hydrogenation in Germany, 1898–1933." *Past and Present* 44 (August, 1969): 106–32.

———. *Elmer Sperry, Inventor and Engineer.* Baltimore: Johns Hopkins University Press, 1971.

———. "The Development Phase of Technological Change: Introduction." *Technology and Culture* 17 (July, 1976): 423–30.

———. "The Electrification of America: The System Builders." *Technology and Culture* 20 (October, 1979): 124–61.

———. "Emerging Themes in the History of Technology." *Technology and Culture* 20 (October, 1979): 697–711.

———. "The Order of the Technological World." In *History of Technology* 1980, ed. A. Rupert Hall and Norman Smith, 2–14. London: Maxwell, 1980.

———. *Networks of Power: Electrification in Western Society, 1880–1930.* Baltimore: Johns Hopkins University Press, 1983.

———. *American Genesis: A Century of Invention and Technological Enthusiasm, 1870–1970.* New York: Viking, 1989.

———. "The Evolution of Large Technological Systems." In *The Social Construction of Technological Systems: New Directions in the Sociology and History of Technology,* ed. Wiebe Bijker, Thomas P. Hughes, and Trevor Pinch, 51–76. Cambridge: MIT Press, 1989.

———. *Rescuing Prometheus.* New York: Pantheon Books, 1998.

———, and Agatha C. Hughes. *Systems, Experts and Computers: The Systems Approach in Management and Engineering, World War II and After.* Cambridge: MIT Press, 2000.

Hunley, J. D., ed. *The Birth of NASA: The Diary of T. Keith Glennan.* Washington, D.C.: U.S. Government Printing Office, NASA SP-4105, 1993.

Jensen, H. H., and R. G. Kramer. "Air Force Satellite Control Facility History." El Segundo, Calif.: Aerospace Corporation, 1970.

Jernigan, Roger A. *Air Force Satellite Control Facility: Historical Brief and Chronology, 1954–Present.* Sunnyvale AFS, Calif.: Air Force Satellite Control Facility History Office, n.d. [ca. 1984].

Johnson, Stephen B. *The Secret of Apollo: Systems Management in American and European Space Programs.* Baltimore: Johns Hopkins University Press, 2002.

——. *The United States Air Force and the Culture of Innovation 1945–1965.* Washington, D.C.: Air Force History and Museums Program, 2002.

Killian, James R., Jr. *Sputnik, Scientists, and Eisenhower: A Memoir of the First Special Assistant to the President for Science and Technology.* Cambridge: MIT Press, 1977.

Klass, Philip J. *Secret Sentries in Space.* New York: Random House, 1971.

Koppes, Clayton R. *JPL and the American Space Program: A History of the Jet Propulsion Laboratory.* New Haven: Yale University Press, 1982.

Kovalchik, Dan. *Range Rats at Sea: Tracking Satellites, Sailing the Tropics, and Searching for the Sybaritic Life.* San Jose: Author's Choice Press, 2001.

Krieger, F. J. *Behind the Sputniks: A Survey of Soviet Space Science.* Washington, D.C.: Public Affairs Press, 1958.

Launius, Roger D., ed. *Organizing for the Use of Space: Historical Perspectives on a Persistent Issue.* San Diego: American Astronautical Society, 1995.

Lewis, Craig. "Mercury Network Offered for Soviet Use." *Space Technology* 3 (January, 1960): 12–13.

Logsdon, John M., ed. *Exploring the Unknown: Selected Documents in the History of the U.S. Civil Space Program.* Vol. 1, *Organizing for Exploration.* Washington, D.C.: Government Printing Office, NASA, SP-4407, 1995.

——. *Exploring the Unknown: Selected Documents in the History of the U.S. Civil Space Program.* Vol. 2, *External Relationships.* Washington, D.C.: Government Printing Office, NASA, SP-4407, 1996.

Lonnquest, John. "The Face of Atlas: General Bernard Schriever and the Development of the Atlas Intercontinental Ballistic Missile, 1953–1960." Ph.D. diss., Duke University, 1996.

Macko, Stanley J. *Satellite Tracking.* New York: John F. Rider, 1962.

Malberg, Carl. "NHS 1962–1966." *Downlink: The Newsletter of the Air Force Space Operations Association* 7 (Summer, 2000): 1–8.

Martin, Donald H. *Communications Satellites, 1958–1992.* El Segundo, Calif.: Aerospace Corp., 1991.

Mayo-Wells, Wilfrid J. "The Origins of Space Telemetry." *Technology and Culture* IV (October, 1963): 499–514.

McCurdy, Howard E. *Inside NASA: High Technology and Organizational Change in the U.S. Space Program.* Baltimore: Johns Hopkins University Press, 1990.

——. *The Space Station Decision: Incremental Politics and Technological Choice.* Baltimore: Johns Hopkins University Press, 1985.

McDougall, Walter A. *The Heavens and the Earth: A Political History of the Space Age.* New York: Basic Books, 1985.

Medaris, John Bruce. *Countdown for Decision.* New York: G. P. Putnam's Sons, 1960.

Mengel, John T., and Paul Herget. "Tracking Satellites by Radio." *Scientific American* 198 (January, 1958): 23–29.

"Mission Transcript Collection: U.S. Human Spaceflight Missions from Mercury Redstone 3 to Apollo 17." Washington, D.C.: Government Printing Office, NASA, SP-4602, 2000.

Morrison, Larry R. *From Flares to Satellites: A Brief History of Air Force Communications.* Scott AFB, Ill.: Air Force Communications Agency Office of History, 1997.

Mudgway, Douglas J. *Uplink/Downlink: A History of the Deep Space Network.* Washington, D.C.: Government Printing Office, NASA, SP-4225, 2002.

Nalty, Bernard C., ed. *Winged Shield, Winged Sword: A History of the United States Air Force.* Vol. 2, *1950–1997.* Washington, D.C.: Air Force History and Museums Program, 1997.

Nammack, John. "C-119's Third Pass Snares Discoverer." *Space Technology* 3(4) (October, 1960): 44–45.

Narducci, Henry M. *Strategic Air Command and the Space Mission, 1977–1984.* Historical monograph no. 209. Offutt AFB, Neb.: Strategic Air Command History Office, 1985.

"National Range Division: A $5 Billion Asset Sings Smoothly into Worldwide Operation." *Armed Forces Management* (June, 1965): 76–79.

Neufeld, Jacob. *The Air Force in Space, 1970–1974.* Washington, D.C.: Office of Air Force History, 1976.

———. *The Development of Ballistic Missiles in the United States Air Force, 1945–1960.* Washington, D.C.: Government Printing Office, Office of Air Force History, 1990.

Newlon, Clarke. "Air Force Satellite Program Gets New Boss." *Missiles and Rockets* (September 5, 1960): 18.

Noble, David F. *Forces of Production: A Social History of Industrial Automation.* Oxford: Oxford University Press, 1984.

Oberg, James E. *Red Star in Orbit: The Inside Story of Soviet Failures and Triumphs in Space.* New York: Random House, 1981.

Pearson, David E. *The World Wide Military Command and Control System: Evolution and Effectiveness.* Maxwell AFB, Montgomery, Ala.: Air University Press, 2000.

Peebles, Curtis. *Guardians: Strategic Reconnaissance Satellites.* Novato, Calif.: Presidio Press, 1987.

———. *The Corona Project: America's First Spy Satellites.* Annapolis: Naval Institute Press, 1997.

———. *High Frontier: The United States Air Force and the Military Space Program.* Washington, D.C.: Air Force History and Museums Program, 1997.

Perry, Robert L. *Management of the National Reconnaissance Program, 1960–1965.* Washington, D.C.: RAND Corp, 1969.

———. *Origins of the USAF Space Program, 1945–1956.* 1960. Reprint, Los Angeles: Space and Missile Systems Center, 1997.

Polmar, Norman. "Here's Looking at You, Boris." *U.S. Naval Institute Proceedings* (December, 1995): 87–88.

Proceedings of the IAS National Tracking and Command of Aerospace Vehicles Symposium. San Francisco, February 19–21, 1962. New York: Institute of the Aerospace Sciences, 1962.

Redmond, Kent C., and Thomas M. Smith. *From Whirlwind to MITRE: The R&D Story of the SAGE Air Defense Computer.* Cambridge: MIT Press, 2000.

Richelson, Jeffrey T. *America's Secret Eyes in Space: The U.S. Keyhole Spy Satellite Program.* New York: Harper and Row, 1990.

———. *America's Space Sentinels: DSP Satellites and National Security.* Lawrence: University Press of Kansas, 1999.

———. "Undercover in Outer Space: The Creation and Evolution of the NRO, 1960–1963." *International Journal of Intelligence and Counterintelligence* 13 (March, 2000): 301–44.

———. *The Wizards of Langley: Inside the CIA's Directorate of Science and Technology.* Boulder: Westview Press, 2001.

Rockefeller, Alfred, Jr. "History of the Evolution of the AFBMD Advanced Ballistic Missile and

Space Program (prior to and Immediately after Sputnik) (1955–1958)." Los Angeles: Air Force Ballistic Missile Division, 1960.

———. "History of THOR, 1955–1959." Los Angeles: Air Force Ballistic Missile Division, 1960.

Rosenberg, Max. *The Air Force in Space, Fiscal Year 1959–1960.* Vol. SHO-S-62/112. Washington, D.C.: USAF Historical Division Liaison Office, 1962.

Ruffner, Kevin C. *Corona: America's First Satellite Program.* Center for the Study of Intelligence. Washington, D.C.: CIA History Staff, n.d., declassified 1995.

Schriever, Bernard A. "The Operational Urgency of R&D." *Air University Quarterly Review* (Winter–Spring, 1960): 235.

Shulman, Seth. "Code Name: Corona." *Technology Review* 99 (July, 1997): 22–33.

Siddiqi, Asif A. *Challenge to Apollo: The Soviet Union and the Space Race, 1945–1974.* Washington, D.C.: Government Printing Office, NASA, SP-4408, 2000.

Singer, S. F. "Studies of a Minimum Orbital Unmanned Satellite of the Earth (MOUSE)." *Astronautica Acta* 1 (1955): 171–84.

Smaker, Tony. *Chiniak.* Http://209.165.152.119/kL7af/kL7af.html. Accessed Feb. 9, 2004.

Spires, David N. *Beyond Horizons: A Half Century of Air Force Space Leadership.* Peterson AFB, Colo.: Government Printing Office, 1997.

Stares, Paul B. *The Militarization of Space: U.S. Policy, 1945–1984.* Ithaca: Cornell University Press, 1984.

Stephenson, Richard G., and R. C. Hansen. "Aerospace Corporation and Satellite Control Engineering." In *Proceedings of the IAS National Tracking and Command of Aerospace Vehicles Symposium.* San Francisco, February 19–21. New York: Institute of the Aerospace Sciences, 1962.

Sturdevant, Rick W. "The United States Air Force Organizes for Space: The Operational Quest." In *Organizing for the Use of Space: Historical Perspectives on a Persistent Issue,* ed. Roger D. Launius. San Diego: American Astronautical Society, 1999.

Sweeny, Richard. "*Discoverer* 2 Orbital Attitude Controlled." *Space Technology* 2 (July, 1959): 26–27.

Swenson Lloyd S., Jr., James M. Grimwood, and Charles C. Alexander. *This New Ocean: A History of Project Mercury.* Washington, D.C.: Government Printing Office, NASA, SP-4201, 1966.

Terhune, Charles H., Jr. "In the 'Soaring Sixties' Man Is on His Way—Up." *Air Force/Space Digest* (April, 1960): 64–71.

Thomas, Shirley. *Satellite Tracking Facilities: Their History and Operation.* New York: Holt, Rinehart and Winston, 1963.

Twining, Nathan F. *Neither Liberty nor Safety.* New York: Holt, Rinehart and Winston, 1966.

Von Kármán, Theodore, with Lee Edson. *The Wind and Beyond: Theodore von Kármán, Pioneer in Aviation and Pathfinder in Space.* Boston: Little, Brown, 1967.

Whalen, David J. *The Origins of Satellite Communications, 1945–1965.* Washington, D.C.: Smithsonian Institution Press, 2002.

White, Thomas D. "At the Dawn of the Space Age." *Air Power Historian* 5 (January, 1958): 15–19.

Wolf, Richard I. *The United States Air Force Basic Documents on Roles and Missions.* Washington, D.C.: Office of Air Force History, 1987.

NEWSPAPERS AND PERIODICALS

Air Force Magazine
Air Force/Space Digest
Airman
Airpower Journal

Aviation Week and Space Technology (July, 1947–present)
Journal of the British Interplanetary Society
Missiles and Rockets (October, 1956–January, 1966)
Missiles and Space (January, 1961–August, 1963)
Missile/Space Daily (May, 1963–January, 1968)
Space Aeronautics (October, 1958–July, 1970)
Space Technology (1958–present)
Space World (1966–1988)
Spaceflight (1956–present)

Index

ISBN 1-58544-385-9

90000

Spying from Space

Book # ___

Arnold, D.

(Name, Rank, Unit)

DATE	ISSUED TO
2 1 SEP 2006	Capt Harvey